Quantitative Data Analysis with Minitab

A guide for social scientists

Alan Bryman and Duncan Cramer

London and New York

MINITAB is a registered trademark of Minitab Inc., 3081 Enterprise Drive, State College, PA 16801-3008, USA, telephone 814-238-3280, fax 814-238-4383.

First published 1996
by Routledge
11 New Fetter Lane, London EC4P 4EE

Simultaneously published in the USA and Canada
by Routledge
29 West 35th Street, New York, NY 10001

Routledge in an International Thomson Publishing company

© 1996 Alan Bryman and Duncan Cramer

Typeset in Times by
Mathematical Composition Setters, Salisbury, Wiltshire

Printed and bound in Great Britain by
T J Press (Padstow) Ltd, Padstow, Cornwall

British Library Cataloguing in Publication Data
A catalogue record for this book is available from the British Library

Library of Congress Cataloguing in Publication Data
Bryman, Alan.
    Quantitative data analysis with minitab: a guide for social scientists/Alan Bryman and Duncan Cramer.
        p.   cm.
    Includes bibliographical references and index.
    1. Social sciences—Statistical methods.   2. Social sciences—Data processing.   3. Social sciences—Computer programs.   4. Minitab.
I. Cramer, Duncan, 1948–   . II. Title.
HA32.B793   1996
300′.1′5195—dc20   95-44812
                                                            CIP

ISBN 0-415-12323-2 (hbk)
ISBN 0-415-12324-0 (pbk)

Contents

Figures

Tables

Preface

In this book, we introduce readers to the main techniques of statistical analysis employed by psychologists and sociologists. However, we do not see the book as a standard introduction to statistics. We see it as distinctively different because we are not concerned to introduce the often complex formulae that underlie the statistical methods covered. Students often find these formulae and the calculations that are associated with them extremely daunting, especially when their background in mathematics is weak. Moreover, in these days of powerful computers and packages of statistical programs, it seems gratuitous to put students through the anxiety of confronting complex calculations when machines can perform the bulk of their work. Indeed, most practitioners employ statistical packages that are run on computers to perform their calculations, so there seems little purpose in treating formulae and their application as a *rite de passage* for social scientists. Moreover, few students come to understand fully the rationale for the formulae that they would need to learn. Indeed, we prefer the term 'quantitative data analysis' to 'statistics' because of the negative image that the latter term has in the minds of many prospective readers.

In view of the widespread availability of statistical packages and computers, we feel that the two areas that students need to get to grips with are, first, how to decide which statistical procedures are suitable for which purpose, and second, how to interpret the ensuing results. We try to emphasize these two elements in this book.

In addition, the student needs to get to know how to operate the computer software needed to perform the statistical procedures described in this book. To this end, we introduce students to a widely-used suite of programs for statistical analysis in the social sciences – Minitab. As such, this book differs from earlier versions of the book, which were based on a different package of statistical programs (Bryman and Cramer, 1990, 1994). Minitab has undergone many revisions over the years and the most recent releases are described in Chapter 2. Moreover, Minitab can be used on mainframe computers and on IBM-compatible personal computers in DOS and Windows environments as well as on Apple Macintosh computers. We have tried to present the workings of Minitab in such a way that it will be useful and accessible to all groups of users.

In order to distinguish methods of quantitative data analysis from Minitab commands, the latter are always in **bold**. We also present some data that students can work on and the names of the variables are also in **bold** (for example, **income**).

There are exercises at the end of each chapter. Answers are provided at the end of the book. We hope that students and instructors alike will find these useful; they can easily be adapted to provide further exercises.

The case for combining methods of quantitative data analysis used by both psychologists and sociologists in part derives from our belief that the requirements of students of the two subjects can often overlap substantially. None the less, instructors can omit particular techniques as they wish.

We are grateful to the Longman Group UK Ltd, on behalf of the Literary Executor of the late Sir Ronald A. Fisher, F.R.S. and Dr Frank Yates, F.R.S. for permission to reproduce a portion of Table VII from *Statistical Tables for Biological and Medical Research* 6/e (1974).

We wish to thank David Stonestreet, formerly of Routledge, for his support for the earlier editions of this book and our current editor Vivien Ward for her support of the present book. We also wish to thank Louis Cohen, Max Hunt, and Tony Westaway for reading the manuscript for the first version of this book and for making many helpful suggestions for improvement of that edition. We accept that they cannot be held liable for any errors in that or the present edition: such errors are entirely of our own making, though we will undoubtedly blame each other for them.

Alan Bryman and Duncan Cramer,
Loughborough University

Chapter 1

Data analysis and the research process

This book largely covers the field that is generally referred to as 'statistics', but as our Preface has sought to establish, we have departed in a number of respects from the way in which this subject is conventionally taught to under- and post-graduates. In particular, our preferences are for integrating data analysis with computing skills and for not burdening the student with formulae. These predilections constitute a departure from many, if not most, treatments of this subject. We prefer the term 'quantitative data analysis' because the emphasis is on the understanding and analysis of data rather than on the precise nature of the statistical techniques themselves.

Why should social science students have to study quantitative data analysis, especially at a time when qualitative research is coming increasingly to the fore (Bryman, 1988a)? After all, everyone has heard of the ways in which statistical materials can be distorted, as indicated by Disraeli's often-quoted dictum: 'There are lies, damn lies and statistics'. Why should serious researchers and students be prepared to get involved in such a potentially unworthy activity? If we take the first issue – why should social science students study quantitative data analysis – it is necessary to remember that an extremely large proportion of the empirical research undertaken by social scientists is designed to generate or draws upon quantitative data. In order to be able to appreciate the kinds of analyses that are conducted in relation to such data and possibly to analyse their own data (especially since many students are required to carry out projects), an acquaintance with the appropriate methods of analysis is highly desirable for social science students. Further, although qualitative research has quite properly become a prominent strategy in sociology and some other areas of the social sciences, it is by no means as pervasive as quantitative research, and in any case many writers recognise that there is much to be gained from a fusion of the two research traditions (Bryman, 1988a).

On the question of the ability of statisticians to distort the analyses that they carry out, the prospects for which are substantially enhanced in many people's eyes by books with such disconcerting titles as *How to Lie with Statistics* (Huff, 1973), it should be recognized that an understanding of the techniques to be covered in our book will greatly enhance the ability to see through the misrepresentations about which many people are concerned. Indeed, the inculcation of a sceptical appreciation of quantitative data analysis is beneficial in the light of the pervasive use of statistical data in everyday life. We are deluged with such data in the form of the results of opinion polls, market research findings, attitude surveys, health and crime statistics, and so on. An awareness of quantitative data analysis greatly enhances the ability to recognise faulty conclusions or potentially biased manipulations of the information. There is even a fair chance that a substantial proportion of the readers of this book will get jobs in which at some point they will have to think about the question of how to analyse and present statistical material. Moreover, quantitative data analysis does not comprise a mechanical application of predetermined techniques by statisticians and others; it is a subject with its own controversies and debates, just like the social sciences themselves. Some of these areas of controversy will be brought to the reader's attention where appropriate.

QUANTITATIVE DATA ANALYSIS AND THE RESEARCH PROCESS

In this section, the way in which quantitative data analysis fits into the research process – specifically the process of quantitative research – will be explored. As we will see, the area covered by this book does not solely address the question of how to deal with quantitative data, since it is also concerned with other aspects of the research process that impinge on data analysis.

Figure 1.1 provides an illustration of the chief steps in the process of quantitative research. Although there are grounds for doubting whether research always conforms to a neat linear sequence (Bryman, 1988a, 1988b), the components depicted in Figure 1.1 provide a useful model. The following stages are delineated by the model.

Theory

The starting point for the process is a theoretical domain. Theories in the social sciences can vary between abstract general approaches (such as functionalism) and fairly low-level theories to explain specific phenomena (such as voting behaviour, delinquency, aggressiveness). By and large, the theories that are most likely to receive direct empirical attention are those which are at a fairly low level of generality. Merton (1967) referred to these as theories of the middle-range, to denote theories that stood between general, abstract theories and empirical findings. Thus, Hirschi (1969), for example, formulated a 'control theory' of juvenile delinquency which proposes that delinquent acts are more likely to occur when the child's

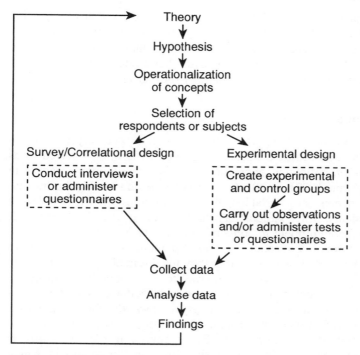

Figure 1.1   The research process

bonds to society are breached. This theory in large part derived from other theories and also from research findings relating to juvenile delinquency.

Hypothesis

Once a theory has been formulated, it is likely that researchers will want to test it. Does the theory hold water when faced with empirical evidence? However, it is rarely possible to test a theory as such. Instead, we are more likely to find that a hypothesis, which relates to a limited facet of the theory, will be deduced from the theory and submitted to a searching enquiry. For example, Hirschi, drawing upon his control theory, stipulates that children who are tied to conventional society (in the sense of adhering to conventional values and participating or aspiring to participate in conventional values) will be less likely to commit delinquent acts than those not so tied. Hypotheses very often take the form of relationships between two or more entities – in this case commitment to conventional society and juvenile delinquency. These 'entities' are usually referred to as 'concepts', that is, categories in which are stored our ideas and observations about common elements in the world. The nature of concepts is discussed in greater detail in Chapter 4. Although hypotheses have the advantage that they force researchers to think systematically about what they want to study and to structure their research plans accordingly, they exhibit a potential disadvantage in that they may divert a researcher's attention too far away from other interesting facets of the data he or she has amassed.

Operationalization of concepts

In order to assess the validity of a hypothesis it is necessary to develop measures of the constituent concepts. This process is often referred to as *operationalization*, following expositions of the measurement process in physics (Bridgman, 1927). In effect, what is happening here is the translation of the concepts into variables, that is, attributes on which relevant objects (individuals, firms, nations, or whatever) differ. Hirschi operationalized the idea of commitment to conventional society in a number of ways. One route was through a question on a questionnaire asking the children to whom it was to be administered whether they liked school. Delinquency was measured in two ways, of which one was to ask about the number of delinquent acts to which children admitted (i.e. self-reported delinquent acts). In much experimental research in psychology, the measurement of concepts is achieved through the observation of people, rather than through the administration of questionnaires. For example, if the researcher is interested in aggression, a laboratory situation may be set up in which variations in aggressive behaviour are observed. Another way in which concepts may be operationalized is through the analysis of existing statistics, of which Durkheim's (1952/1898) classic analysis of suicide rates is an example. A number of issues to do with the process of devising measures of concepts and some of the properties that measures should possess are discussed in Chapter 4.

Selection of respondents or subjects

If a survey investigation is being undertaken, the researcher must find relevant people to whom the research instrument that has been devised (e.g. self-administered questionnaire, interview schedule) should be administered. Hirschi, for example, randomly selected over 5,500 school children from an area in California. The fact of random selection is important here because it reflects a commitment to the production of findings that can be generalized beyond the confines of those who participate in a study. It is rarely possible to contact all units in a population, so that a *sample* invariably has to be selected. In order to be able to generalize to a wider population, a *representative sample*, such as one that can be achieved through random sampling, will be required. Moreover, many of the statistical techniques to be covered in this book are *inferential statistics*, which allow the researcher to demonstrate the probability that the results deriving from a sample are likely to be found in the population from which the sample was taken, but only if a random sample has been selected. These issues are examined in Chapter 6.

Setting up a research design

There are two basic types of research design that are employed by psychologists and sociologists. The former tend to use *experimental* designs in which the researcher actively manipulates aspects of a setting, either in the laboratory or in a field situation, and observes the effects of that manipulation on experimental subjects. There must also be a 'control group' which acts as a point of comparison with the group of subjects who receive the experimental manipulation. With a *survey/correlational* design, the researcher does not manipulate any of the variables of interest and data relating to all variables are collected simultaneously. The term *correlation* also refers to a technique for analysing relationships between variables (see Chapter 8), but is used in the present context to denote a type of research design. The researcher does not always have a choice regarding which of the two designs can be adopted. For example, Hirschi could not *make* some children committed to school and other's less committed and observe the effects on their propensity to commit delinquent acts. Some variables, like most of those studied by sociologists, are not capable of manipulation. However, there are areas of research in which topics and hypotheses are addressed with both types of research design (e.g. the study of the effects of participation at work on job satisfaction and performance – see Bryman, 1986; Locke and Schweiger, 1979). It should be noted that in most cases, therefore, the nature of the research design – whether experimental or survey/correlational – is known at the outset of the sequence signified by Figure 1.1, so that research design characteristics permeate and inform a number of stages of the research process. The nature of the research design has implications for the kinds of statistical manipulation that can be performed on the resulting data. The differences between the two designs are given greater attention in the next section.

Collect data

The researcher collects data at this stage, by interview, questionnaire, observation, or whatever. The technicalities of the issues pertinent to this stage are not usually associated with a book such as this. Readers should consult a text-book concerned with social and psychological research methods if they are unfamiliar with the relevant issues.

Analyse data

This stage connects very directly with the material covered in this book. At a minimum, the researcher is likely to want to describe his or her subjects in terms of the variables deriving from the study. For example, the researcher might be interested in the proportion of children who claim to have committed no, just one, or two or more delinquent acts. The various ways of analysing and presenting the information relating to a single variable (sometimes called *univariate analysis*) are examined in Chapter 5. However, the analysis of a single variable is unlikely to suffice and the researcher will probably be interested in the connection between that variable and each of a number of other variables, i.e. *bivariate analysis*. The examination of connections among variables can take either of two forms. A researcher who has conducted an experiment may be interested in the extent to which experimental and control groups differ in some respect. For example, the researcher might be interested in examining whether watching violent films increases aggressiveness. The experimental group (which watches the violent films) and the control group (which does not) can then be compared to see how far they differ. The techniques for examining differences are explored in Chapter 7. The researcher may be interested in relationships between variables – are two variables connected with each other so that they tend to vary together? For example, Hirschi (1969: 121) presents a table which shows how liking school and self-reported delinquent acts are inter-connected. He found that whereas only 9 per cent of children who say they like school have committed two or more delinquent acts, 49 per cent of those who say they dislike school have committed as many delinquent acts. The ways in which relationships among pairs of variables can be elucidated can be found in Chapter 8. Very often the researcher will be interested in exploring connections among more than two variables, i.e. *multivariate analysis*. Chapter 9 examines such analysis in the context of the exploration of differences, while Chapter 10 looks at the multivariate analysis of relationships among more than two variables. The distinction between studying differences and studying relationships is not always clear-cut. We might find that boys are more likely than girls to commit delinquent acts. This finding could be taken to mean that boys and girls differ in terms of propensity to engage in delinquent acts or that there is a relationship between gender and delinquency.

Findings

If the analysis of data suggests that a hypothesis is confirmed, this result can be fed back into the theory that prompted it. Future researchers can then concern themselves either with seeking to replicate the finding or with other ramifications of the theory. However, the refutation of a hypothesis can be just as important in that it may suggest that the theory is faulty or at the very least in need of revision. Sometimes, the hypothesis may be confirmed in some respects only. For example, a multivariate analysis may suggest that a relationship between two variables pertains only to some members of a sample, but not others (e.g. women but not men, or younger but not older people). Such a finding will require a reformulation of the theory. Not all findings will necessarily relate directly to a hypothesis. With a social survey, for example, the researcher may collect data on topics whose relevance only becomes evident at a later juncture.

As suggested above, the sequence depicted in Figure 1.1 constitutes a model of the research process, which may not always be reproduced in reality. None the less, it does serve to pinpoint the importance to the process of quantitative research of developing measures of concepts and the thorough analysis of subsequent data. One point that was not mentioned in the discussion is the *form* that the hypotheses and findings tend to assume. One of the main aims of much quantitative research in the social sciences is the demonstration of *causality* – that one variable has an impact upon another. The terms *independent variable* and *dependent variable* are often employed in this context. The former denotes a variable that has an impact upon the dependent variable. The latter, in other words, is deemed to be an effect of the independent variable. This causal imagery is widespread in the social sciences and a major role of multivariate analysis is the elucidation of such causal relationships (Bryman, 1988a). The ease with which a researcher can establish cause and effect relationships is strongly affected by the nature of the research design and it is to this topic that we shall now turn.

CAUSALITY AND RESEARCH DESIGN

As suggested in the last paragraph, one of the chief preoccupations among quantitative researchers is to establish causality. This preoccupation in large part derives from a concern to establish findings similar to those of the natural sciences, which often take a causal form. Moreover, findings which establish cause-and-effect can have considerable practical importance: if we know that one thing affects another, we can manipulate the cause to produce an effect. In much the same way that our knowledge that smoking may cause a number of illnesses, such as lung cancer and heart disease, the social scientist is able to provide potentially practical information by demonstrating causal relationships in appropriate settings.

To say that something causes something else is not to suggest that the dependent variable (the effect) is totally influenced by the independent variable (the cause). You do not necessarily contract a disease if you smoke and many of the diseases contracted by people who smoke afflict those who never smoke. 'Cause' here should be taken to mean that variation in the dependent variable is affected by variation in the independent variable. Those who smoke a lot are more likely than those who smoke less, who in turn are more likely than those who do not smoke at all, to contract a variety of diseases that are associated with smoking. Similarly, if we find that watching violence on television induces aggressive behaviour, we are not saying that only people who watch televised violence will behave aggressively, nor that only those people who behave aggressively watch violent television programmes. Causal relationships are invariably about the likelihood of an effect occurring in the light of particular levels of the cause: aggressive behaviour may be more likely to occur when a lot of television violence is watched and people who watch relatively little television violence may be less likely to behave aggressively.

Establishing causality

In order to establish a causal relationship, three criteria have to be fulfilled. First, it is necessary to establish that there is an apparent relationship between two variables. This means that it is necessary to demonstrate that the distribution of values of one variable corresponds to the distribution of values of another variable. Table 1.1. provides information for ten children on the number of aggressive acts they exhibit when they play in two groups of five for two hours per group. The point to note is that there is a relationship between the two variables in that the distribution of values for number of aggressive acts coincides with the distribution for the amount of televised violence watched – children who watch more violence exhibit more aggression than those who watch little violence. The relationship is not

Table 1.1 Data on television violence and aggression

Child	Number of hours of violence watched on television per week	Number of aggressive acts recorded
1	9.50	9
2	9.25	8
3	8.75	7
4	8.25	7
5	8.00	6
6	5.50	4
7	5.25	4
8	4.75	5
9	4.50	3
10	4.00	3

perfect: three pairs of children – 3 and 4, 6 and 7 and 9 and 10 – record the same number of aggressive acts, even though they watch different amounts of television violence. Moreover, 8 exhibits more aggression than 6 or 7, even though the latter watch more violence. None the less, a clear pattern is evident which suggests that there is a relationship between the two variables.

Second, it is necessary to demonstrate that the relationship is *non-spurious*. A spurious relationship occurs when there is not a 'true' relationship between two variables that appear to be connected. The variation exhibited by each variable is affected by a common variable. Imagine that the first five children are boys and the second five are girls. This would suggest that gender has a considerable impact on both variables. Boys are more likely than girls both to watch more television violence *and* to exhibit greater aggressiveness. There is still a slight tendency for watching more violence and aggression to be related for both boys and girls, but these tendencies are far less pronounced than for the ten children as a whole. In other words, gender affects each of the two variables. It is because boys are much more likely than girls both to watch more television violence and to behave aggressively that Figure 1.2 illustrates the nature of such a spurious relationship.

Third, it is necessary to establish that the cause precedes the effect, i.e. the *time order* of the two related variables. In other words, we must establish that aggression is a consequence of watching televised violence and not the other way around. An effect simply cannot come before a cause. This may seem an extremely obvious criterion that is easy to demonstrate, but as we will see, it constitutes a very considerable problem for non-experimental research designs.

Causality and experimental designs

A research design provides the basic structure within which an investigation takes place. While a number of different designs can be found, a basic

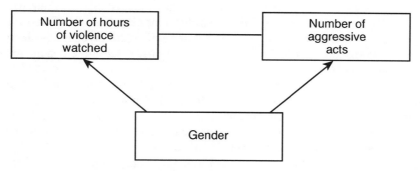

Figure 1.2 A spurious relationship

distinction is that between experimental and non-experimental research designs of which the survey/correlational is the most prominent. In an experiment, the elucidation of cause-and-effect is an explicit feature of the framework. The term *internal validity* is often employed as an attribute of research and indicates whether the causal findings deriving from an investigation are relatively unequivocal. An internally valid study is one which provides firm evidence of cause and effect. Experimental designs are especially strong in respect of internal validity; this attribute is scarcely surprising in view of the fact that they have been developed specifically in order to generate findings which indicate cause and effect.

Imagine that we wanted to establish that watching violence on television enhances aggression in children, we might conceive of the following study. We bring together a group of ten children. They are allowed to interact and play for two hours, during which the number of aggressive acts committed by each child is recorded by observers, and the children are then exposed to a television programme with a great deal of violence. Such exposure is often called the experimental treatment. They are then allowed a further two-hour period of play and interaction. Aggressive behaviour is recorded in exactly the same way. What we have here is a sequence which runs

$$\text{Obs}_1 \ \text{Exp} \ \text{Obs}_2$$

where Obs_1 is the initial measurement of aggressive behaviour (often called the *pre-test*), Exp is the experimental treatment which allows the independent variable to be introduced, and Obs_2 is the subsequent measurement of aggression (often called the *post-test*).

Let us say that Obs_2 is 30 per cent higher than Obs_1, suggesting that aggressive behaviour has increased substantially. Does this mean that we can say that the increase in aggression was caused by the violence? We cannot make such an attribution because there are alternative explanations of the presumed causal connection. The children may well have become more aggressive over time simply as a consequence of being together and becoming irritated by each other. The researchers may not have given the children enough food or drink and this may have contributed to their bad humour. There is even the possibility that different observers were used for the pre- and post-tests who used different criteria of aggressiveness. So long as we cannot discount these alternative explanations, a definitive conclusion about causation cannot be proffered.

Anyone familiar with the natural sciences will know that an important facet of a properly conducted experiment is that it is controlled so that potentially contaminating factors are minimized. In order to control the contaminating factors that have been mentioned (and therefore to allow the alternative explanations to be rejected), a *control group* is required. This group has exactly the same cluster of experiences as the group which receives the first treatment − known as the *experimental group* − but it does not receive the experimental treatment. In the context of our imaginary television study, we now have two groups of children who are exposed to exactly the same conditions, except that one group watches the violent films (the experimental group) and the second group has no experimental treatment (the control group). This design is illustrated in Figure 1.3. The two groups' experiences have to be as similar as possible, so that only the experimental group's exposure to the experimental treatment distinguishes them.

It is also necessary to ensure that the members of the two groups are as similar as possible. This is achieved by taking a sample of children and *randomly assigning* them to either the experimental or the control group. If random assignment is not carried out, there is always the possibility that differences between the two groups can be attributed to divergent personal or other characteristics. For example, there may be more boys than girls in one group, or differences in the ethnic composition of the two groups. Such differences in personal or background characteristics would mean that the ensuing findings could not be validly attributed to the independent variable, and that factor alone.

Let us say that the difference between Obs_1 and Obs_2 is 30 per cent and between Obs_3 and Obs_4 is 28 per cent. If this were the case, we would conclude that the difference between the two groups is so small that it appears that the experimental treatment (Exp) has made no difference to the increase in aggression; in other words, aggression in the experimental group would probably have increased anyway. The frustration of being together too long or insufficient food or drink or some other factor probably accounts for the $Obs_2 - Obs_1$ difference. However, if the difference between Obs_3 and Obs_4 was only 3 per cent, we would be much more prepared to say that watching violence has increased aggression in the experimental group. It would suggest that around 27 per cent of the increase in aggressive behaviour in the experimental group (i.e. $30 - 3$) can be attributed to the experimental treatment. Differences between experimental and control groups are not usually as clear cut as in this illustration, since often the difference between the groups is fairly small. Statistical tests are necessary

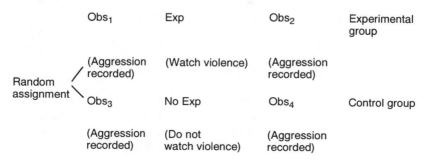

Figure 1.3 An experiment

in this context to determine the probability of obtaining such a difference by chance. Such tests are described in Chapters 7 and 9.

In this imaginary investigation, the three criteria of causality are met, and therefore if we did find that the increase in the dependent variable was considerably greater for the experimental group than the control group we could have considerable confidence in saying that watching television violence caused greater aggression. First, a relationship is established by demonstrating that subjects watching television violence exhibited greater aggression than those who did not. Second, the combination of a control group and random assignment allows the possibility of the relationship being spurious to be eliminated, since other factors which may impinge on the two variables would apply equally to the two groups. Third, the time order of the variables is demonstrated by the increase in aggressive behaviour succeeding the experimental group's exposure to the television violence. Precisely because the independent variable is manipulated by the researcher, time order can be easily demonstrated, since the effects of the manipulation can be directly gauged. Thus, we could say confidently that Watching television violence → Aggressive behaviour since the investigation exhibits a high degree of internal validity.

There is a variety of different types of experimental design. These are briefly summarized in Figure 1.4. In the first design, there is no pre-test, just a comparison between the experimental and control groups in terms of the dependent variable. With the second design, there is a number of groups. This is a frequent occurrence in the social sciences where one is more likely

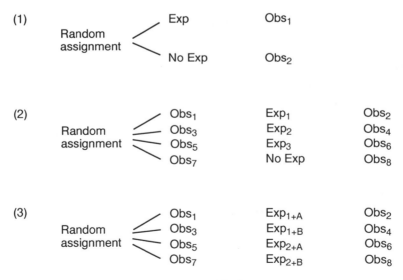

Figure 1.4   Three types of experimental design

to be interested in different levels or types of the independent variable rather than simply its presence or absence. Thus, in the television violence context, we could envisage four groups consisting of different degrees of violence. The third design, a *factorial* design, occurs where the researcher is interested in the effects of more than one independent variable on the dependent variable. The researcher might be interested in whether the presence of adults in close proximity reduces children's propensity to behave aggressively. We might then have four possible combinations deriving from the manipulation of each of the two independent variables. For example, Exp_{1+A} would mean a combination of watching violence and adults in close proximity; Exp_{1+B} would be watching violence and no adults in close proximity.

SURVEY DESIGN AND CAUSALITY

When a social survey is carried out, the nature of the research design is very different from the experiment. The survey usually entails the collection of data on a number of variables at a single juncture. The researcher might be interested in the relationship between people's political attitudes and behaviour on the one hand, and a number of other variables such as each respondent's occupation, social background, race, gender, age, and various non-political attitudes. But none of these variables is manipulated as in the experiment. Indeed, many variables cannot be manipulated and their relationships with other variables can only be examined through a social survey. We cannot make some people old, others young, and still others middle-aged and then observe the effects of age on political attitudes. Moreover, not only are variables not manipulated in a social-survey study, data on variables are simultaneously collected so that it is not possible to establish a time order to the variables in question. In an experiment, a time order can be discerned in that the effect of the manipulated independent variable on the dependent variable is directly observed. These characteristics are not solely associated with research using interviews or questionnaires. Many studies using archival statistics, such as those collected by governments and organizations, exhibit the same characteristics, since data are often available in relation to a number of variables for a particular year.

Survey designs are often called *correlational* designs to denote the tendency for such research to be able to reveal relationships between variables and to draw attention to their limited capacity in connection with the elucidation of causal processes. Precisely because in survey research variables are not manipulated (and often are not capable of manipulation), the ability of the researcher to impute cause and effect is limited. Let us say that we collect data on manual workers' levels of job satisfaction and productivity in a firm. We may find, through the kinds of techniques examined in Chapter 8 of this book, that there is a strong relationship between the two, suggesting that workers who exhibit high levels of job satisfaction also have high levels of productivity. We can say that there is a relationship between the two variables (see Figure 1.5), but as we have seen, this is only a first step in the demonstration of causality. It is also necessary to confirm that the relationship is non-spurious. For example, could it be that workers who have been with the firm a long time are both more satisfied and more productive (see Figure 1.6)? The ways in which the possibility of non-spuriousness can be checked are examined in Chapter 10.

However, the third hurdle – establishing that the putative cause precedes the putative effect – is extremely difficult. The problem is that either of the two possibilities depicted in Figure 1.7 may be true. Job satisfaction may cause greater productivity, but it has long been recognized that the causal connection may work the other way around (i.e. if you are good at your job you often enjoy it more). Because data relating to each of the two variables have been simultaneously collected, it is not possible to arbitrate between the two versions of causality presented in Figure 1.7. One way of dealing with this problem is through a reconstruction of the likely causal order of the variables involved. Sometimes this process of inference can be fairly uncontroversial. For example, if we find a relationship between race and

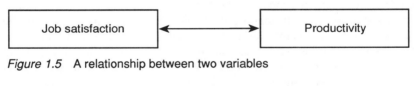

Figure 1.5   A relationship between two variables

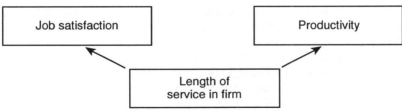

Figure 1.6   Is the relationship spurious?

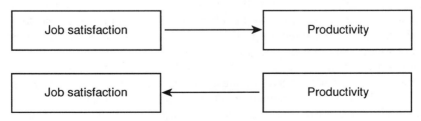

Figure 1.7   Two possible causal interpretations of a relationship

number of years spent in formal schooling, we can say that the former affects the latter. However, this modelling of likely causal connections is more fraught when it is not obvious which variable precedes the other, as with the relationship between job satisfaction and productivity. When such difficulties arise, it may be necessary to include a second wave of data collection in relation to the same respondents in order to see, for example, whether the impact of job satisfaction on subsequent productivity is greater than the impact of productivity on subsequent job satisfaction. Such a design is known as a *panel design* (Cramer, 1994a), but is not very common in the social sciences. The bulk of the discussion in this book about non-experimental research will be concerned with the survey/correlational design in which data on variables are simultaneously collected.

The procedures involved in making causal inferences from survey data are examined in Chapter 10 in the context of the multivariate analysis of relationships among variables. The chief point to be gleaned from the preceding discussion is that the extraction of causal connections among variables can be undertaken with greater facility in the context of experimental research than when survey data are being analysed.

EXERCISES

1. What is the chief difference between univariate, bivariate and multivariate quantitative data analysis?

2. Why is random assignment crucial to a true experimental design?

3. A researcher collects data by interview on a sample of households to find out if people who read 'quality' daily newspapers are more knowledgeable about politics than people who read 'tabloid' newspapers daily. The hunch was confirmed. People who read the quality newspapers were twice as likely to respond accurately to a series of questions designed to test their political knowledge. The researcher concludes that the quality dailies induce higher levels of political knowledge than the tabloids. Assess this reasoning.

Chapter 2

Analysing data with computers
First steps with Minitab

Since the different kinds of statistics to be described in this book will be carried out with one of the most widely used and comprehensive statistical programs in the social sciences, Minitab, we will begin by outlining what it entails. This program is available for both personal and mainframe (or multi-user) computers. It is being continuously updated and so there are various versions in existence. Currently there are two main kinds of *operating system* for computers. The traditional system, still employed by mainframe (or multi-user) computers, requires *commands* to be typed in. The more recent system uses *menus* from which commands can be selected by *keys* or a *mouse*, although commands can also be typed in. This latter system was originally developed for Macintosh personal computers and is now available for a Windows environment on IBM-compatible personal computers having a 386 or higher processor. At the time of writing, the latest revision of Minitab is *Release 10Xtra for Windows and Macintosh* (Minitab Inc., 1995). *Release 9* is available for some kinds of mainframe (or multi-user) computers (Minitab Inc., 1992) and *Release 7* (Minitab Inc., 1989) for others. There is also a *Release 8* (Minitab Inc., 1991) for certain types of IBM-compatible personal computers and a *Release 7* for others. Apart from the operating systems, the differences between these releases are few and relatively minor for the purposes of this book. Consequently, any differences are described as they arise.

The great advantage of using a package like Minitab is that it will enable you to score and to analyse quantitative data very quickly and in many different ways once you have learned how. In other words, it will help you to eliminate those long hours spent working out scores, carrying out involved calculations, and making those inevitable mistakes that so frequently occur. It will also provide you with the opportunity for using more complicated and often more appropriate statistical techniques which you would not have dreamt of attempting otherwise.

There is, of course, what may seem to be a strong initial disadvantage in using computer programs to analyse data and that is you will have to learn how to run these programs. The time spent doing this, however, will be much less than doing these same calculations by hand. In addition, you will have picked up some knowledge which should be of value to you in a world where the use of computers is fast becoming increasingly common. The ability to do things quickly and with little effort is also much more fun and often easier than you might at first imagine.

When mastering a new skill, like Minitab, it is inevitable that you will make mistakes which can be frustrating and off-putting. While this is something we all do, it may seem that we make many more mistakes when learning to use a computer than we do carrying out other activities. The reason for this is that programs require instructions to be given in a very precise form and usually in a particular sequence for them to work. This precision may be less obvious or true of other everyday things we do. It is worth remembering, however, that these errors will not harm the computer or its program in any way.

To make as few mistakes as possible, it is important at this stage to follow precisely the instructions laid down for the examples in this and subsequent chapters in terms of the characters and spaces that go to make up each line. Although 'bugs' do sometimes occur, errors are usually the result of something you have done and not the fault of the machine or the program. The program will tell you what the error is if there is something wrong with the form of the instructions you have given it, but not if you have told it to add up the wrong set of numbers. In other words, it questions the presentation but not the objectives of the instructions.

GAINING ACCESS TO MINITAB

To use Minitab, it is necessary to have access to it via a personal computer or a *terminal* connected to a mainframe (or multi-user) computer. Both a computer terminal and a personal computer consist of a *keyboard* on which you type in your instructions and usually a video display unit (VDU) or television-like *screen* which shows you what you have typed. While the amount of information shown at any one moment on the screen is necessarily limited, further information can be brought into view with the appropriate use of the keys or the mouse. The computer you are connected to will have a *high speed* printer which you can instruct to print out any information you have stored in it. Indeed, if you want to keep a record of what you have done when using a screen, then this usually can be carried out by typing a few instructions. It should be relatively easy to find out what these are from someone familiar with your computer.

Keyboards are used to type or put in (hence the term *input*) the data that you want to analyse. If you have a small amount of data, it is most probably quicker to do this yourself. If, however, you are intending to collect and analyse a large amount of data, then it may be more convenient to have this done for you by people who provide such a service. You can also use the keyboard to type in or write any Minitab commands that you want to run.

Since different makes of computers have different instructions or programs for operating them which also change from time to time, it is not possible in a book of this size to provide you with all the information you need to use them. Your local expert should be able to show you how to do this. However, you might find it helpful to have a general idea of how to operate a computer.

First, if you are using a mainframe (or multi-user) computer, you usually have to register as a user just as you do when using a library or bank. You will be given an identification label or *ID* which may be your surname and initials, a *password* which you can change so that only you will know it, and some space to store information in, which is sometimes referred to as your *directory* or *file space*. Every time you want to use a terminal, you have to quote your ID followed by your password. This is often called *logging on* or *in*. The idea of the password is to prevent unauthorized people from using the computer and having access to your file space.

Second, you will have to learn how to store or to file information in this space as well as how to change it and get rid of or delete it. In other words, you will need to know how to use an *editor* or editing system which does this. The information is stored in *files* which will generally consist of your data and any Minitab programs or *macros* you want to run. In order to work with them, it is necessary to give each of them a short name. The name should be of a form which helps you remember what is contained in the file to which it refers.

Third, you will need to learn the few commands necessary to run Minitab and to print any results of which you wish to keep a hard copy. While this might seem like a lot to learn at first, you will soon get the hang of it.

THE DATA FILE

Before you can analyse your data, you need to create a file which holds them. The data have to be put into a file space which consists of a large number of rows, comprising a maximum of eighty columns in many computers. The data for the same variable are always placed in the same column(s) in a row and a row always contains the data of the same object of analysis or *case*. Cases are often people, but can be any unit of interest such as families, schools, hospitals, regions or nations.

To illustrate the way in which these files are created, we will use an imaginary set of data from a questionnaire study referred to as the Job Survey. The data relating to this study derive from two sources: a questionnaire study of employees who answer questions about themselves and a questionnaire study of their supervisors who answer questions relating to each of the employees. The questions asked are shown in Appendix 2.1 at the end of this chapter, while the coding of the information collected is presented in Table 2.1. The cases consist of people, traditionally called *respondents* by sociologists and *subjects* by psychologists whose preferred term now is *participants*. Although questionnaire data have been used as an example, it should be recognized that Minitab and the data analysis

Table 2.1 The Job Survey data (see text and Appendix 2.1, p. 35, for explanation)

01	1	1	8300	29	01	4	*	3	4	4	2	4	2	2	2	2	3	2	2	3	*	1	07
02	2	1	7300	26	05	2	*	*	2	3	2	2	1	2	3	4	4	4	1	3	4	4	08
03	3	1	8900	40	05	4	4	4	4	1	2	1	2	2	2	1	2	3	1	4	3	4	00
04	3	1	8200	46	15	2	2	5	2	4	1	2	2	2	3	2	2	3	2	3	3	4	04
05	2	2	9300	63	36	4	3	4	4	1	2	3	3	3	4	5	5	4	1	3	5	3	00
06	1	1	8000	54	31	2	2	5	3	3	2	1	1	2	4	4	4	1	1	3	4	01
07	1	1	8300	29	02	*	3	3	2	3	2	2	3	2	3	5	4	2	2	3	5	2	00
08	3	1	8800	35	02	5	2	2	4	2	3	4	3	2	3	3	3	2	2	3	4	4	02
09	2	2	8800	33	04	3	3	1	2	4	2	3	4	1	2	2	3	2	2	2	1	1	05
10	2	2	6900	27	06	4	3	2	3	3	2	1	3	2	3	4	3	5	1	2	2	4	04
11	1	1	7100	29	04	2	2	4	1	4	2	1	1	2	5	4	3	4	2	2	2	3	08
12	2	1	*	19	02	1	1	5	2	4	1	1	1	1	3	4	3	3	1	3	2	3	04
13	4	1	9000	55	35	3	3	3	4	2	2	2	3	2	5	5	5	4	1	4	3	5	01
14	1	2	8500	29	01	2	3	4	2	4	2	2	3	1	4	3	4	4	1	1	2	2	00
15	3	1	9100	48	08	3	3	2	2	1	3	2	4	4	2	3	3	3	2	4	5	5	01
16	2	1	7900	32	07	3	3	4	2	2	2	3	1	2	4	2	2	2	2	2	2	3	04
17	1	1	8300	48	14	3	3	3	2	4	1	2	2	2	4	5	4	4	1	2	5	3	01
18	1	2	6700	18	01	2	2	4	2	4	2	3	2	2	5	5	5	1	1	2	3	3	06
19	3	2	7500	28	02	4	4	2	3	2	3	4	3	3	3	2	3	2	2	3	4	4	03
20	3	2	8800	37	01	3	2	3	3	3	3	2	1	2	5	4	4	5	1	1	4	1	03
21	1	1	*	43	16	1	4	4	3	3	3	2	3	3	3	2	4	4	2	4	5	2	06
22	1	1	8700	39	06	3	2	3	2	3	3	2	2	3	4	3	5	3	2	1	1	5	05
23	1	1	9000	53	05	1	4	3	4	4	4	3	2	2	3	5	4	2	1	3	3	5	13
24	2	2	8000	34	09	1	3	4	1	5	1	2	1	1	3	4	4	3	2	1	3	3	09
25	3	2	8500	43	17	4	3	4	5	3	3	1	3	2	3	2	4	4	1	3	5	2	02
26	1	1	7000	21	01	4	4	2	2	3	4	3	3	4	2	3	2	2	1	2	5	5	03
27	1	1	8100	50	28	3	2	3	3	4	2	1	1	2	5	5	5	4	1	2	2	4	08
28	1	2	6200	31	09	1	2	5	1	4	2	2	1	2	4	4	5	4	2	3	5	5	00
29	1	1	6800	31	12	3	4	3	3	4	3	2	3	2	3	1	2	1	3	5	4	06
30	2	2	8200	52	21	2	3	2	3	2	3	3	3	3	2	2	2	2	4	4	3	10
31	1	1	7200	54	12	3	5	3	3	3	3	2	3	2	4	3	4	4	2	4	4	2	*
32	3	2	6200	28	10	2	2	4	1	5	1	2	2	2	3	3	3	2	1	2	4	4	09
33	2	2	8300	50	23	4	4	3	4	3	4	2	3	4	3	3	3	3	2	3	4	5	05
34	2	2	8000	52	21	5	4	3	3	3	4	3	3	2	3	3	2	1	3	2	5	04
35	1	2	7500	40	21	1	1	3	4	3	3	2	3	2	3	2	2	1	2	2	3	06
36	2	1	5900	19	01	2	2	5	2	4	2	1	2	2	5	5	5	5	2	2	3	2	03
37	2	1	8800	38	04	5	4	1	4	3	5	3	3	3	2	1	2	1	2	4	4	4	08
38	2	1	9000	61	41	5	3	2	4	1	3	2	2	2	2	1	2	2	3	5	4	03
39	1	2	7800	37	08	3	2	4	2	3	2	3	3	2	4	5	4	5	1	3	4	4	08
40	2	1	6700	31	05	2	2	5	2	5	2	2	2	1	5	5	5	4	2	1	1	2	05
41	2	2	7500	43	21	4	3	2	2	2	3	4	2	3	3	3	3	3	1	1	4	2	00
42	3	1	6800	23	03	1	2	5	3	5	1	1	2	1	4	4	4	5	1	3	2	2	08
43	2	2	7000	27	05	1	1	4	1	4	1	1	1	2	4	5	4	4	2	1	2	1	09
44	1	1	7500	28	07	3	3	1	3	3	3	5	3	3	1	2	2	1	1	2	4	3	09
45	1	1	6600	00	10	1	1	4	1	4	2	2	2	4	2	5	5	1	4	1	3	10
46	3	1	6700	18	01	4	2	3	4	2	2	3	3	2	4	5	4	1	4	3	4	03
47	1	2	10300	48	23	3	4	3	3	3	2	2	3	2	1	3	2	2	4	4	3	08
48	1	2	6800	29	10	2	3	5	4	4	2	2	1	3	4	2	2	1	3	4	4	11
49	1	2	7300	42	10	2	2	3	3	3	2	2	1	2	5	5	5	2	1	4	4	00

(Continued)

Table 2.1   Continued

50	1	1	9100	53	12	4	5	2	5	1	4	5	3	4	2	2	2	2	2	4	4	4	01
51	1	1	7600	32	12	3	2	4	1	4	3	2	2	3	3	3	4	2	1	2	3	2	01
52	1	2	6500	31	02	1	3	5	1	5	2	2	3	2	5	4	4	5	2	1	3	1	08
53	1	1	9500	55	19	5	4	3	5	3	5	4	3	3	3	4	3	3	1	3	4	3	00
54	3	2	7400	26	08	4	4	1	3	3	4	5	2	3	1	2	1	2	2	4	3	3	02
55	1	2	8600	53	22	3	4	2	3	1	3	4	4	3	2	1	2	2	1	3	5	5	00
56	1	1	7800	51	31	2	3	3	3	3	3	2	4	4	5	4	5	5	1	4	1	1	08
57	1	1	7700	48	23	3	1	4	3	4	2	2	2	2	5	5	4	5	1	1	3	2	06
58	1	2	6900	48	28	1	1	4	1	5	2	2	2	1	5	5	5	5	2	1	4	3	04
59	2	2	7900	62	40	1	2	3	2	5	2	2	3	2	5	4	4	5	2	1	1	5	07
60	2	1	8700	57	13	2	3	4	2	3	2	3	1	2	3	3	4	3	1	4	4	1	04
61	1	2	8900	42	20	5	4	2	2	2	3	3	3	3	2	1	2	4	2	3	3	3	02
62	1	1	7100	21	02	1	2	3	1	4	2	3	2	1	3	3	3	3	1	4	2	2	00
63	3	2	6400	26	08	3	1	3	2	4	1	2	1	1	2	3	3	2	1	4	1	1	04
64	1	2	6800	46	00	1	2	5	2	4	3	1	2	2	5	5	5	5	2	2	3	4	05
65	1	2	10500	59	21	4	3	2	4	2	2	2	3	3	2	3	2	2	2	4	5	1	04
66	4	2	7100	30	08	0	3	3	2	4	2	3	2	2	5	4	4	4	1	2	2	3	02
67	1	1	7300	29	08	3	2	2	3	3	2	3	2	1	5	3	4	3	2	1	4	5	10
68	3	1	6900	45	09	2	3	4	3	4	3	3	3	3	4	3	3	2	2	3	4		09
69	3	1	8000	53	30	3	2	5	3	2	2	1	2	2	4	5	3	4	2	2	1	4	02
70	1	1	6900	47	22	2	3	4	2	5	2	3	4	2	4	3	5	4	1	2	4	4	11

procedures described in this book may be used with other forms of quantitative data, such as official statistics or observational measures.

Since it is easier to analyse data consisting of numbers rather than a mixture of numbers and other characters such as alphabetic letters, all of the variables or answers in the Job Survey have been coded as numbers. So, for instance, each of the five possible answers to the first question has been given a number varying from 1 to 5. If the respondent has put a tick against White/European, then this response is coded as 1. (Although the use of these ethnic groups may be questioned, as may many of the concepts in the social sciences, this kind of information is sometimes collected in surveys and is used here as an example of a categorical variable. We shall shorten the name of the first category to 'white' throughout the book to simplify matters.) It is preferable in designing questionnaires that, wherever possible, numbers should be clearly assigned to particular answers so that little else needs to be done to the data before it is typed in by someone else. Before multiple copies of the questionnaire are made it is always worth checking with the person who types in this information that this has been adequately done. Missing values in Minitab should be represented with an asterisk (*).

It is advisable to give each subject an identifying number to be able to refer to them if necessary. This number should be placed in the first few columns of each row or line. Since there are seventy subjects, only columns 1 and 2 need to be used for this purpose. If there were 100 subjects, then the first three columns would be required to record this information as the largest number consists of three digits.

As previously mentioned, there are two main kinds of operating system. The first requires commands to be typed in after a *prompt* appears on the screen. Prompts in Minitab are short or abbreviated words written in capitals followed by a right facing arrow (e.g. **MTB >**). To call up this version of Minitab, we usually have to type its name and press the *Return* or *Enter* key. On many keyboards, the Return key is identified by having a ↵ sign on it. After the title of the program has been shown, the prompt **MTB >** together with a flashing *cursor* will appear. The cursor is the sign which indicates your position on the screen where you may initiate an action such as typing in a command.

The second system allows commands to be selected from words or *icons* presented as a menu in a window on the screen. Commands can usually be selected by moving the cursor on to them with either the keys or, more normally, the mouse, and then pressing the Return key or the left button on the mouse, or in Windows 95 by simply selecting the next option. Choosing options with the mouse is generally easier than doing this with keys since it simply involves moving the mouse appropriately. With keys, however, some options are chosen by pressing the relevant cursor keys while others are selected by pressing up to two keys other than the cursor keys. The cursor keys are usually on the right hand side of the keyboard and have arrows on them pointing in the direction in which the cursor is to be moved. You may prefer to use the mouse for some operations and the keys for others.

However, in the Windows version of Minitab, commands can also be typed in if the window called **Session** is selected. To invoke the Windows version when in the windows environment, select the appropriate **Minitab** icon. In *Release 9* two overlapping windows appear as shown in Figure 2.1. The front one is the **Data** window while immediately behind it is the **Session** window. To select the

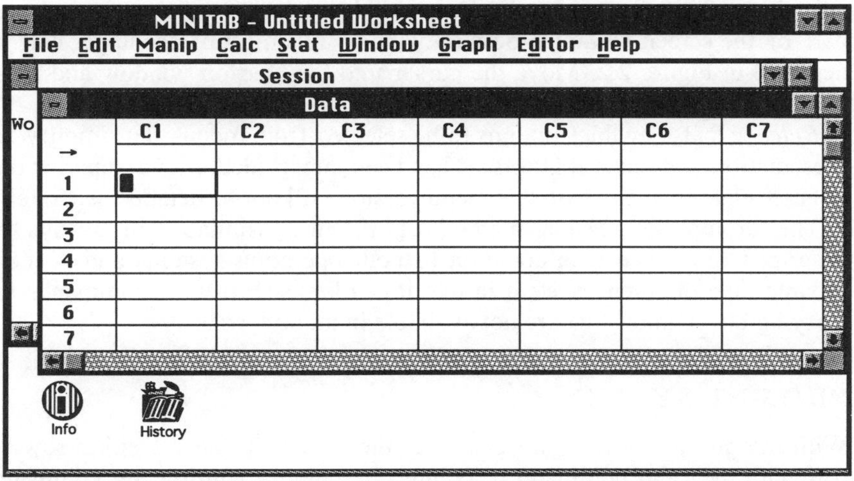

Figure 2.1 Opening **Session** and **Data** window in *Release 9*

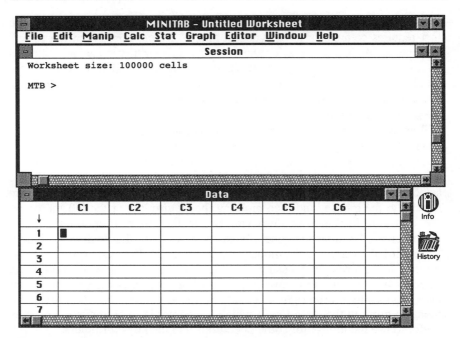

Figure 2.2   Opening **Session** and **Data** window in *Release 10*

Session window with the mouse, move the cursor on to the *bar* containing this word or title and then either pressing the left button on the mouse or the Return key when the **MTB** > prompt will be presented together with the cursor. The key strokes for carrying out this action are described in Appendix 2.2.

In *Release 10*, however, the **Data** window occupies most of the lower half of the screen while the **Session** window fills most of the upper half as depicted in Figure 2.2. Move the cursor into the **Session** window and press the left button on the mouse.

Release 8 also enables options to be selected from menus. To simplify the presentation and since this format has been superseded with a superior one in later releases, the use of this menu version will not be detailed separately.

The prompt or session method of running Minitab will always be described first since it is common to both operating systems and is more flexible than the menu system in that it can be used to write commands for carrying out routines that are not available in menu format.

PROMPT SYSTEM

With the prompt system, we can enter the data in Table 2.1 either row by row with the **read** command or column by column with the **set** command. Note that columns in Minitab refer to the values of a variable and are specified by the letter **c** followed by their respective number so that the first column is called **c1**, the second **c2** and so on. The number of columns (or variables) per row (or case) is restricted to 1,000 in *Releases 7* to *10*.

With the **read** command we need to list the columns for each case. Since in this example we have 24 columns of data, we can list the 24 columns on the **read** command by naming each one separately. Each column label needs to be separated by a blank space or a comma. Consequently, after the **MTB >** prompt, we can type

MTB > read c1,c2,c3,c4,c5,c6,c7,c8,c9,c10,c11,c12,c13,c14,c15, c16,c17,c18,c19,c20,c21,c22,c23,c24

Alternatively, as the columns are consecutive, we can list them implicitly by specifying only the first and last column (with a hyphen between the two), so that the **read** command becomes shortened to

MTB > read c1-c24

Note that Minitab commands have been printed in small letters throughout the book to distinguish them from Minitab prompts which are displayed on the screen in capital letters followed by a right facing arrow. The command is completed by pressing the Return key, when the **DATA>** prompt will appear.

If, before pressing the Return key, you type the wrong information (say, **a1** instead of **c1**), use the backspace delete key to delete back to and including the mistake (**a**) and type in the correct details. The backspace delete key usually has a leftward facing arrow sign [←] on it to identify it. If, after pressing the Return key, you realize you have made a mistake (say, **a1** instead of **c1**) type in the correct command when the **MTB >** prompt reappears. If, on the other hand, you typed in the wrong column (say, **c2** instead of **c1**), the **DATA>** prompt will appear in which case you need to type **end** after it when the **MTB >** prompt will be shown. You then type in the correct command.

After listing the appropriate column numbers, we type in the first row of data (separating each datum with either a blank space or a comma) as follows

DATA> 01 1 1 8300 29 01 4 ∗ 3 4 4 2 4 2 2 2 2 3 2 2 3 ∗ 1 07

To enter this line of data, we press the Return key. We proceed in this way until we have typed in all 70 rows of data.

If in a row you type in fewer values than the number of columns, you will receive the following error message

∗ ERROR ∗ INCOMPLETE ROW -REENTER

whereas if you type in too many values, the error message will be

∗ ERROR ∗ TOO MANY VALUES -REENTER ROW

Simply type in the values again after the **DATA>** prompt.

When we have finished typing in the data, we indicate this by typing **end** after the **DATA>** prompt

DATA> end

A message will appear which reads

70 ROWS READ

To display the data we have typed in, we simply type **print** after the **MTB >** prompt and the columns we want to see. So, to show the first, third and fifth columns, we need only type

MTB > print c1 c3 c5

Note that the output also gives the row number so that you may feel it unnecessary to input the case number if it is the same as the row number.

If you realize you have typed in a wrong value (say, 27 instead of 29 in column 5 for the age of case 1), you can correct this by typing

MTB > let c5 (1) = 29

where the value in brackets refers to the row number and the value after the equals sign is the correct value. You can check that this has been done by printing **c5**

MTB > print c5

To type in data with the **set** command, we first specify the column (say, **c5**)

MTB > set c5

after which we press the Return key when the **DATA>** prompt appears. We type in the values for that column, i.e.

DATA> 29 26 40 46 63 54 29 35 33 27 29 19 55 29 48 32 48 18 28 37 43 39 53 34 43 21 50 31 31 52 54 28 50 52 40 19 38 61 37 31 43 23 27 28 ∗ 18 48 29 42 53 32 31 55 26 53 51 48 48 62 57 42 21 26 46 59 30 29 45 53 47

Then we press the Return key, and type **end** after the **DATA>** prompt.

If we had more than ninety-six cases, we would have to add an ampersand (**&**) after entering the age of the ninety-sixth case, press Return when another **DATA>** prompt would appear and then continue to add more ages. If we added the ampersand after the ninety-seventh case, the data in the previous row will be ignored. In other words, when entering a long column of data, make sure that you add the ampersand at least two spaces before the end of the row.

You can name your columns with the **name** command on which you list the column number and a name in single quotes of up to eight characters.

So, the command for calling **c5 'age'** and **c7 'commit'** (for organizational commitment) is

MTB > name c5 'age' c7 'commit'

Once a column is named we can refer to it either by the name in single quotation marks or the column number. So, we can print **c5** and **c7** by typing

MTB > print 'age' 'commit'

If we do not save the set of data we have just typed in we will lose it when we leave Minitab and we will have to type it in again should we wish to carry out some further analyses on a later occasion. Since alternative ways of analysing data often occur to us later on either as the result of our own thoughts or the suggestions of others, it is almost always desirable to save data. Information in computers is stored in *files* which we have to name in order to retrieve them. To save a set of data we use the **save** command followed by the name we wish to call it placed within single quotation marks. The name consists of a prefix or *stem* of up to eight characters followed by a full stop and a suffix or *extension* of up to three characters. To remind us of the content and the nature of the file, it is conventional to have the stem name refer to the content of the file and the extension name to the kind of file it is.

The **save** command stores the data as a *worksheet* which is written in binary code and which cannot be read as simple text. If we do not give this worksheet an extension name, then Minitab will automatically add the extension **.MTW** which is short for **M**initab **w**orksheet. Consequently, we shall follow this practice and use the extension **.mtw** for naming our worksheets. As the data in our example refer to the raw data of our job survey, the stem name could be **jsrd** which is an abbreviation of '**j**ob **s**urvey **r**aw **d**ata'. Since Minitab accepts letters written in capitals or upper case (for example, JSRD.MTW) and small or lower case (for example, jsrd.mtw), lower-case letters will be used to make typing easier for you. The command for saving these data as a worksheet is

MTB > save 'jsrd.mtw'

If we are working on a personal computer, it is worthwhile storing a copy of the data file on a separate *floppy disk* in case the file stored in our computer is deleted or lost. The floppy disk is inserted into a slot called a *drive*. This is done only after the computer has been switched on. The disk may first have to be *formatted* if it is new or if its present format is not compatible with the machine. It is preferable to do this before entering Minitab so that any files can be stored direct on to the floppy disk when you are using Minitab. To store a file on to a floppy disk, use the same **save** command but insert the letter of the drive followed by a colon after the opening quote of the name and before the stem. So, to store this file on the floppy disk in drive *a*, the command would be

MTB > save 'a:jsrd.mtw'

In a session of Minitab we may wish to work on a number of different data files. To call up a different file in the same session or to call a file in a new session we use the **retrieve** command followed by the name of the file (including the disk drive if it is on a floppy disk). So, to call up the file **jsrd.mtw** on the floppy disk in drive *a*, the command would be

MTB > retrieve 'a:jsrd.mtw'

Note that full command words longer than four letters can generally be shortened to the first four letters of the word as the subsequent letters are ignored. Thus, for example, the word **retrieve** will work if shortened to **retr** or misspelt as **retrive**.

A full listing of the variables and their Minitab names is given in Table 2.2. It is important to remember that the same name cannot be used for different files or variables. Thus, for example, you could not use the name **'satis'** to refer to all four of the questions which measure job satisfaction. You would need to distinguish them in some way such as calling the answer to the first question **'satis1'**, the answer to the second one **'satis2'**, and so on. Of course, it is possible to shorten them further. However, to make it easier for you to remember what we are referring to, we have kept them as long and as meaningful as possible. Since it is easier to work with names than with column numbers, we will name all the columns as shown in Table 2.2 and save the names in the worksheet **'jsrd.mtw'**. If you forget the column number or name for any variable you can always obtain the complete list with the prompt command **info**. The output for this command is displayed in Table 2.3. This output also gives the overall number of values for each variable and the number of missing values.

Data are often stored in a simple text or *ASCII* file. ASCII stands for *A*merican *S*tandard *C*ode for *I*nformation *I*nterchange and is widely used for transferring information from one computer to another. If, for example, we had collected a large amount of data and if we had access to a service which typed in those data for us, then this information may be stored for us in a text file which we can transfer to the computer we are using. The conventional extension name of such files is often **dat** which is short for **dat**a. If the data in Table 2.1 had been stored as a text file, then we might call it **jsr.dat**. To read such a file from our computer into a Minitab session, we would use the **read** command which lists the name of the file in single quotes together with the columns of data we want to read. So if we wanted to read all 24 columns, the command would be

MTB > read 'jsr.dat' into c1-c24

Table 2.2   The Minitab names and column numbers of the Job Survey variables

Variable name	Minitab name	Column number
Identification number	**id**	**c1**
Ethnic group	**ethnicgp**	**c2**
Gender	**gender**	**c3**
Gross annual income	**income**	**c4**
Age	**age**	**c5**
Years worked	**years**	**c6**
Organizational commitment	**commit**	**c7**
Job-satisfaction scale		
Item 1	**satis1**	**c8**
Item 2	**satis2**	**c9**
Item 3	**satis3**	**c10**
Item 4	**satis4**	**c11**
Job-autonomy scale		
Item 1	**autonom1**	**c12**
Item 2	**autonom2**	**c13**
Item 3	**autonom3**	**c14**
Item 4	**autonom4**	**c15**
Job-routine scale		
Item 1	**routine1**	**c16**
Item 2	**routine2**	**c17**
Item 3	**routine3**	**c18**
Item 4	**routine4**	**c19**
Attendance at meeting	**attend**	**c20**
Rated skill	**skill**	**c21**
Rated productivity	**prody**	**c22**
Rated quality	**qual**	**c23**
Absenteeism	**absence**	**c24**

Note that the word **into** can be omitted. If we find it easier, we can then name the column numbers as before and save the text file as a worksheet.

To leave Minitab, we use the command **stop**

MTB > stop

In the Windows version, the program will ask you if you wish to save the data as a worksheet if you have not already done so.

MENU SYSTEM

The opening windows differ slightly for *Releases 9* and *10* of Minitab for Windows. In *Release 9*, two overlapping windows appear. The front one is the **Data** window while immediately behind it is the **Session** window (see Figure 2.1). In *Release 10*, however, the **Data** window occupies most of the lower half of the screen while the **Session** window fills most of the upper half (see Figure 2.2).

Table 2.3 **Info** listing of column numbers and names of variables in **jsrd.mtw**

COLUMN	NAME	COUNT	MISSING
C1	id	70	
C2	ethnicgp	70	
C3	gender	70	
C4	income	70	2
C5	age	70	1
C6	years	70	
C7	commit	70	
C8	satis1	70	2
C9	satis2	70	1
C10	satis3	70	
C11	satis4	70	
C12	autonom1	70	
C13	autonom2	70	
C14	autonom3	70	
C15	autonom4	70	
C16	routine1	70	
C17	routine2	70	
C18	routine3	70	
C19	routine4	70	
C20	attend	70	
C21	skill	70	
C22	prody	70	1
C23	qual	70	
C24	absence	70	1

CONSTANTS USED: NONE

The **Data** window consists of a matrix of numbered columns and rows. The cursor will be in the *cell* in the first row of the first column. The *frame* of this cell will be shown in bold to denote that it is the *active* cell. To enter a value in any one cell, make that cell active by moving to it with either the cursor keys or the mouse, type in the value and then move to the next cell into which you want to put a value. To change any value already entered, move to the cell containing that value, remove that value with the backspace key and type in the new value. If you delete the entry with the backspace key and move to another cell, an asterisk (*) will be left denoting a missing value. To name any particular column move to the cell just below its column number and type in the name.

To increase the size of the **Data** (or the **Session**) window with the mouse, place the cursor on the triangle pointing upward in the right-hand corner of the window and press the left button. To return the window to its original size, place the pointer on the square in the right-hand corner containing the upward and downward facing triangle and press the left button. The key

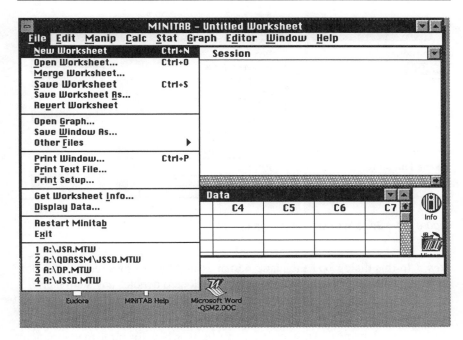

Figure 2.3   Options on the **File** drop-down menu

strokes for carrying out the actions described in this section are given in Appendix 2.2.

To save the data as a worksheet, carry out the following steps.

Step 1   Select **File** from the bar on the **Worksheet** window by pressing the left button on the mouse which will cause a menu to drop down. The options on this menu are shown in Figure 2.3. To cancel the *drop-down* menu, place the pointer anywhere outside the option and press the left button.

Step 2   Select **Save Worksheet As** ... when a *dialog box* will appear as illustrated in Figure 2.4.

Note that in *Release 9* an intermediate dialog box is presented in which the **Minitab worksheet** option is ready to be selected. This is indicated by this option being encased in a rectangle drawn with a dashed line. So select it to produce the dialog box shown in Figure 2.4.

The ellipse or three dots after an option term (**...**) signifies a dialog box will appear if this option is chosen. A right facing arrowhead >, on the other hand, indicates that a further submenu will appear to the right of the drop-down menu. An option with neither of these signs means that there are no further drop-down menus to select.

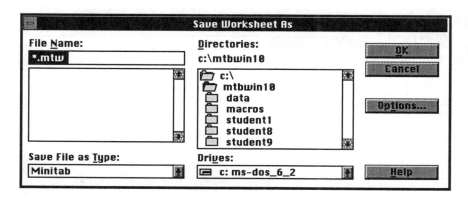

Figure 2.4   **Save Worksheet As** dialog box

Step 3 In this dialog box the name ***.mtw** is highlighted in a rectangular box under the label **File Name**:. The asterisk or wildcard denotes any stem name.

Step 4   Type in the name of your file and press the Return key or select **OK**. When using the menu system you do not have to put single quotation marks around names. An exception to this is when forming mathematical expressions which will be described in the next chapter.

To save the file on a floppy disk in a disk drive, select the appropriate drive (e.g. **a**) from those in the box below the label **Drives:** by putting the cursor on the downward button, pressing the left button and highlighting the **a** drive.

When carrying out procedures with the menu system, the prompt commands for performing the same procedure will be displayed in the **Session** window once the procedure has been executed. The first letter after the **MTB** > prompt is capitalized.

We will use a particular notation to describe the steps involved in using the menu system. The selection of a step or option will be indicated with a right facing arrow → pointing to the term(s) on the menu or dialog box to be chosen. Any explanations will be placed in square parentheses after the option shown. Thus, the notation for saving data as a worksheet using the menu system in Release 10 is

→**File** →**Save Worksheet As** ... →box under **Drives** → drive [e.g. **a**] from options listed → box under **File Name** and in it type file name [e.g. **jsrd.mtw**] →**OK**

In the rest of this chapter we will initially explain the steps involved in using the menu system and give the notation whereas in subsequent chapters we will simply present the notation.

To retrieve this file at a later stage when it is no longer the current file, select **File** from the bar of the window, **Open Worksheet...**, the appropriate drive if it is not already present and either type in the name or select the name from the files listed. To call up this file, highlight it and either press the left button once and select **OK** or press the left button twice.

→**File** →**Open Worksheet...** →box under **Drives** →drive [e.g. **a**] from options listed →box under **File Name** →file name [e.g. **jsrd.mtw**] →press the left button once and select **OK** or press the left button twice

In *Release 9* an intermediate **Open Worksheet** dialog box appears in which the **Type of Worksheet** is first selected before choosing **Select File**.

To read in a data text ASCII file, you need to use the prompt system in the **Session** window, as in the following example

MTB > read 'a:jsr.dat' c1-c24

The data will be displayed in the **Data** window.

To remind yourself of the column numbers and any names for the variables in your current worksheet, choose **File, Get Worksheet Info...** and **OK**.

→**File** →**Get Worksheet Info ...** →**OK**

To display a column in the **Session** window, select **File** and **Display Data....** Then select or type the variable(s) into the box entitled **Columns, constants, and matrices to display**: and select **OK**. You can move the appropriate column or variable name into such a box by first highlighting it and then choosing **Select**. To carry out the procedure, choose **OK** or press Return.

→**File** →**Display Data...** →variable(s) →**Select** [this puts the relevant variable(s) in the box beside **Columns, constants, and matrices to display:**] →**OK**

To leave Minitab with the menu system, select **File** and **Exit**.

→**File** →**Exit**

STATISTICAL PROCEDURES

At this stage, you may be ready to analyse your data. The rest of the book describes numerous ways in which you can do this. To show you how this is generally done, we will ask Minitab to calculate the average or *mean* age of the sample. This can be performed with a number of Minitab commands, but we shall use the one called **mean**. All we have to do is to add after the word **mean** the column number (**c5**) or name we have given this variable (**age**), making sure to leave one space between them. So, to provide these descriptive statistics for **c5** (or **'age'**), we type

MTB > mean c5

The output from this command is displayed on the screen when this command is run and is shown below.

MEAN = 39.188

To do this with the menu system, first select the **Calc** option from the menu bar when a drop-down menu will appear listing various statistics as illustrated in Figure 2.5. To calculate the mean of a column, select the **Column Statistics...** option when a dialog box will be shown as depicted in Figure 2.6. Select **Mean** and type in or select into the box labelled **Input variables:** the column number (**c5**) or the name of the variable (**age**) whose mean you want.

→**Calc** →**Column Statistics...** →**Mean** →box beside **Input variables:** →variables [e.g. **age**] →**Select** [this will put the relevant variable in this box] →**OK**

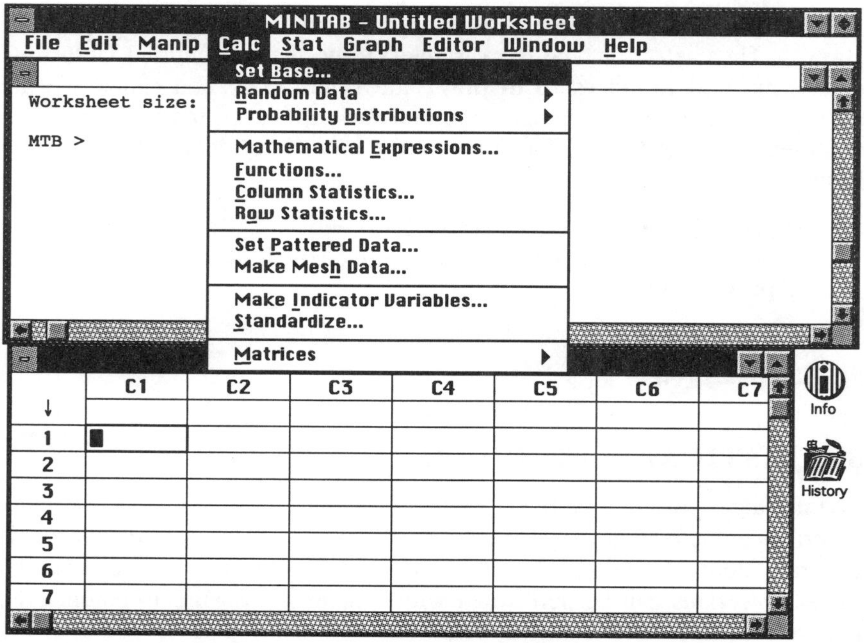

Figure 2.5   Options on the **Calc** drop-down menu

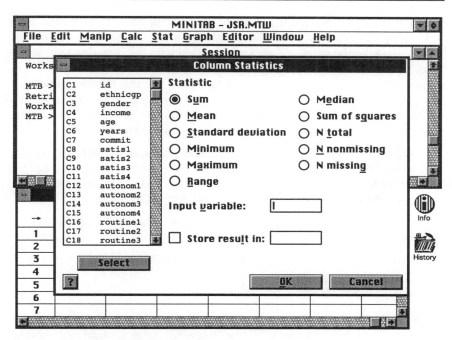

Figure 2.6 **C̲olumn Statistics** dialog box

KEEPING MINITAB OUTPUT

To keep a listing of what you will do in a session, type the command **outfile** followed by the name you want to call that file in single quotes at the point you want the record to begin. The default extension name is **.lis** which is short for **lis**ting. If we wished to call our output or listing file **'sess1.lis'**, we would use the following command

MTB > outfile = 'sess1.lis'

There is normally no need to save this file on to your floppy disk as we will want to print it out immediately after we have left Minitab. If this is not the case, store the file on to your floppy disk.

We can control the width of that output file from 30 to 132 spaces with the **ow** command (**o**utput **w**idth), although some commands cannot make their output narrower than 70. So, the command for requesting a width of 70 spaces is

MTB > ow = 70

Output is saved in this file until the command **nooutfile** is typed. Output may be saved in different listing files if desired. If the same listing file is called up later in the session, then the output will be added to the end of that file.

In the Windows version of Minitab, the **Session** window keeps up to 25 half-full pages, after which it automatically discards the first half of the output. To save the output of an entire session with the menu system, select **File, Other Files** and **Start Recording Session...** when a dialog box will appear. The default option of **Record output in file and display in Session window** is already selected. Specify the output width if necessary in the box entitled **Set output width to** and then select **Select File**. In the dialog box, select the drive if necessary, name the file and select **OK**.

>**File** →**Other Files** →**Start Recording Session...** →**Record output in file and display in Session window** →box to the left of **Set output width to** [optional e.g. →**70** in the box to its right] →**Select File** →box under **File Name** →filename [e.g. **sess1.lis**] →**OK**

To stop saving the output, select **File, Other Files** and **Stop Recording Session**.

>**File** →**Other Files** →**Stop Recording Session**

EXERCISES

1. You need to collect information on the religious affiliation of your respondents. You have thought of the following options: Agnostic, Atheist, Buddhist, Catholic, Jewish, Hindu, Muslim, Protestant and Taoist. Which further category has to be included?

2. You want to record this information in a data file to be stored in a computer. How would you code this information?

3. Looking through your completed questionnaires, you notice that on one of them no answer has been given to this question. What are you going to put in your data file for this person?

4. Suppose that on another questionnaire two categories had been ticked by the respondent. How would you deal with this situation?

5. The first two of your sample of fifty subjects describe themselves as agnostic and the second two as atheists. The ages of these four subjects are 25, 47, 33, and 18. How would you arrange this information in your data file?

6. If data are available for all the options of the religious affiliation question, how many columns would be needed to store this information in Minitab?

7. How many columns to a line are there in most computers for listing data or commands?

8. What is the maximum number of characters that can be used for the name of a variable in Minitab?

Appendix 2.1: The Job Survey questions

EMPLOYEE QUESTIONNAIRE

This questionnaire is designed to find out a few things about yourself and your job. Please answer the questions truthfully. There are no right or wrong answers.

                                                                Code   Col
1. To which one of the following racial or ethnic groups do you belong? (Tick one)   4
                    __ White/European   1
                    __ Asian   2
                    __ West Indian   3
                    __ African   4
                    __ Other   5

2. Are you male or female   6
                    __ Male   1
                    __ Female   2

3. What is your current annual income before tax and other deductions?
                                        £_____   8–12

4. What was your age last birthday (in years)?
                                        __ years   14–15

5. How many years have you worked for this firm?
                                        __ years   17–18

6. Please indicate whether you (1) strongly disagree, (2) disagree, (3) are undecided, (4) agree, or (5) strongly agree with each of the following statements. Circle one answer only for each statement.

		SD	D	U	A	SA	
(a)	I would not leave this firm even if another employer could offer me a little more money	1	2	3	4	5	20
(b)	My job is like a hobby to me	1	2	3	4	5	22
(c)	Most of the time I have to force myself to go to work	1	2	3	4	5	24
(d)	Most days I am enthusiastic about my work	1	2	3	4	5	26
(e)	My job is pretty uninteresting	1	2	3	4	5	28
(f)	I am allowed to do my job as I choose	1	2	3	4	5	30
(g)	I am able to make my own decisions about how I do my job	1	2	3	4	5	32

(h)	People in my section of the firm are left to do their work as they please		1	2	3	4	5	34
(i)	I do not have to consult my supervisor if I want to perform my work slightly differently		1	2	3	4	5	36
(j)	I do my job in much the same way every day		1	2	3	4	5	38
(k)	There is little variety in my work		1	2	3	4	5	40
(l)	My job is repetitious		1	2	3	4	5	42
(m)	Very few aspects of my job change from day to day		1	2	3	4	5	44

7. Did you attend the firm's meeting this month?   46
                     __ Yes   1
                     __ No   2

SUPERVISOR QUESTIONNAIRE

I would be grateful if you could answer the following questions about one of the people for whom you act as supervisor – [Name of Employee]

1. Please describe the skill level of work that this person performs. Which one of the following descriptions best fits his/her work? (Tick one)   48
                     __ Unskilled   1
                     __ Semi-skilled   2
                     __ Fairly skilled   3
                     __ Highly skilled   4

2. How would you rate his/her productivity? (Tick one)   50
                     __ Very poor   1
                     __ Poor   2
                     __ Average   3
                     __ Good   4
                     __ Very good   5

3. How would you rate the quality of his/her work? (Tick one)   52
                     __ Very poor   1
                     __ Poor   2
                     __ Average   3
                     __ Good   4
                     __ Very good   5

4. How many days has he/she been absent in the last twelve months?
                     __ days   54–55

Appendix 2.2: Operating within Windows using keys

To select the **Sessions** window, press the Tab key while holding down the Ctrl key. The Tab key is usually on the leftmost side of the keyboard and may have two arrows on it pointing leftwards and rightwards respectively.

To expand a window, press Alt and the key with the hyphen (-) on it which will produce a drop-down menu; select **Maximise**. To return the window to its original size, press the Alt and hyphen key and select either the **Restore** or **Minimise** option from the drop-down menu.

To save the data as a worksheet, carry out the following steps.

Step 1 Select **File** from the bar on the **Worksheet** window when a menu will drop down. To select any of these options, press the Alt key and the key of the letter underlined in the option, which is **F** in this case. To cancel the drop-down menu, press the Esc key.

Step 2 Select **Save Worksheet As** pressing either the downward cursor key or the key of the letter underlined in the option, which is **A**. A dialog box will appear.

In *Release 9* an intermediate dialog box appears in which the **Minitab worksheet** option is ready to be and should be selected.

Step 3 In this dialog box the name ***.MTW** is highlighted in a rectangular box under the label **File Name:**.

Step 4 Type in the name of your file and press the Return key or select **OK**. To save it on a floppy disk in a disk drive, select the appropriate drive from those in the box below the label **Drives:**.

The cursor may be moved in a dialog box with the following keys. To move forwards to the box entitled **Drives:**, press the Tab key. To move backwards to it, press the Tab key while holding down the Shift key. Alternatively, press Alt and the letter underlined in the title which in this case is **v**. To move the cursor within a box, use the cursor keys.

To retrieve this file at a later stage when it is no longer the current file, select **File** from the bar of the window, **Open Worksheet**, the appropriate drive if it is not already present and either type in the name or select the name from the files listed. To select a file, use the downward cursor key until the right file has been underlined, press the upward cursor key and the Return key.

Chapter 3

Analysing data with computers
Further steps with Minitab

Now that you know some of the basics of how to run Minitab, we can introduce you to some further commands which you may find very useful. These commands will enable you to carry out the following kinds of operations: select certain cases (such as all white men under the age of 40) for separate analyses; recode values; and create new variables (such as scoring an attitude or personality scale) and new files for storing them.

SELECTING CASES

To select cases with certain characteristics, we can copy the data of those cases into other columns with the **copy** command and select particular cases with the **use** subcommand. For example, if you wanted to find out the average age of only the men in the Job Survey sample, you could first copy 'age' with the **copy** command into a new column **c25** which we shall first call 'agec' (for **age c**opy)

MTB > name c25 'agec'
MTB > copy 'age' 'agec';

Then with the **use** subcommand you would select 'gender' (which contains the code for gender) and specify **1** which is the code for men

SUBC> use 'gender' = 1.

Note that the line before a subcommand must end in a semi-colon (;) and the last subcommand must finish with a full stop (.).

The menu procedure for doing this is

→**Manip** →**Copy Columns...** →variable or column to be copied [e.g. age] →**Select** [this puts the variable in the box under **Copy from columns:**] →box under **To columns:** →type column or name of variable to be copied [e.g. **agec**] →**Use Rows...** [this opens a second dialog box] →**Use rows with column [equal to (eg, −4.5 −2:3 14):]** →box beside it →variable for selection [e.g. **gender**] →**Select** →type value for selection [e.g. **1**] which goes in the box below →**OK** [this closes the second dialog box] →**OK**

Options on the **Manip** menu are depicted in Figure 3.1 whereas the **Copy** and **Copy – Use Rows** dialog boxes are shown in Figures 3.2 and 3.3 respectively.

To calculate the average age of the men with the prompt system we would simply use the **mean** command

MTB > mean 'agec'

The menu procedure for doing this is

→**Calc** →**Column Statistics...** →**Mean** →box beside **Input variables:** [this will display variables which can be selected] →**agec** →**Select** [this puts **agec** in this box] →**OK**

The output for this command is displayed below:

MEAN = 39.211

To work out the average age of the women we would repeat the procedure substituting **2** for **1** in the **use** subcommand. The data for women overwrites the data for men in **'agec'**.

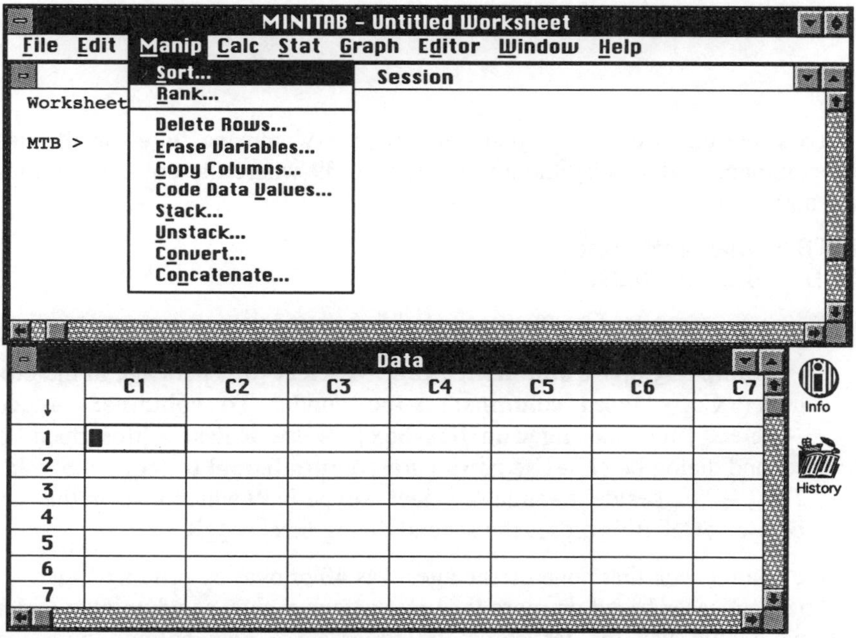

Figure 3.1 **Manip** menu options

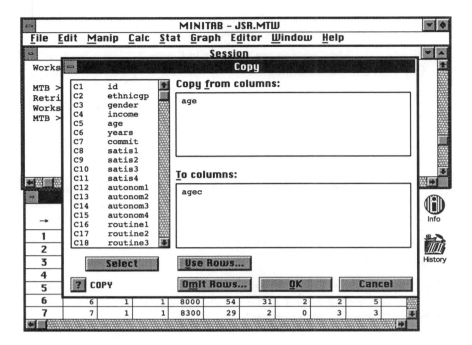

Figure 3.2   **Copy** dialog box

To select cases under 40 years of age, we would list **'age'** on the **use** subcommand and specify the age range **0** to **39** where the colon **:** signifies the notion of 'to'

MTB > copy 'age' 'agec';
SUBC> use 'age' 0:39.

The menu procedure for doing this is

> →**Manip** →**Copy Columns...** →**age** →**Select** [this puts **age** in the box under **Copy from columns:**] →box under **To columns:** →**agec** →**Select** [this puts **agec** in this box] →**Use Rows...** [this opens a second dialog box] →**Use rows with column [equal to (eg, −4.5 −2:3 14):]** →box beside it →**age** →**Select** →type **0:39** which goes in the box below →**OK** [this closes the second dialog box] →**OK**

We could check that none of the ages was 40 or over by printing **'agec'**.
To select cases based on more than one category such as white men under 40, we would use the **let** command to create a new column with the appropriate categories which we then use to copy the variables we wish to

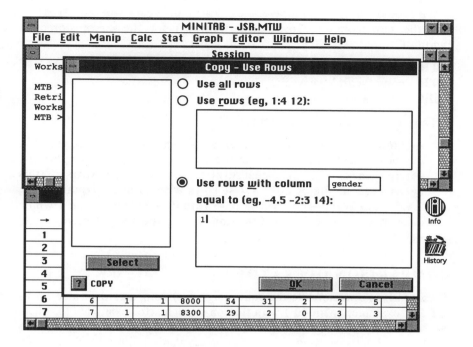

Figure 3.3 **Copy – Use Rows** dialog box

analyse. Suppose we want to calculate the average number of years worked (**'years'**) for white men under 40. We would first specify on the **let** command that the new column **c25** (which we shall first name **'wmu40'**) holds the relevant categories, namely whites coded as **1** in **'ethnicgp'** containing the ethnic categories, men coded as **1** in **'gender'** comprising the gender categories and values less than (**lt**) 40 in **'age'** storing age

MTB > name c25 'wmu40'
MTB > let 'wmu40' = ('ethnicgp' = 1) and ('gender' = 1) and ('age' lt 40)

The **let** command assigns **1** to cases which are white, male and under 40 and puts them into **'wmu40'**.

The menu procedure for doing this is

→**Calc** →**Mathematical Expressions...** →type the variable name [e.g. **wmu40**] in the box beside **Variable [new or modified]:** →box beneath **Expression:** and type in it the required expression [e.g. **('ethnicgp' = 1) and ('gender' = 1) and ('age' lt 40)**] →**OK**

We would then copy the average number of years worked (**'years'**) into the new column **c26** (called **'yearsc'**) for the cases stored in **'wmu40'**.

MTB > name c26 'yearsc'
MTB > copy 'years' 'yearsc';
SUBC > use 'wmu40' = 1.

The menu sequence for doing this is

→<u>M</u>anip →<u>C</u>opy Columns... →years →Select [this puts **years** in the box under **Copy <u>f</u>rom columns:**] →box under **<u>T</u>o columns:** →type **yearsc** [this puts **yearsc** in this box] →<u>U</u>se Rows... [this opens a second dialog box] →**Use rows <u>w</u>ith column [equal to (eg, −4.5 −2:3 14):**] →box beside it →**wmu40** →**Select** →type **1** which goes in the box below →**<u>O</u>K** [this closes the second dialog box] →**<u>O</u>K**

COMPARISON OPERATORS

A comparison operator like the equals sign (=) compares the value on its left (for example, **'wmu40'**) with that on its right (for example, **1**). There are six such operators, which can be represented by the following symbols (with or without spaces on either side) or keywords (with a blank space on either side):

= or **eq**	equal to
~= or **ne**	not equal to
< or **lt**	less than
<= or **le**	less than or equal to
> or **gt**	greater than
>= or **ge**	greater than or equal to

If the comparison is true (for example, if the age of a particular case is less than 40), the result is set to **1**. If the comparison is not true (for example, age is 40 or greater), the result is set to **0**. If the datum is missing, then the result is set to **∗**.

LOGICAL OPERATIONS

We can combine comparison operations with one of three logical operators using the following symbols or keywords:

& or **and**
| or **or**
~ or **not**

In other words, the three comparison operations of (**'ethnicgp'** = **1**), (**'gender'** = **1**) and (**'age' lt 40**) are added together with the logical operator **and**.

To select people of only West Indian and African origin, we would have to use the **or** logical operator since people cannot have been born in both the West Indies and Africa:

MTB > let c25 = ('ethnicgp' = 3 or 'ethnicgp' = 4)

The menu procedure for doing this is

→**C̲alc** →**Mathematical E̲xpressions...** →**c25** →**Select** [this puts **c25** in the box beside **V̲ariable [new or modified]:**] →box under **Expression:** and in it type (**'ethnicgp' = 3 or 'ethnicgp' = 4**) →**O̲K**

Note that it is necessary to repeat the full logical relation. It is *not* permissible to abbreviate this expression as:

(**'ethnicgp' = 3 or = 4**)

To select people between the ages of 30 and 40 inclusively, we can use the expression:

(**'age' ge 30 and 'age' le 40**)

Here, we have to use the **and** logical operator. If we used **or**, we would in effect be selecting the whole sample since everybody is either above 30 or below 40 years of age.

RECODING THE VALUES OF VARIABLES

Sometimes it is necessary to change or to recode the values of some variables. For example, it is recommended that the wording of questions which go to make up a scale or index should be varied in such a way that people who say yes to everything (*yeasayers*) or no (*naysayers*) do not end up with an extreme score. To illustrate this, we have worded two of the four questions assessing job satisfaction in the Job Survey ('6c. Most of the time I have to force myself to go to work.' and '6e. My job is pretty uninteresting.') in the opposite direction from the other two ('6b. My job is like a hobby to me.' and '6d. Most days I am enthusiastic about my work.'). These questions are answered in terms of a 5-point scale ranging from 1 ('strongly disagree') to 5 ('strongly agree'). While we could reverse the numbers for the two negatively worded items (6c and 6e) on the questionnaire, this would draw the attention of our respondents to what we were trying to accomplish. It is simpler to reverse the coding when we come to analyse the data. Since we want to indicate greater job satisfaction with a higher number, we will recode the answers to the two negatively worded questions, so that 1 becomes 5, 2 becomes 4, 4 becomes 2, and 5 becomes 1. We can do this in the following way with the **code** command where the column values for 6c are named as **'satis2'** and those for 6e as **'satis4'**:

MTB > code (1) 5 (2) 4 (4) 2 (5) 1 'satis2' 'satis4' c25 c26

The values to be changed precede the column number or variable names. The original values in **'satis2'** and **'satis4'** are placed in the new columns **c25** and **c26** when recoded which we could name **'satis2r'** and **'satis4r'** where the **r** stands for **r**ecoded. The values to be changed must always be placed in parentheses. Any number of values can be changed but only to one value. For example, if we wished to form a 3-point scale with only one 'agree', one 'disagree', and one 'undecided' answer, we could do this in the following way:

MTB > code (2) 1 (3) 2 (4 5) 3 'satis1'-'satis4' c25-c28

If we then wanted to recode the two negatively worded items, we could do this with a further **code** command:

MTB > code (1) 3 (3) 1 c26 c28-c30

We can specify a range of values with the colon symbol **:**. For example, we could recode ethnic group into whites (code unchanged) and nonwhites (recoded as 2) with this symbol as follows:

MTB > code (3:5) 2 'ethnicgp' c31

Similarly, we could recode cases into those 40 years old or above and those below:

MTB > code (0:39) 1 (40:99) 2 'age' c32

If we had ages which were not whole numbers and which fell between 39 and 40, such as 39.9, they would not be recoded. To avoid this problem, we would use overlapping end-points:

MTB > code (0:40) 1 (40:99) 2 'age' c32

In this example all people aged 40 and less would be coded as **1**. Since values are recoded consecutively and once only, age 40 will not also be recoded as **2**.

The menu action for recoding is

→**Manip** →**Code Data Values...** →variable(s) to be changed [e.g. age] →**Select** [this puts the variable(s) in the box beneath **Code data from columns:**] →box under **Into columns** and in it type new variable [e.g. **c32**] →first box under **Original values [eg, 1:4 12]:** and type first values to be changed [e.g. **0:40**] →first corresponding box under **New:** and in it type first new value [e.g. **1**] →second box under **Original values [eg, 1:4 12]:** and in it type second values to be changed [e.g.

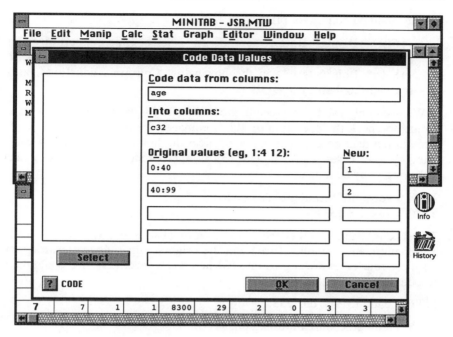

Figure 3.4 **Code Data Values** dialog box

40:99] →second corresponding box under **New:** and in it type second new value [e.g. **2**] →**OK**

The **Code Data Values** dialog box is presented in Figure 3.4.

CHECKING RECODED VALUES AND NEW VARIABLES

It is always good practice to check what you have done, particularly when you are learning a new skill. So far, we have asked you to accept on trust what we have said about recoding values. Let us now see whether some of these examples do what we have described. To check this, we use the command **print** and list the columns containing the original data and the recoded data. So, to check the original and new values of the ethnic group variable

MTB > code (3:5) 2 'ethnicgp' c31

we use the following command:

MTB > print 'ethnicgp' c31

The menu procedure for printing is

→**File** →**Display Data...** →**ethnicgp** →**Select** [this puts **ethnicgp** in the box under **Columns, constants, and matrices to display:**] →**c31** →**Select** [this puts **c31** in the box below **Columns, constants, and matrices to display:**] →**OK**

We need only ask for the recoding of one case for each of the four ethnic groups to check the operation of this command. We could, therefore, look through the data on ethnic group and select the first representative of each category (i.e. cases 1, 2, 3, and 13) as appropriate examples using the following **copy** command:

MTB > copy 'id' 'ethnicgp' c31 c32;
SUBC> use 1:3 13.

The subcommand specifies the rows or cases (**1** to **3** and **13**) to be copied. The identification number (**'id'**) and the original ethnic code (**'ethnicgp'**) for these four cases are copied into **c31** and **c32** respectively. We could then recode **c32** and store it as **c33**:

MTB > code (3:5) 2 c32 c33

The menu procedure for doing this is

→**Manip** →**Copy** Columns... →**id** →**Select** [this puts **id** in the box under **Copy from columns:**] →**ethnicgp** →**Select** →box under **To columns:** and in it type **c31** and **c32** →**Use Rows...** →**Use rows** [eg, 1:4 12]: →box under it and in this box type **1:3 13** →**OK** →**OK**

We then **print c31-c33** which gives the following output:

ROW	C31	C32	C33
1	1	1	1
2	2	2	2
3	3	3	2
4	13	4	2

As we can see, values 1 and 2 remain the same, while 3 and 13 are recoded as 2. Once we are satisfied that the command does what we want, we can then recode the values for all 70 cases.

COMPUTING A NEW VARIABLE

Sometimes we want to create a new variable. For example, we have used four items to assess what may be slightly different aspects of job satisfaction. Rather than treat these items as separate measures, it may be preferable and reasonable to combine them into one index. To do this, we can use the **rsum** command to create a new column or variable which is the four job satisfaction items **'satis1'**, 'satis2', 'satis3' and 'satis4' added together. In other words, this command sums specified columns across rows. Before doing this, however, we have to remember to recode two of the items ('satis2' and 'satis4') because the answers to them are scored in the reverse way. The two commands, then, which are needed for creating the new variable in c27 which we shall call 'satis' are:

MTB > code (1) 5 (2) 4 (4) 2 (5) 1 'satis2' 'satis4' 'satis2r' 'satis4r'
MTB > name c27 'satis'
MTB > rsum 'satis1' 'satis2r' 'satis3' 'satis4r' 'satis'

The menu action for doing this is

→Manip →Code Data Values... →satis2 →Select [this puts satis2 in the box beneath Code data from columns:] →satis4 →Select [this puts satis4 in the box beneath Code data from columns:] →box under Into columns: and type satis2r satis4r in it →first box under Original values [eg, 1:4 12]: and in it type 1 →first corresponding box under New: and in it type 5 →second box under Original values [eg, 1:4 12]: and in it type 2 →second corresponding box under New: and in it type 4 →third box under Original values [eg, 1:4 12]: and in it type 4 →third corresponding box under New: and in it type 2 →fourth box under Original values [eg, 1:4 12]: and in it type 5 →fourth corresponding box under New: and in it type 1 →OK
→Calc →Row Statistics... →Sum →box under Input variables: →satis1 →Select [this puts satis1 in this box] →satis2r →Select →satis3 →Select →satis4r →Select →box beside Store result in: and in it type satis →OK

To check that these commands do what we want, we will try them out initially on the first three cases in the data file. To select these cases, we can use the following command:

MTB > copy c1 c8-c11 c30-c34;
SUBC> use 1:3.

We could then recode c9 and c11 which for the three cases are now in c32 and c34 and store the recoded values in c35 and c36.

MTB > code (1) 5 (2) 4 (4) 2 (5) 1 c32 c34-c36

Next we sum these four values to create the new variable c37:

MTB > rsum c31 c33 c35-37

We then print c30-c37 which produces the following output:

ROW	C30	C31	C32	C33	C34	C35	C36	C37
1	1	*	3	4	4	3	2	9
2	2	*	*	2	3	*	3	5
3	3	4	4	4	1	2	5	15

If we look at the first case, we can see that **4** in **c34** has been recoded as **2** in **c36**. We can also see that the **9** in **c37** is the sum of * in **c31**, **4** in **c33**, **3** in **c35** and **2** in **c36**.

We can carry out these actions with the menu system by

→**Manip** →**Copy Columns...** →**c1** →**Select** [this puts **c1** in the box under **Copy from columns:**] →**c8 c9 c10 c11** →**Select** →box under **To columns:** and in it type **c30-c34** →**Use Rows...** →**Use rows [eg, 1:4 12]:** →box under it and in this box type **1:3** →**OK** →**OK**
→**Manip** →**Code Data Values...** →**c32** →**Select** [this puts **c32** in the box beneath **Code data from columns:**] →**c34** →**Select** →box under **Into columns:** and in it type **c35 c36** →type **1, 2, 4** and **5** in the appropriate boxes beneath **Original values [eg, 1:4 12]:** →type **5, 4, 2** and **1** in the corresponding boxes beneath **New:** →**OK**
→**Calc** →**Row Statistics...** →**Sum** →box beside **Input variables:** →**c31** →**Select** [this puts **c31** in this box] →**c33** →**Select** →**c35 c36** →**Select** →box beside **Store result in:** and in it type **c37** →**OK**
→**File** →**Display Data...** →**c30 c31 c32 c33 c34 c35 c36 c37** →**Select** [this puts **c30-c37** in the box beneath **Columns, constants, and matrices to display:**] →**OK**

An alternative way of summing these four items is to use the **let** command as follows:

MTB > let 'satis' = 'satis1' + 'satis2r' + 'satis3' + 'satis4r'

The menu action for doing this is

→**Calc** →**Mathematical Expressions...** →type **satis** in the box beside **Variable [new or modified]:** →box beneath **Expression:** and in it type **('satis1' + 'satis2r' + 'satis3' + 'satis4r')** →**OK**

Other arithmetic operations available with **let** are subtraction (−), multiplication (*), division (/) and exponentiation (* *).

MISSING DATA AND COMPUTING SCORES TO FORM NEW MEASURES

This section may be difficult for some readers to follow and, if so, can be skipped. It describes how new measures can be created by adding scores together such as the responses to the four job satisfaction questions.

As we have seen, the answer to the first job satisfaction item for the first subject and to the first and second job satisfaction items for the second subject are missing. In research, it is quite common for some scores to be missing. Participants may omit to answer questions, they may circle two different answers to the same question, the experimenter may forget to record a response and so on. It is important to consider carefully how you are going to deal with missing data. If many of the data for one particular variable are missing, this suggests that there are problems with its measurement which need to be sorted out. Thus, for example, it may be a question which does not apply to most people in which case it is best omitted. If many scores for an individual are missing, it is most probably best to omit this person from the sample since there may be problems with the way in which these data were collected. Thus, for example, it could be that the participant was not paying attention to the task at hand.

When computing scores to form a new measure, a rule of thumb is sometimes applied to the treatment of missing data such that if 10 per cent or more of them are missing for that index, the index itself is then defined as missing for that subject. If we applied this principle to the two subjects in this case, no score for job satisfaction would be computed for them, although they would have scores for job routine and autonomy. To operate this rule, we would first have to count the number of missing values to see whether they exceeded 10 per cent. We would then have to set the job satisfaction total score as missing for subjects with more than this number of items missing, which in this case is if one or more of the items are absent.

When computing scores to form an index, we may want to form an average total score by dividing the total score by the number of available individual scores. One such situation is where we have a variable which is made up of more than ten items and we want to assign it as missing when the scores for 10 per cent or more of its items are not available. Suppose we have a variable which is made up of 100 items. If ten or more of the scores for these items are missing, this variable will be coded as zero. If nine or fewer of them are missing, we have to take account of the fact that the total score may be based on numbers of items ranging from ninety-one to 100. We can control for this by using the average rather than the total score, which is obtained by dividing the total score by the number of items for which data are available. One advantage of doing this is that the averaged scores now correspond to the answers on the Job Survey questionnaire, so that an average score of 4.17 on job satisfaction means that that person generally answers 'agree' to the job-satisfaction items.

To illustrate how this can be done, we will use the four job-satisfaction items. With only four items, we cannot use a cut-off point of 10 per cent for exclusion as missing. Therefore, we will adopt a more lenient criterion of 50 per cent. If 50 per cent or more (i.e. two or more) of the scores for the job-satisfaction items are missing, we will code that variable for subjects as missing.

We first count the number of valid or non-missing values in each row for the four items using the **rn** command and store this number in **c27** which we shall call **'nvsatis'** (for **n**umber of **v**alid job-**satis**faction items):

MTB > name c27 'nvsatis'
MTB > rn 'satis1' 'satis2r' 'satis3' 'satis4r' 'nvsatis'

The menu system for doing this is

→**Calc** →**Row Statistics...** →**N total** →box beside **Input variables:**
→**satis1** →**Select** [this puts **satis1** in this box] →**satis2r** →**Select**
→**satis3** →**Select** →**satis4r** →**Select** →box beside **Store result in:** and
in it type **nvsatis** →**OK**

With the **code** command we then recode **'nvsatis'** as missing (∗) for
cases which have two, one or no valid values and store these in **c28** which
we shall call **'cvsatis'** (for the criterion of valid job-**satis**faction items):

MTB > name c28 'cvsatis'
MTB > code (0:2) ∗ 'nvsatis' 'cvsatis'

The menu procedure for doing this is

→**Manip** →**Code Data Values...** →**nvsatis** →**Select** [this puts **nvsatis**
in the box under **Code data from columns:**] →box under **Into**
columns: and in it type **cvsatis** →first box under **Original values** [eg,
1:4 12]: and in it type **0:2** →first corresponding box under **New:** and in
it type ∗ →**OK**

Next we sum with the **rsum** command the four job-satisfaction items and put
these into **c29** which we shall call **'ssatis'** (for sum of job-**satis**faction items):

MTB > name c29 'ssatis'
MTB > rsum 'satis1' 'satis2r' 'satis3' 'satis4r' 'ssatis'

The menu action for this is

→**Calc** →**Row Statistics...** →**Sum** →box beside **Input variables:**
→**satis1** →**Select** [this puts **satis1** in this box] →**satis2r** →**Select**
→**satis3** →**Select** →**satis4r** →**Select** →box beside **Store result in:** and
in it type **ssatis** →**OK**

In other words, a mean job-satisfaction score will only be computed for
cases on the basis of valid answers to three or four job-satisfaction items.
We use the **let** command to divide the sum of the job-satisfaction items
(**'ssatis'**) by the criterion of valid job-satisfaction items (**'cvsatis'**) to give
the mean job-**satis**faction score which we put in **c30** and which we name
'msatis'.

MTB > name c30 'msatis'
MTB > let 'msatis' = 'ssatis'/'cvsatis'

The menu procedure for doing this is

→**Calc** →**Mathematical Expressions...** →type **msatis** in the box
beside **Variable [new or modified]:** →box under **Expression:** and in it
type **'ssatis'/'cvsatis'** →**OK**

Finally, if we want to convert this mean score back into a total score (which takes into account numbers of valid scores that might vary between three and four), we use the **let** command to multiply the mean score by four and store it in **c31** which we shall call **'tsatis'** (for **t**otal job-**satis**faction score):

MTB > name c31 'tsatis'
MTB > let 'tsatis' = 'msatis' ∗ 4

The menu procedure for doing this is

→**C**alc →**M**athematical **E**xpressions... →type **tsatis** in the box beside **V**ariable [**new or modified**]: →box beneath **E**xpression: and in it type **'msatis' ∗ 4** →**O**K

To check that these commands have done what we wanted them to do we will print **'satis1'**, **'satis2r'**, **'satis3'**, **'satis4r'**, **'nvsatis'**, **'cvsatis'**, **'ssatis'**, **'msatis'** and **'tsatis'** for the first three cases as shown below:

ROW	satis1	satis2r	satis3	satis4r	nvsatis	cvsatis	ssatis	msatis
1	∗	3	4	2	3	3	9	3.00
2	∗	∗	2	3	2	∗	5	∗
3	4	2	4	5	4	4	15	3.75

> tsatis

12	∗	15

Because the last column (**tsatis**) could not fit on to the screen, it is printed as a row. We can see that for the first two cases who have missing values, a mean and total job satisfaction score have been worked out for the first case who has only one missing job-satisfaction item score but not for the second case who has two such missing scores.

We need to save **'msatis'** on our worksheet and we also have to calculate and save the mean job-autonomy and job-routine scores for subsequent analyses.

If we want to check whether these items have missing values which we need to take into account or values which do not constitute valid scores such as 6 or 7, we would use the **tally** command to give us the frequencies of the values for those variables. We would use the following command to give these frequencies for the job-autonomy items:

MTB > tally 'autonom1' – 'autonom4'

The menu action for this is

→**S**tat →**T**ables →**T**ally... →autonom1 autonom2 autonom3 autonom4 →**S**elect [this puts **autonom1-autonom4** in the box under **V**ariables:] →**O**K

The options available on the **S**tat menu are shown in Figure 3.5.

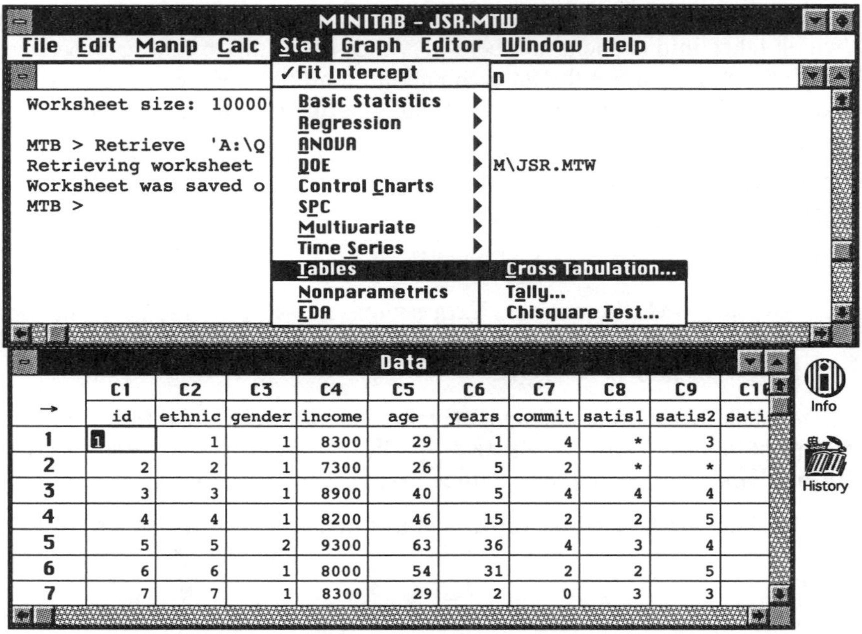

```
┌──────────────────────────────────────────────────────────────────┐
│ ▣              MINITAB – JSR.MTW                            ▣▣ │
│ File  Edit  Manip  Calc  Stat  Graph  Editor  Window  Help         │
│ ▣                          ✓Fit Intercept          n         ▣▣ │
│ Worksheet size: 10000   Basic Statistics  ▶                  ▣ │
│                         Regression        ▶                      │
│ MTB > Retrieve  'A:\Q   ANOVA             ▶                      │
│ Retrieving worksheet    DOE               ▶ M\JSR.MTW            │
│ Worksheet was saved o   Control Charts    ▶                      │
│ MTB >                   SPC               ▶                      │
│                         Multivariate      ▶                      │
│                         Time Series       ▶                      │
│                        ┌─Tables──────────┬─Cross Tabulation...─┐ │
│                         Nonparametrics      Tally...             │
│                         EDA                 Chisquare Test...    │
└──────────────────────────────────────────────────────────────────┘
```

	C1	C2	C3	C4	C5	C6	C7	C8	C9	C1
→	id	ethnic	gender	income	age	years	commit	satis1	satis2	sati
1	1		1	8300	29	1	4	*	3	
2	2	2	1	7300	26	5	2	*	*	
3	3	3	1	8900	40	5	4	4	4	
4	4	4	1	8200	46	15	2	2	5	
5	5	5	2	9300	63	36	4	3	4	
6	6	6	1	8000	54	31	2	2	5	
7	7	7	1	8300	29	2	0	3	3	

Figure 3.5 **Stat** menu options

The output from this command is shown below:

autonom1	COUNT	autonom2	COUNT	autonom3	COUNT	autonom4	COUNT
1	8	1	12	1	13	1	11
2	34	2	31	2	25	2	37
3	21	3	17	3	27	3	17
4	5	4	7	4	5	4	5
5	2	5	3	N =	70	N =	70
N =	70	N =	70				

As we can see, there are no missing or invalid values for these items and that there was no 'strongly agree' response (coded as 5) for the third and fourth items.

When you no longer need variables, you may find it more convenient to delete them with the **erase** command. For example, once we have created a composite job-satisfaction score such as **'msatis'** or **'tsatis'**, it is unlikely that we will need the variables that we used to produce it such as **'nvsatis'**, **'cvsatis'** and **'ssatis'**. Consequently, we could erase these as follows

MTB > erase 'nvsatis' 'cvsatis' 'ssatis'

The menu action for doing this is

→**Manip** →**Erase variables...** →**nvsatis** →**Select** [this puts **nvsatis** in the box under **Columns, constants, and matrices to erase:**] →**cvsatis** →**Select** →**ssatis** →**Select** →**OK**

Indeed, you may find it more useful to create a new worksheet which just contains the variables we want to analyse. For example, once we have formed the new variables of mean job satisfaction (**'msatis'**), mean job autonomy (**'mautonom'**) and mean job routine (**'mroutine'**), we could delete the variables we used to create them including the individual items such as **'satis1'** and **'satis2'**. We could save these mean scores together with the remaining variables of the Job Survey such as **'ethnicgp'** and **'gender'** in a new worksheet which we could call **'jssd.mtw'** (for **j**ob **s**cored **s**urvey **d**ata) and use this file in subsequent analyses.

Aggregate measures of job satisfaction, job autonomy and job routine used in subsequent chapters have been based on summing the four items within each scale and assigning the summed score as missing where 10 per cent or more of the items were missing. Since two of the seventy cases in the Job Survey had one or two of the answers to the individual job satisfaction items missing, the number of cases for whom a summed job satisfaction score could be computed is sixty-eight. The summed scores for job satisfaction, job autonomy and job routine have been called **'satis'**, **'autonom'** and **'routine'** respectively.

HELP SYSTEM

Minitab has a Help system which you may like to use to avoid having to refer to a book like this one or to find out more about the program. The Help systems are meant to be self-explanatory and so you should be able to learn to use them yourself after a little experience. Consequently, only the way to access the Help system will be described here.

In *Release 7* of Minitab, type **help** after the **MTB >** prompt to find out how Help is organised. Basically, you can obtain general information about how Minitab works by typing **help overview** and details of the commands available by typing **help commands**. If you want help on a particular command such as **read**, type **help** followed by the name of the command.

In *Release 8* you can obtain information about Minitab as follows. For example, for information about the **read** command, type **help read**. The information will quickly *scroll* or move down the screen. To read it once it has stopped, move up it using either the cursor keys or the mouse. The cursor key with Pg Dn on it will take you down a page or a screenful at a time while the key with Pg Up on it will take you up a screenful at a time. To move through the text with the mouse, move the cursor to the bottom of the scroll bar on the right-hand side if you want to go down and to the top if you want to go up. Alternatively, you can access a window of **Help** by either pressing the H key while holding down Alt or pressing the F1 *function key*. The function keys are usually on either the top of the keyboard or the left-hand side. To remove this window, press Return.

In the *Windows* version, there are three ways of accessing **Help**. In the **Session** window you may type **help** and the name of the command with which you want help. In a dialog box, select the **Help** or **?** option in the dialog box. When not in a dialog box, you may obtain help by pressing F1 when you will be presented with the **Contents** of the Help system. Alternatively, you may select the **Help** option from the menu bar, when you may then choose from a drop-down menu of **Contents**, **Getting Started...**, **How do I...**, **Search for Help on...** and **How to Use Help**. Ignore **About Minitab** which simply displays the Minitab title page.

There are a number of different routes for selecting these options. The **Contents** option also contains **Using Help**, **Getting Started** and **How do I...?** which are the same as **How to Use Help**, **Getting Started...** and **How do I...**. When you select any of these options, a second horizontal menu bar will appear below the one containing the **Help** option. This menu bar will always offer **Contents**, **Search**, **Back** and **History**. In addition, when the **How to Use Help** option is chosen, a further **Glossary** menu bar option is offered. The **Search** option is the same as **Search for Help on...**.

The **Search** or **Search for Help on...** option enables you to type in a topic you want help on or to choose one from those listed. The **Back** option takes you back to the **Contents** option when you have chosen the **Contents** option. The **History** option keeps a record of the **Help** options you have selected. The **Glossary** option offers you information on a number of topics.

EXERCISES

1. What is the appropriate Minitab command for selecting men and women who are of African origin in the Job Survey data?

2. Write a Minitab command to select women of Asian or West Indian origin who are 25 years or younger in the Job Survey data.

3. Recode the Job Survey variable **'skill'** so that there are only two categories (unskilled/semi-skilled vs fairly/highly skilled).

4. Recode the variable **'income'** into three groups of those earning less than £5,000, between £5,000 and under £10,000, and £10,000 and under £50,000.

5. Using the arithmetic operator ∗ , express the variable **'weeks'** as **'days'**. In other words, convert the number of weeks into the number of days.

Chapter 4

Concepts and their measurement

Concepts form a linchpin in the process of social research. Hypotheses contain concepts which are the products of our reflections on the world. Concepts express common elements in the world to which we give a name. We may notice that some people have an orientation in which they dislike people of a different race from their own, often attributing to other races derogatory characteristics. Still others are highly supportive of racial groups, perhaps seeing them as enhancing the 'host' culture through instilling new elements into it and hence enriching it. Yet others are merely tolerant, having no strong views one way or the other about people of other racial groups. In other words, we get a sense that people exhibit a variety of positions in regard to racial groups. We may want to suggest that there is a common theme to these attitudes, even though the attitudes themselves may be mutually antagonistic. What seems to bind these dispositions together is that they reflect different positions in regard to 'racial prejudice'. In giving the various dispositions that may be held regarding persons of another race a name, we are treating it as a concept, an entity over and above the observations about racial hostility and supportiveness that prompted the formulation of a name for those observations. Racial prejudice has acquired a certain abstractness, so that it transcends the reflections that prompted its formulation. Accordingly, the concept of racial prejudice becomes something that others can use to inform their own reflections about the social world. In this way, hypotheses can be formulated which postulate connections between racial prejudice and other concepts, such as that it will be related to social class or to authoritarianism.

Once formulated, a concept and the concepts with which it is purportedly associated, such as social class and authoritarianism, will need to be *operationally defined*, in order for systematic research to be conducted in relation to it. An operational definition specifies the procedures (operations) that will permit differences between individuals in respect of the concept(s) concerned to be precisely specified. What we are in reality talking about here is *measurement*, that is, the assignment of numbers to the units of analysis – be they people, organizations, or nations – to which a concept refers.

Measurement allows small differences between units to be specified. We can say that someone who actively speaks out against members of other races is racially prejudiced, while someone who actively supports them is the obverse of this, but it is difficult to specify precisely the different positions that people may hold in between these extremes. Measurement assists in the specification of such differences by allowing systematic differences between people to be stipulated.

In order to provide operational definitions of concepts, *indicators* are required which will stand for those concepts. It may be that a single indicator will suffice in the measurement of a concept, but in many instances it will not. For example, would it be sufficient to measure 'religious commitment' by conducting a survey in which people are asked how often they attend church services? Clearly it would not, since church attendance is but one way in which an individual's commitment to his or her religion may be expressed. It does not cover personal devotions, behaving as a religious person should in secular activities, being knowledgeable about one's faith, or how far they adhere to central tenets of faith (Glock and Stark, 1965). These reflections strongly imply that more than one indicator is likely to be required to measure many concepts; otherwise our findings may be open to the argument that we have only tapped one facet of the concept in question.

If more than one indicator of a concept can be envisaged, it may be necessary to test hypotheses with each of the indicators. Imagine a hypothesis in which 'organizational size' was a concept. We might measure (i.e. operationally define) this concept by the number of employees in a firm, its turnover or its net assets. While these three prospective indicators are likely to be inter-connected, they will not be perfectly related (Child, 1973), so that hypotheses about organizational size may need to be tested for each of the indicators. Similarly, if religious commitment is to be measured, it may be necessary to employ indicators which reflect all of the facets of such commitment in addition to church attendance. For example, individuals may be asked how far they endorse central aspects of their faith in order to establish how far they adhere to the beliefs associated with their faith.

When questionnaires are employed to measure concepts, as in the case of religious commitment, researchers often favour multiple-item measures. In the Job Survey data, **'satis'** is an example of a multiple-item measure. It entails asking individuals their positions in relation to a number of indicators, which stand for one concept. Similarly, there are four indicators of both **'autonom'** and **'routine'**. One could test a hypothesis with each of the indicators. However, if one wanted to use the Job Survey data to examine a hypothesis relating to **'satis'** and **'autonom'**, each of which contains four questions, sixteen separate tests would be required. The procedure for analysing such multiple-item measures is to aggregate each individual's response in relation to each question and to treat the overall measure as a scale in relation to which each unit of analysis has a score. In the case of **'satis'**, **'autonom'** and **'routine'**, the scaling procedure is *Likert Scaling*, which is a popular approach to the creation of multiple-item measures. With Likert scaling, individuals are presented with a number of statements which appear to relate to a common theme; they then indicate their degree of agreement or disagreement on a five- or seven-point range. The answer to each constituent question (often called an *item*) is scored, for example from 1 for Strongly Disagree to 5 for Strongly Agree if the range of answers is in terms of five points. The individual scores are added up to form an overall score for each respondent. Multiple-item scales can be very long; the four **'satis'** questions are taken from an often-used scale developed by Brayfield and Rothe (1951) which comprised eighteen questions.

These multiple-item scales are popular for various reasons. First, a number of items is more likely to capture the totality of a broad concept like job satisfaction than a single question. Second, we can draw finer distinctions between people. The **'satis'** measure comprises four questions which are scored from 1 to 5, so that respondents' overall scores can vary between 4 and 20. If only one question was asked, the variation would be between 1 and 5 – a considerably narrower range of potential variation. Third, if a question is misunderstood by a respondent, when only one question is asked that respondent will not be appropriately classified; if a few questions are asked, a misunderstood question can be offset by those which are properly understood.

It is common to speak of measures as *variables*, to denote the fact that units of analysis differ in respect to the concept in question. If there is no variation in a measure, it is a *constant*. It is fairly unusual to find concepts whose measures are constants. On the whole, the social sciences are concerned with variables and with expressing and analysing the variation that variables exhibit. When *univariate analysis* is carried out, we want to know how individuals are distributed in relation to a single variable. For example, we may want to know how many cases can be found in each of the categories or levels of the measure in question, or we may be interested in what the average response is, and so on. With *bivariate analysis* we are interested in the connections between two variables at a time. For example, we may want to know whether the variation in **'satis'** is associated with variation in another variable like **'autonom'** or whether men and women differ in regard to **'satis'**. In each case, it is variation that is of interest.

TYPES OF VARIABLE

One of the most important features of an understanding of statistical operations is an appreciation of when it is permissible to employ particular tests. Central to this appreciation is an ability to recognise the different forms that variables take, because statistical tests presume certain kinds of variable, a point that will be returned to again and again in later chapters.

The majority of writers on statistics draw upon a distinction developed by Stevens (1946) between nominal, ordinal and interval/ratio scales or levels of measurement. First, *nominal* (sometimes called *categorical*) scales entail the classification of individuals in terms of a concept. In the Job Survey data, the variable **'ethnicgp'**, which classifies respondents in terms of five categories – White, Asian, West Indian, African and Other – is an example of a nominal variable. Individuals can be allocated to each category, but the measure does no more than this and there is not a great deal more that we can say about it as a measure. We cannot order the categories in any way, for example.

This inability contrasts with *ordinal* variables, in which individuals are categorized but the categories can be ordered in terms of 'more' and 'less' of the concept in question. In the Job Survey data, **'skill'**, **'prody'** and **'qual'** are all ordinal variables. If we take the first of these, **'skill'**, we can see that people are not merely categorized into each of four categories – highly skilled, fairly skilled, semi-skilled and unskilled – since we can see that someone who is fairly skilled is at a higher point on the scale than someone who is semi-skilled. We cannot make the same inference with **'ethnicgp'** since we cannot order the categories that it comprises. Although we can order the categories comprising **'skill'**, we are still limited in the things that we can say about it. For example, we cannot say that the skill difference between being highly skilled and fairly skilled is the same as the skill difference between being fairly skilled and semi-skilled. All we can say is that those rated as highly skilled have more skill than those rated as fairly skilled, who in turn have greater skill than the semi-skilled, and so on. Moreover, in coding semi-skilled as 2 and highly skilled as 4, we cannot say that people rated as highly skilled are twice as skilled as those rated as semi-skilled. In other words, care should be taken in attributing to the categories of an ordinal scale an arithmetic quality that the scoring seems to imply.

With *interval/ratio variables*, we can say quite a lot more about the arithmetic qualities. In fact, this category subsumes two types of variable – interval and ratio. Both types exhibit the quality that differences between categories are identical. For example, someone aged 20 is one year older than someone aged 19, and someone aged 50 is one year older than someone aged 49. In each case, the difference between the categories is identical – one year. A scale is called an interval scale because the intervals between categories are identical. Ratio measures have a fixed zero point. Thus **'age'**, **'absence'** and **'income'** have logical zero points. This quality means that one can say that somebody who is aged 40 is twice as old as someone aged 20. Similarly, someone who has been absent from work six times in a year has been absent three times as often as someone who has been absent twice. However, the distinction between interval and ratio scales is often not examined by writers because in the social sciences, true interval variables frequently are also ratio variables (e.g. income, age). In this book, the term *interval variable* will sometimes be employed to embrace ratio variables as well.

Interval/ratio variables are recognized to be the highest level of measurement because there is more that can be said about them than with the other two types. Moreover, a wider variety of statistical tests and procedures is available to interval/ratio variables. It should be noted that if an interval/ratio variable like age is grouped into categories – such as 20–29, 30–39, 40–49, 50–59 and so on – it becomes an ordinal variable. We cannot really say that the difference between someone in the 40–49 group and someone in the 50–59 group is the same as the difference between someone in the 20–29 group and someone in the 30–39 group, since we no longer know the points within the groupings at which people are located. On the other hand, such groupings of individuals are sometimes useful for the presentation and easy assimilation of information. It should be noted too, that the position of *dichotomous* variables within the three-fold classification of types of variable is somewhat ambiguous. With such variables, there are only two categories, such as male and female for the variable gender. A dichotomy is usually thought of as a nominal variable, but sometimes it can be considered an ordinal variable. For example, when there is an inherent ordering to the dichotomy, such as passing and failing, the characteristics of an ordinal variable seem to be present.

Strictly speaking, measures like **'satis'**, **'autonom'** and **'routine'**, which derive from multiple-item scales, are ordinal variables. For example, we do not know whether the difference between a score of 20 on the **'satis'** scale and a score of 18 is the same as the difference between 10 and 8. This poses a problem for researchers since the inability to treat such variables as interval means that methods of analysis like correlation and regression (see Chapter 8), which are both powerful and popular, could not be used in their connection since these techniques presume the employment of interval variables. On the other hand, most of the multiple-item measures created by researchers are treated by them as though they are interval variables because these measures permit a large number of categories to be stipulated. When a variable allows only a small number of ordered categories, as in the case of **'commit'**, **'prody'**, **'skill'** and **'qual'** in the Job Survey data, each of which comprises only either four or five categories, it would be unreasonable in most analysts' eyes to treat them as interval variables. When the number of categories is considerably greater, as in the case of **'satis'**, **'autonom'** and **'routine'**, each of which can assume sixteen categories from 5 to 20, the case for treating them as interval variables is more compelling.

Certainly, there seems to be a trend in the direction of this more liberal treatment of multiple-item scales as having the qualities of an interval variable. On the other hand, many purists would demur from this position.

Moreover, there does not appear to be a rule of thumb which allows the analyst to specify when a variable is definitely ordinal and when interval. None the less, in this book it is proposed to reflect much of current practice and to treat multiple-item measures such as **'satis'**, **'autonom'** and **'routine'** as though they were interval scales. Labovitz (1970) goes further in suggesting that almost all ordinal variables can and should be treated as interval variables. He argues that the amount of error that can occur is minimal, especially in relation to the considerable advantages that can accrue to the analyst as a result of using techniques of analysis like correlation and regression which are both powerful and relatively easy to interpret. However, this view is controversial (Labovitz, 1971) and whereas many researchers would accept the treatment of variables like **'satis'** as interval, they would cavil about variables like **'commit'**, **'skill'**, **'prody'** and **'qual'**. Table 4.1 summarizes the main characteristics of the types of scale discussed in this section, along with examples from the Job Survey data.

In order to help with the identification of whether variables should be classified as nominal, ordinal, dichotomous, or interval/ratio, the steps articulated in Figure 4.1 can be followed. We can take some of the job survey

Table 4.1   Types of variable

Type	Description	Example in Job Survey data
Nominal	A classification of objects (people, firms, nations, etc.) into discrete categories.	**ethnicgp**
Ordinal	The categories associated with a variable can be rank-ordered. Objects can be ordered in terms of a criterion from highest to lowest.	**commit** **skill** **prody** **qual**
Interval (a)	With 'true' interval variables, categories associated with a variable can be rank-ordered, as with an ordinal variable, but the distances between categories are equal.	**income** **age** **years** **absence**
Interval (b)	Variables which strictly speaking are ordinal, but which have a large number of categories, such as multiple-item questionnaire measures. These variables are assumed to have similar properties to 'true' interval variables.	**satis** **routine** **autonom**
Dichotomous	A variable that comprises only two categories.	**gender** **attend**

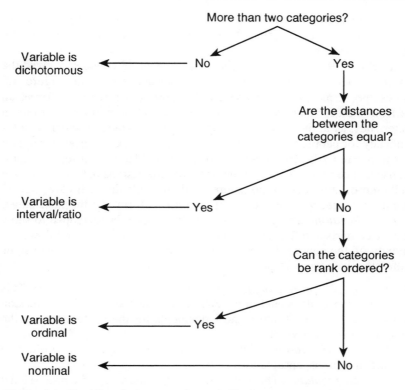

Figure 4.1   Deciding the nature of a variable

variables to illustrate how this table can be used. First, we can take **'skill'**. This variable has more than two categories; the distances between the categories are not equal; the categories *can* be rank ordered; therefore the variable is ordinal. Now **income**. This variable has more than two categories; the distances between them are equal; therefore the variable is interval/ratio. Now **gender**. This variable does not have more than two categories; therefore it is dichotomous. Finally, we can take **'ethnicgp'**. This variable has more than two categories; the distances between the categories are not equal; the categories cannot be rank ordered; therefore, the variable is nominal.

DIMENSIONS OF CONCEPTS

When a concept is very broad, serious consideration needs to be given to the possibility that it comprises underlying dimensions which reflect different aspects of the concept in question. Very often it is possible to specify those dimensions on *a priori* grounds, so that possible dimensions are established in advance of the formation of indicators of the concept. There is much to recommend deliberation about the possibility of such underlying dimensions, since it encourages systematic reflection on the nature of the concept that is to be measured.

Lazarsfeld's (1958) approach to the measurement of concepts viewed the search for underlying dimensions as an important ingredient. Figure 4.2 illustrates the steps that he envisaged. Initially, the researcher forms an image from a theoretical domain. This image reflects a number of common characteristics, as in the previous example of job satisfaction which denotes the tendency for people to have a distinctive range of experiences in relation to their jobs. Similarly, Hall (1968) developed the idea of 'professionalism' as a consequence of his view that members of professions have a distinctive constellation of attitudes to the nature of their work. In each case, out of this *imagery* stage, we see a concept starting to form. At the next stage, *concept specification* takes place, whereby the concept is developed to show whether it comprises different aspects or dimensions. This stage allows the complexity of the concept to be recognized. In Hall's case, five dimensions of professionalism were proposed:

1 *The use of the professional organization as a major reference* This means that the professional organization and members of the profession are the chief source of ideas and judgements for the professional in the context of his or her work.
2 *A belief in service to the public* According to this aspect, the profession is regarded as indispensable to society.
3 *Belief in self-regulation* This notion implies that the work of a professional can and should only be judged by other members of the profession, because only they are qualified to make appropriate judgements.
4 *A sense of calling to the field* The professional is someone who is dedicated to his or her work and would probably want to be a member of the profession even if material rewards were less.
5 *Autonomy* This final dimension suggests that professionals ought to be able to make decisions and judgements without pressures from either clients, the organizations in which they work, or any other non-members of the profession.

Not only is the concept specification stage useful in order to reflect and to capture the full complexity of concepts, but it also serves as a means of bridging the general formulation of concepts and their measurement, since the establishment of dimensions reduces the abstractness of concepts.

The next stage is the *selection of indicators*, in which the researcher searches for indicators of each of the dimensions. In Hall's case, ten indicators of each dimension were selected. Each indicator entailed a statement in relation to which respondents had to answer whether they believed that it agreed Very Well, Well, Poorly, or Very Poorly in the light of how they felt and behaved as members of their profession. A neutral category

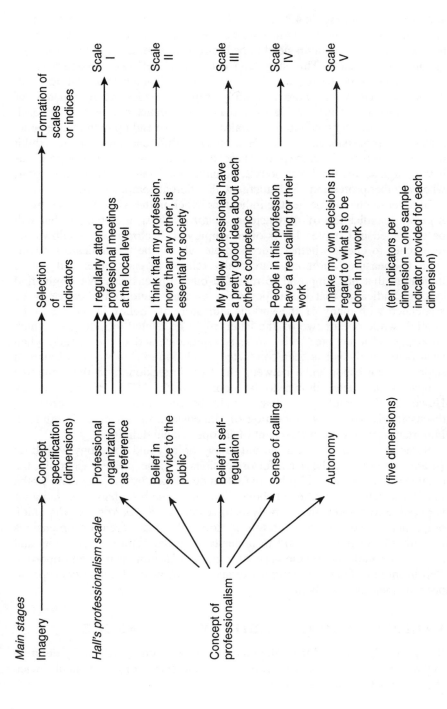

Figure 4.2 Concepts, dimensions and measurements
Sources: Lazarsfeld (1958); Hall (1968); Snizek (1972)

was also provided. Figure 4.2 provides both the five dimensions of professionalism and one of the ten indicators for each dimension. Finally, Lazarsfeld proposed that the indicators need to be brought together through the *formation of indices* or *scales*. This stage can entail either of two possibilities. An overall scale could be formed which comprised all indicators relating to all dimensions. However, more frequently, separate scales are formulated for each dimension. Thus, in Hall's research, the indicators relating to each dimension were combined to form scales, so that we end up with five separate scales of professionalism. As Hall shows, different professions exhibit different 'profiles' in respect of these dimensions – one may emerge as having high scores for dimensions 2, 3, and 5, moderate for 1, and low for 4, whereas other professions will emerge with different combinations.

In order to check whether the indicators bunch in the ways proposed by an *a priori* specification of dimensions, *factor analysis*, a technique that will be examined in Chapter 11, is often employed. Factor analysis allows the researcher to check whether, for example, all of the ten indicators developed to measure 'autonomy' are really related to each other and not to indicators that are supposed to measure other dimensions. We might find that an indicator that is supposed to measure autonomy seems to be associated with many of the various indicators of 'belief in service to the public', while one or two of the latter might be related to indicators which are supposed to denote 'belief in self-regulation', and so on. In fact, when such factor analysis has been conducted in relation to Hall's professionalism scale, the correspondence between the five dimensions and their putative indicators has been shown to be poor (Snizek, 1972; Bryman, 1985). However, the chief point that should be recognized in the foregoing discussion is that the specification of dimensions for concepts is often an important step in the development of an operational definition.

Some measurement is carried out in psychology and sociology with little (if any) attention to the quest for dimensions of concepts. For example, the eighteen-item measure of job satisfaction developed by Brayfield and Rothe (1951), which was mentioned above, does not specify dimensions, though it is possible to employ factor analysis to search for *de facto* ones. The chief point that can be gleaned from this section is that the search for dimensions can provide an important aid to understanding the nature of concepts and that when established on the basis of *a priori* reasoning can be an important step in moving from the complexity and abstractness of many concepts to possible measures of them.

VALIDITY AND RELIABILITY OF MEASURES

It is generally accepted that when a concept has been operationally defined, in that a measure of it has been proposed, the ensuing measurement device should be both reliable and valid.

Reliability

The reliability of a measure refers to its consistency. This notion is often taken to entail two separate aspects – external and internal reliability. External reliability is the more common of the two meanings and refers to the degree of consistency of a measure over time. If you have kitchen scales which register different weights every time the same bag of sugar is weighed, you would have an externally unreliable measure of weight, since the amount fluctuates over time in spite of the fact that there should be no differences between the occasions that the item is weighed. Similarly, if you administered a personality test to a group of people, re-administered it shortly afterwards and found a poor correspondence between the two *waves* of measurement, the personality test would probably be regarded as externally unreliable because it seems to fluctuate. When assessing external reliability in this manner, that is by administering a test on two occasions to the same group of subjects, *test–retest reliability* is being examined. We would anticipate that people who scored high on the test initially will also do so when retested; in other words, we would expect the relative position of each person's score to remain relatively constant. The problem with such a procedure is that intervening events between the test and the retest may account for any discrepancy between the two sets of results. For example, if the job satisfaction of a group of workers is gauged and three months later is re-assessed, it might be found that in general respondents exhibit higher levels of satisfaction than previously. It may be that in the intervening period they have received a pay increase or a change to their working practices or some grievance that had been simmering before has been resolved by the time job satisfaction is retested. Also, if the test and retest are too close in time, subjects may recollect earlier answers, so that an artificial consistency between the two tests is created. However, test–retest reliability is one of the main ways of checking external reliability.

Internal reliability is particularly important in connection with multiple-item scales. It raises the question of whether each scale is measuring a single idea and hence whether the items that make up the scale are internally consistent. A number of procedures for estimating internal reliability exist. One of the most common is *split-half reliability*. The researcher divides the items in a scale into two groups (either randomly or on an odd-even basis) and examines the relationship between respondents' scores for the two halves. Thus, the Brayfield–Rothe job satisfaction measure, which contains eighteen items, would be divided into two groups of nine, and the relationship between respondents' scores for the two halves would be estimated. A correlation coefficient is then generated (see Chapter 8), which varies between 0 and 1 and the nearer the result is to 1 – and preferably at or over 0.8 – the more internally reliable is the scale. This can be done in Minitab through the **correlation** procedure which is described in Chapter 8. Other methods for examining internal reliability exist and are described in Zeller and Carmines (1980; see also Cramer, 1994b, chapter 12).   Two other aspects of reliability, that is in addition to internal and external reliability, ought to be mentioned. First, when material is being coded for themes, the reliability of the coding scheme should be tested. This problem can occur when a researcher needs to code people's answers to interview questions that have not been pre-coded, in order to search for general underlying themes to answers or when a content analysis of newspaper articles is conducted to elucidate ways in which news topics tend to be handled. When such exercises are carried out, more than one coder should be used and an estimate of *inter-coder reliability* should be provided to ensure that the coding scheme is being consistently interpreted by coders. This exercise would entail gauging the degree to which coders agree on the coding of themes deriving from the material being examined. Second, when the researcher is classifying behaviour an estimate of *inter-observer reliability* should be provided. For example, if aggressive behaviour is being observed, an estimate of inter-observer reliability should be presented to ensure that the criteria of aggressiveness are being consistently interpreted. Methods of bivariate analysis (see Chapter 8) can be used to measure inter-coder and inter-observer reliability. A discussion of some methods which have been devised specifically for the assessment of inter-coder or inter-observer reliability can be found in Cramer (1994b).

Validity

The question of validity draws attention to how far a measure really measures the concept that it purports to measure. How do we know that our measure of job satisfaction is really getting at job satisfaction and not at something else? At the very minimum, a researcher who develops a new measure should establish that it has *face validity*, that is, that the measure apparently reflects the content of the concept in question.

The researcher might seek also to gauge the *concurrent validity* of the concept. Here the researcher employs a criterion on which people are known to differ and which is relevant to the concept in question. For example, some people are more often absent from work (other than through illness) than others. In order to establish the concurrent validity of our job satisfaction measure we may see how far people who are satisfied with their jobs are less likely than those who are not satisfied to be absent from work. If a lack of correspondence was found, such as frequent absentees being just as likely to be satisfied as not satisfied, we might be tempted to question whether our measure is really addressing job satisfaction. Another possible test for the validity of a new measure is *predictive validity*, whereby the researcher uses a future criterion measure, rather than a contemporaneous one as in the case of concurrent validity. With predictive validity, the researcher would take later levels of absenteeism as the criterion against which the validity of job satisfaction would be examined.

Some writers advocate that the researcher should also estimate the *construct validity* of a measure (Cronbach and Meehl, 1955). Here, the researcher is encouraged to deduce hypotheses from a theory that is relevant to the concept. For example, drawing upon ideas about the impact of technology on the experience of work (e.g. Blauner, 1964), the researcher might anticipate that people who are satisfied with their jobs are less likely to work on routine jobs; those who are not satisfied are more likely to work on routine jobs. Accordingly, we could investigate this theoretical deduction by examining the relationship between job satisfaction and job routine. On the other hand, some caution is required in interpreting the absence of a relationship between job satisfaction and job routine in this example. First, the theory or the deduction that is made from it may be faulty. Second, the measure of job routine could be an invalid measure of the concept.

All of the approaches to the investigation of validity that have been discussed up to now are designed to establish what Campbell and Fiske (1959) refer to as *convergent validity*. In each case, the researcher is concerned to demonstrate that the measure harmonizes with another measure. Campbell and Fiske argue that this process usually does not go far enough in that the researcher should really be using different measures of the same concept to see how far there is convergence. For example, in addition to devising a questionnaire-based measure of job routine, a researcher could use observers to rate the characteristics of jobs in order to distinguish between degrees of routineness in jobs in the firm (e.g. Jenkins *et al.*, 1975). Convergent validity would entail demonstrating a convergence between the two measures, although it is difficult to interpret a lack of convergence since either of the two measures could be faulty. Many of the examples of convergent validation that have appeared since Campbell and Fiske's (1959) article have not involved different methods, but have employed different questionnaire research instruments (Bryman, 1989). For example, two questionnaire-based measures of job routine might be used, rather than two different methods. Campbell and Fiske went even further in suggesting that a measure should also exhibit *discriminant validity*. The investigation of discriminant validity implies that one should also search for *low* levels of correspondence between a measure and other measures which are supposed to represent other concepts. Although discriminant validity is an important facet of the validity of a measure, it is probably more important for the student to focus upon the various aspects of convergent validation that have been discussed. In order to investigate both the various types of convergent validity and discriminant validity, the various techniques covered in Chapter 8, which are concerned with relationships between pairs of variables, can be employed.

EXERCISES

1. Which of the following answers is true? A Likert scale is (a) a test for validity; (b) an approach to generating multiple-item measures; (c) a test for reliability; or (d) a method for generating dimensions of concepts?
2. When operationalizing a concept, why might it be useful to consider the possibility that it comprises a number of dimensions?
3. Consider the following questions which might be used in a social survey about people's drinking habits and decide whether the variable is nominal, ordinal, interval/ratio or dichotomous:

    a. Do you ever consume alcoholic drinks?
        Yes __
        No   __ (go to question 5)

    b. If you have ticked **Yes** to the previous question, which of the following alcoholic drinks do you consume most frequently (tick one category only)?
        Beer __
        Spirits __
        Wine __
        Liquors __
        Other __

    c. How frequently do you consume alcoholic drinks? Tick the answer that comes closest to your current practice.
        Daily __
        Most days __
        Once or twice a week __
        Once or twice a month __
        A few times a year __
        Once or twice a year __

    d. How many units of alcohol did you consume last week? (We can assume that the interviewer would help respondents to translate into units of alcohol)

        number of units __

4. In the Job Survey data, is **absence** a nominal, an ordinal, an interval/ratio, or a dichotomous variable?

5. Is test–retest reliability a test of internal or external reliability?

6. A researcher computes the split-half reliability for **'autonom'**. Would this be a test of internal or external reliability?

7. A researcher develops a new multiple-item measure of 'political conservatism'. He/she administers the measure to a sample of individuals and also

asks them how they voted at the last general election in order to validate the new measure. The researcher relates respondents' scores to how they voted. Which of the following is the researcher assessing: (a) the measure's concurrent validity; (b) the measure's predictive validity; or (c) the measure's discriminant validity?

Chapter 5

Summarizing data

When researchers are confronted with a bulk of data relating to each of a number of variables, they are faced with the task of summarizing the information that has been amassed. If large amounts of data can be summarized, it becomes possible to detect patterns and tendencies that would otherwise be obscured. It is fairly easy to detect a pattern in a variable when, say, we have data on ten cases. But once we go beyond about twenty, it becomes difficult for the eye to catch patterns and trends unless the data are treated in some way. Moreover, when we want to present our collected data to an audience, it would be extremely difficult for readers to take in the relevant information. This chapter is concerned with the various procedures that may be employed to summarize a variable.

FREQUENCY DISTRIBUTIONS

Imagine that we have data on fifty-six students regarding which faculty they belong to at a university (see Table 5.1). The university has only four faculties: engineering, pure sciences, arts, and social sciences. Even though fifty-six is not a large number on which to have data, it is not particularly easy to see how students are distributed across the faculties. A first step that might be considered when summarizing data relating to a nominal variable such as this (since each faculty constitutes a discrete category) is the construction of a *frequency distribution* or *frequency table*. The idea of a frequency distribution is to tell us the number of cases in each category. By 'frequency' is simply meant the number of times that something occurs. Very often we also need to compute percentages, which tell us the proportion of cases contained within each frequency, i.e. *relative frequency*. In Table 5.2, the number 11 is the frequency relating to the arts category, i.e. there are eleven arts students in the sample, which is 20 per cent of the total number of students.

The procedure for generating a frequency distribution with Minitab will be addressed in a later section, but in the meantime it should be realized that all that is happening in the construction of a frequency table is that the number of cases in each category is added up. Additional information in the

Table 5.1   The faculty membership of fifty-six students (imaginary data)

Case No.	Faculty	Case No.	Faculty
1	Arts	29	Eng
2	PS	30	SS
3	SS	31	PS
4	Eng	32	SS
5	Eng	33	Arts
6	SS	34	SS
7	Arts	35	Eng
8	PS	36	PS
9	Eng	37	Eng
10	SS	38	SS
11	SS	39	Arts
12	PS	40	SS
13	Eng	41	Eng
14	Arts	42	PS
15	Eng	43	SS
16	PS	44	PS
17	SS	45	Eng
18	Eng	46	Arts
19	PS	47	Eng
20	Arts	48	PS
21	Eng	49	Eng
22	Eng	50	Arts
23	PS	51	SS
24	Arts	52	Eng
25	Eng	53	Arts
26	PS	54	Eng
27	Arts	55	SS
28	PS	56	SS

Note: Eng = Engineering   PS = Pure Sciences   SS = Social Sciences

Table 5.2   Frequency table for data on faculty membership

	n	Per cent
Engineering	18	32
Pure Sciences	13	23
Arts	11	20
Social Sciences	14	25
Total	56	100

form of the percentage that the number of cases in each category constitutes is usually provided. This provides information about the relative frequency of the occurrence of each category of a variable. It gives a good indication of the relative preponderance of each category in the sample. Table 5.2 provides the frequency table for the data in Table 5.1. Percentages have been rounded up or down to a whole number (using the simple rule that 0.5 and above are rounded up and below 0.5 are rounded down) to make the table easier to read. The letter n is often employed to refer to the number of cases in each category (i.e. the frequency). An alternative way of presenting a frequency table for the data summarized in Table 5.2 is to omit the frequencies for each category and to present only the relative percentages. This approach reduces the amount of information that the reader must absorb. When this option is taken, it is necessary to provide the total number of cases (i.e. $n = 56$) beneath the column of percentages.

Table 5.2 can readily be adapted to provide a diagrammatic version of the data. Such diagrams are usually called *bar charts* or *bar diagrams* and are often preferred to tables because they are more easily assimilated. A bar chart presents a column for the number or percentage of cases relating to each category. Figure 5.1 presents a bar chart for the data in

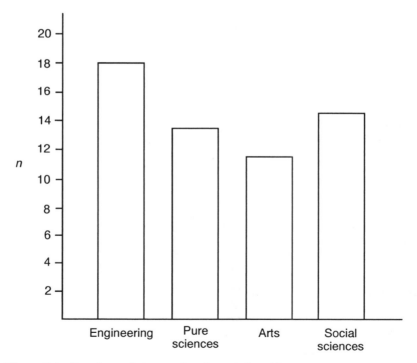

Figure 5.1   Bar chart of data on faculty membership

Table 5.1 in terms of the number of cases. On the horizontal axis the name of each category is presented. There is no need to order them in any way (e.g. short to long bars). The bars should not touch each other but should be kept clearly separate. It should be realized that the bar chart does not provide more information than Table 5.2; indeed, some information is lost – the percentages. Its main advantage is the ease with which it can be interpreted, a characteristic that may be especially useful when data are being presented to people who may be unfamiliar with statistical material.

When a variable is at the interval/ratio level, the data will have to be grouped in order to be presented in a frequency table. The number of cases in each grouping must then be calculated. As an example, the Job Survey data on **'income'** may be examined. We have data on sixty-eight individuals (two are missing), but if the data are not grouped there are thirty-three categories which are far too many for a frequency table. Moreover, the frequencies in each category would be far too small. In Table 5.3, a frequency table is presented of the data on **'income'**. Six categories are employed. In constructing categories such as these a number of points should be borne in mind. First, it is sometimes suggested that the number of categories should be between six and twenty, since too few or too many categories can distort the shape of the distribution of the underlying variable (e.g. Bohrnstedt and Knoke, 1982). However, it is not necessarily the case that the number of categories will affect the shape of the distribution. Also, when there are relatively few cases the number of categories will have to fall below six in order for there to be a reasonable number of cases in each category. On the other hand, a large number of categories will not be easy for the reader to assimilate and in this regard Bohrnstedt and Knoke's rule of thumb that the upper limit should be twenty categories seems slightly high. Second, the categories must be discrete. You should never group so that you have categories like: 5,500–6,500; 6,500–7,500; 7,500–8,500 and so on. Which categories

Table 5.3 Frequency table for **income** (Job Survey data)

Income (£)	n	Percentage
6499 and below	4	5.9
6500–7499	23	33.8
7500–8499	21	30.9
8500–9499	17	25.0
9500–10499	2	2.9
10500 and over	1	1.5
	68	100.0

Note: Two cases are missing

would incomes of £6,500 and £7,500 belong to? Categories must be discrete, as in Table 5.3, so that there can be no uncertainty about which one a case should be allocated to. Note that in Table 5.3, the reader's attention is drawn to the fact that there are two missing cases. The presence of two missing cases raises the question of whether percentages should be calculated in terms of all seventy cases in the Job Survey sample or the sixty-eight on whom we have income data. Most writers prefer the latter since the inclusion of all cases in the base for the calculation of the percentage can result in misleading interpretations, especially when there might be a large number of missing cases in connection with a particular variable.

The information in Table 5.3 can be usefully presented diagrammatically as a *histogram*. A histogram is like a bar chart, except that the bars are in contact with each other to reflect the continuous nature of the categories of the variable in question. Figure 5.2 presents a histogram produced in professional graphics in Minitab for Windows for the **'income'** data. Its advantages are the same as those for the bar chart.

If an ordinal variable is being analysed, grouping of categories is rarely necessary. In the case of the Job Survey data, a variable like **'skill'**, which can assume only four categories will not need to be grouped. The number of cases in each of the four categories can simply be added up and the percentages computed. A histogram can be used to display such data since the categories of the variable are ordered.

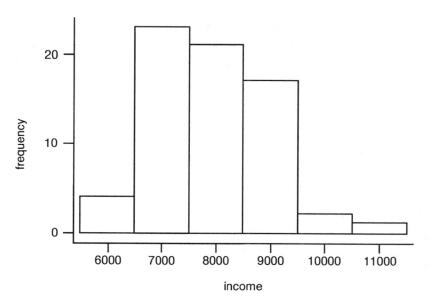

Figure 5.2 Histogram for **income** (Minitab Professional Graphics)

Using Minitab to produce frequency tables and histograms

In order to generate a frequency table for **'income'**, we will need to group the data. Otherwise we will get a frequency count and percentage for every single income in the sample. Similarly, we will have separate bars for each income within the sample. In a large sample, that could represent a lot of bars. To group the data, we will need to use the **code** procedure. This is probably done most easily with the prompt system. In order to group the data for the frequency table to be the same as the grouping for the histogram, we will need the following to be typed in after the **MTB** > prompt:

MTB > code (5500:6499)1 (6500:7499)2 (7500:8499)3 (8500:9499)4 (9500:10499)5 (10500:11499)6 c4 c30

This creates six **'income'** groups: the first is all members of the sample whose incomes lie between £5,500 and £6,499; the second is all those between £6,500 and £7,499 and so on. These categories have been chosen because they are consistent with the way in which a histogram is automatically configured for the variable **'income'**. The new variable, which we might want to call **'incgrp'**, has been placed in **c30**. Note that it is important that income groups do not overlap.

The new variable can be named as follows:

MTB > name c30 'incgrp'

In order to create the frequency table in the prompt system, the following commands are required:

MTB > tally 'incgrp';
SUBC> counts;
SUBC> percents.

This will give the frequencies (counts) for each category and the percentage of the sample in each category. To achieve the same end with the menu system, the following steps can be followed:

→**S**tat →**T**ables →**T**ally... →incgrp →**Select** [this will bring **incgrp** into the window. If frequency tables for other variables are required, simply click on each variable and then click on **Select**] → [for a frequency table with both frequencies **(counts)** and percentages make sure that there is a cross in the relevant boxes in the windows. If crosses are not present, simply click once in each or either box.] →**OK**

The resulting output can be found in Table 5.4.

The histogram of **'income'** in Figure 5.2 was generated with the Professional Graphics facility within Minitab for Windows. If this is unavailable, Standard Graphics must be enabled. Figure 5.3 shows what the

Table 5.4   Frequency table for **incgrp** (Minitab output)

Summary Statistics for Discrete Variables

incgrp	Count	Percent
1	4	5.88
2	23	33.82
3	21	30.88
4	17	25.00
5	2	2.94
6	1	1.47
N =	68	
* =	2	

resulting histogram of **'income'** will look like. In order to generate a histogram in the prompt system, the following step should be taken:

MTB > histogram 'income'

If Professional Graphics are available and are enabled, the histogram will look like Figure 5.2. If only Standard Graphics are available, it will look like Figure 5.3.

To achieve the same end with the menu system, we need to follow the following steps:

→**Graph** →**Histogram...** →income →**Select** [this will bring **income** into the **Graph variables:** box] → [in the **Data display:** box you should have **Bar** in the cell by **Item 1** in the column labelled **Display**. In the cell to the right of this cell you should have **Graph** in the column labelled **For each**. These can be changed, if necessary, by clicking on the downward pointing arrow to the immediate right of **Display** and/or **For each**] → [a title for the histogram can be inserted by clicking on

Character Histogram

Histogram of incgrp   N = 68   N* = 2

Midpoint	Count	
1	4	* * * *
2	23	* *
3	21	* *
4	17	* * * * * * * * * * * * * * * * *
5	2	* *
6	1	*

Figure 5.3   Histogram for **incgrp** (Minitab Standard Graphics)

the downward pointing arrow to the right of **Annotation** and inserting the title at the appropriate point] → [to produce more than one histogram, highlight further variables and click on **Select** for each variable selected] →**OK**

This sequence will generate the output presented in Figure 5.2. or 5.3 depending on whether Professional Graphics are available and enabled. Note that the diagram in Figure 5.2 provides the mid-point for each of the bars on the horizontal axis.

MEASURING CENTRAL TENDENCY

One of the most important ways of summarizing a distribution of values for a variable is to establish its *central tendency* – the typical value in a distribution. Where, for example, do values in a distribution tend to concentrate? To many readers this may mean trying to find the 'average' of a distribution of values. However, statisticians mean a number of different measures when they talk about averages. Three measures of average (i.e. central tendency) are usually discussed in text-books: the arithmetic mean, the median and the mode. Stephen J. Gould, a palaeontologist who is well known for his popular writings on science, illustrates the first two of these measures of average when he writes:

> A politician in power might say with pride, 'The mean income of our citizens is $15,000 per year.' The leader of the opposition might retort, 'But half our citizens make less than $10,000 per year.' Both are right, but neither cites a statistic with impassive objectivity. The first invokes a mean, the second a median.
>
> 1991: 473

While this comment does little to reassure us about the possible misuse of statistics, it does illustrate well the different ways in which average can be construed.

The arithmetic mean

The arithmetic mean is a method for measuring the average of a distribution which conforms to most people's notion of what an average is. Consider the following distribution of values:

12 10 7 9 8 15 2 19 7 10 8 16

The arithmetic mean consists of adding up all of the values (i.e. 123) and dividing by the number of values (i.e. 12), which results in an arithmetic mean of 10.25. It is this kind of calculation which results in such seemingly bizarre statements as 'the average number of children is 2.37'. However, the arithmetic mean, which is often symbolised as $\bar{x}$, is by far the most commonly used method of gauging central tendency. Many of the statistical tests encountered later in this book are directly concerned with comparing means deriving from different samples or groups of cases (e.g. analysis of variance – see Chapter 7). The arithmetic mean is easy to understand and to interpret, which heightens its appeal. Its chief limitation is that it is vulnerable to extreme values, in that it may be unduly affected by very high or very low values which can respectively increase or decrease its magnitude. This is particularly likely to occur when there are relatively few values; when there are many values, it would take a very extreme value to distort the arithmetic mean. For example, if the number 59 is substituted for 19 in the previous distribution of twelve values, the mean would be 13.58, rather than 10.25, which constitutes a substantial difference and could be taken to be a poor representation of the distribution as a whole. Similarly, in Table 8.11 in Chapter 8, the variable 'size of firm' contains an outlier (case number 20) which is a firm of 2,700 employees whereas the next largest has 640 employees. The mean for this variable is 499, but if we exclude the outlier it is 382.6. Again, we see that an outlier can have a very large impact on the arithmetic mean, especially when the number of cases in the sample is quite small.

The median

The median is the mid-point in a distribution of values. It splits a distribution of values in half. Imagine that the values in a distribution are arrayed from low to high, e.g. 2, 4, 7, 9, 10, the median is the middle value, i.e. 7. When there is an even number of values, the average of the two middle values is taken. Thus, in the former group of twelve values, to calculate the mean we need to array them as follows

2 7 7 8 8 <u>9 10</u> 10 12 15 16 19.

Thus in this array of twelve values, we take the two underlined values – the sixth and seventh – and divide their sum by 2, i.e. $(9 + 10)/2 = 9.5$. This is slightly lower than the arithmetic mean of 10.25, which is almost certainly due to the presence of three fairly large values at the upper end – 15, 16, 19. If we had the value 59 instead of 19, although we know that the mean would be higher at 13.58 the median would be unaffected, because it emphasizes the middle of the distribution and ignores the ends. For this reason, many writers suggest that when there is an outlying value which may distort the mean, the median should be considered because it will engender a more representative indication of the central tendency of a group of values. On the other hand, the median is less intuitively easy to understand and it does not use all of the values in a distribution in order for it to be calculated. Moreover, the mean's vulnerability to distortion as a consequence of extreme values is less pronounced when there is a large number of cases.

The mode

This final indicator of central tendency is rarely used in research reports, but is often mentioned in text-books. The mode is simply the value that occurs most frequently in a distribution. In the foregoing array of twelve values, there are three modes – 7, 8, and 10. Unlike the mean, which strictly speaking should only be used in relation to interval variables, the mode can be employed at any measurement level. The median can be employed in relation to interval and ordinal, but not nominal, variables. Thus, although the mode appears more flexible, it is infrequently used, in part because it does not use all of the values of a distribution and is not easy to interpret when there is a number of modes.

MEASURING DISPERSION

In addition to being interested in the typical or representative score for a distribution of values, researchers are usually interested in the amount of variation shown by that distribution. This is what is meant by *dispersion* – how widely spread a distribution is. Dispersion can provide us with important information. For example, we may find two roughly comparable firms in which the mean income of manual workers is identical. However, in one firm the salaries of these workers are more widely spread, with both considerably lower and higher salaries than in the other firm. Thus, although the mean income is the same, one firm exhibits much greater dispersion in incomes than the other. This is important information that can usefully be employed to add to measures of central tendency.

The most obvious measure of dispersion is to take the highest and lowest value in a distribution and to subtract the latter from the former. This is known as the *range*. While easy to understand, it suffers from the disadvantage of being susceptible to distortion from extreme values. This point can be illustrated by the imaginary data in Table 5.5, which shows the marks out of a hundred achieved on a mathematics test by two classes of twenty students, each of which was taught by a different teacher. The two classes exhibit similar means, but the patterns of the two distributions of values are highly dissimilar. Teacher A's class has a fairly bunched distribution, whereas that of Teacher B's class is much more dispersed. Whereas the lowest mark attained in Teacher A's class is 57, the lowest for Teacher B is 45. Indeed, there are eight marks in Teacher B's class that are below 57. However, whereas the highest mark in Teacher A's class is 74, three of Teacher B's class exceed this figure – one with a very high 95. Although the latter distribution is more dispersed, the calculation of the range seems to

Table 5.5 Results of a test of mathematical ability for
the students of two teachers (imaginary data)

	Teacher (A)	Teacher (B)
	65	57
	70	49
	66	46
	59	79
	57	72
	62	54
	66	66
	71	65
	58	63
	67	76
	61	45
	68	95
	63	62
	65	68
	71	50
	69	53
	67	58
	74	65
	72	69
	60	72
Arithmetic mean	65.55	63.2
Standard deviation	4.91	12.37
Median	66	64

exaggerate its dispersion. The range for Teacher A is 74−57, i.e. a range of
17. For teacher B, the range is 95−45, i.e. 50. This exaggerates the amount
of dispersion since all but three of the values are between 72 and 45,
implying a range of 27 for the majority of the values.

One solution to this problem is to eliminate the extreme values. The *inter-
quartile range*, for example, is sometimes recommended in this connection
(see Figure 5.4). This entails arraying a range of values in ascending order.
The array is divided into four equal portions, so that the lowest 25 per cent
are in the first portion and the highest 25 per cent are in the last portion.
These portions are used to generate quartiles. Take the earlier array from
which the median was calculated.

2 7 7 8 8 9 10 10 12 15 16 19
    ⇑   ⇑
    1st   3rd
  Quartile   Quartile

The first quartile (Q1), often called the 'lower quartile' will be between 7 and
8 and is calculated as $([3 \times 7]+8)/4$, i.e. 7.25. The third quartile (Q3), often

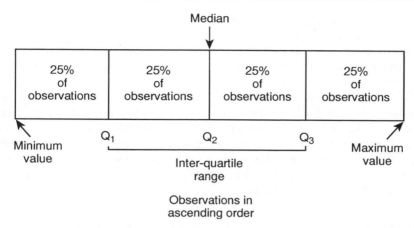

Figure 5.4 The inter-quartile range

called the 'upper quartile', will be $(12+[3 \times 15])/4$, i.e. 14.25. Therefore the inter-quartile range is the difference between the third and first quartiles, i.e. $14.25 - 7.25 = 7$. As Figure 5.4 indicates, the median is the second quartile, but is not a component of the calculation of the inter-quartile range. The main advantage of this measure of dispersion is that it eliminates extreme values, but its chief limitation is that in ignoring 50 per cent of the values in a distribution, it loses a lot of information. A compromise is the *decile range*, which divides a distribution into ten portions (deciles) and, in a similar manner to the inter-quartile range, eliminates the highest and lowest portions. In this case, only 20 per cent of the distribution is lost.

By far the most commonly used method of summarizing dispersion is the *standard deviation*. In essence, the standard deviation calculates the average amount of deviation from the mean. Its calculation is somewhat more complicated than this definition implies. A further description of the standard deviation can be found in Chapter 7. The standard deviation reflects the degree to which the values in a distribution differ from the arithmetic mean. The standard deviation is usually presented in tandem with the mean, since it is difficult to determine its meaning in the absence of the mean.

We can compare the two distributions in Table 5.5. Although the means are very similar, the standard deviation for Teacher B's class (12.37) is much larger than that for Teacher A (4.91). Thus, the standard deviation permits the direct comparison of degrees of dispersal for comparable samples and measures. A further advantage is that it employs all of the values in a distribution. It summarizes in a single value the amount of dispersion in a distribution, which, when used in conjunction with the mean, is easy to interpret. The standard deviation can be affected by extreme values, but since its calculation is affected by the number of cases, the distortion is less pronounced than with the range. On the other hand, the possibility of distortion from extreme values must be borne in mind. None the less, unless there are very good reasons for not wanting to use the standard deviation, it should be used whenever a measure of dispersion is required. It is routinely reported in research reports and widely recognized as the main measure of dispersion.

This consideration of dispersion has tended to emphasize interval variables. The standard deviation can only be employed in relation to such variables. The range and inter-quartile range can be used in relation to ordinal variables, but this does not normally happen, while tests for dispersion in nominal variables are also infrequently used. Probably the best ways of examining dispersion for nominal and ordinal variables is through bar charts, histograms and frequency tables.

Measuring central tendency and dispersion with MINITAB

All of these statistics can be generated in Minitab. When using the prompt system, the following commands should be used for generating these basic statistics for the variables **'satis'** and **'income'**:

MTB > describe 'satis' 'income'

With the Minitab for Windows menu system, the following sequence will achieve the same end:

→**Stat** →**Basic Statistics** →**Descriptive Statistics...** →satis →**Select** [**satis** will now appear in the **Variables:** box] →income →**Select** [**income** will now appear in the **Variables:** box below **satis**] →**OK**

This procedure will generate the following information that has been covered above: number in sample, excluding those for whom there is missing data (**N**); number for whom there is missing data (**N∗**); the arithmetic mean (**Mean**); the median (**Median**); the standard deviation (**StDev**); the minimum value (**Min**); the maximum value (**Max**); the first quartile (**Q1**); and the third quartile (**Q3**). Other information is provided, but can be ignored for present purposes. Sample output can be found in Table 5.6.

Table 5.6 Central tendency and dispersion analysis for **income** and **satis** (Minitab for Windows *Release 10* output)

Variable	N	N∗	Mean	Median	TrMean	StDev	SEMean
income	68	2	7819	7800	7792	998	121
satis	68	2	10.838	11.000	10.790	3.304	0.401

Variable	Min	Max	Q1	Q3
income	5900	10500	6925	8675
satis	5.000	19.000	8.000	14.000

STEMS AND LEAVES, BOXES AND WHISKERS

In 1977, John Tukey published a highly influential book entitled *Exploratory Data Analysis*, which sought to introduce readers to a variety of techniques he had developed which emphasize simple arithmetic computation and diagrammatic displays of data. Although the approach he advocates is antithetical to many of the techniques conventionally employed by data analysts, including the bulk of techniques examined in this book, some of Tukey's displays can be usefully appended to more orthodox procedures. Two diagrammatic presentations of data are very relevant to the present discussion – the *stem and leaf display* and the *boxplot* (sometimes called the *box and whisker plot*).

The stem and leaf display

The stem and leaf display is an extremely simple means of presenting data on an interval variable in a manner similar to a histogram, but without the loss of information that a histogram necessarily entails. It can be easily constructed by hand, although this would be more difficult with very large amounts of data. In order to illustrate the stem and leaf display, data on one indicator of local authority performance are taken. For a number of years, the British government has given the Audit Commission the task of collecting data on the performance of local authorities, so that their performance can be compared. One of the criteria of performance relates to the percentage of special needs reports issued within six months. A good deal of variation could be discerned with respect to this criterion, as the author of an article in *The Times* noted:

> If a child in Sunderland needs a report drawn up on its special educational needs, it has no chance of receiving this within six months. If the child moved a mile or two down the road into Durham, there would be an 80 per cent chance that the report would be issued in that time.
>
> Murray, 1995: 32

Whether such data really measure efficiency is, of course, a matter of whether the measure is *valid* (see Chapter 4), but there is no doubt that there is a great deal of variation with respect to the percentage of reports issued within six months. As Table 5.7 shows, the percentage varies between 0 and 95 per cent.

Figure 5.5 provides a stem and leaf display for this variable which we call 'needs'. The display has two main components. First, the digits in the middle column make up the stem. These constitute the starting parts for presenting each value in a distribution. Each of the digits that form the stem represents age in tens, i.e. 0 refers to single digit numbers; 1 to tens; 2 to twenties; 3 to thirties and so on. To the right of the stem are the leaves, each

Table 5.7 Percentage of special needs reports issued within six months in local authorities in England and Wales, 1993–4

London Boroughs		English Counties		Metropolitan Authorities	
Inner London		Avon	11	**Greater Manchester**	
City of London	*	Bedfordshire	25	Bolton	9
Camden	48	Berkshire	16	Bury	16
Greenwich	14	Buckinghamshire	69	Manchester	35
Hackney	36	Cambridgeshire	7	Oldham	50
Ham & Fulham	6	Cheshire	25	Rochdale	0
Islington	44	Cleveland	32	Salford	10
Ken & Chelsea	8	Cornwall	3	Stockport	16
Lambeth	4	Cumbria	35	Tameside	16
Lewisham	12	Derbyshire	17	Trafford	11
Southwark	10	Devon	55	Wigan	21
Tower Hamlets	37	Dorset	33	**Merseyside**	
Wandsworth	4	Durham	72	Knowsley	8
Westminster	63	East Sussex	8	Liverpool	95
Outer London		Essex	29	St Helens	21
Barking & Dag	22	Gloucestershire	45	Sefton	37
Barnet	40	Hampshire	12	Wirral	13
Bexley	37	Hereford & Worcs	3	**South Yorkshire**	
Brent	23	Hertfordshire	61	Barnsley	15
Bromley	24	Humberside	14	Doncaster	1
Croydon	27	Isle of Wight	60	Rotherham	10
Ealing	3	Kent	15	Sheffield	4
Enfield	2	Lancashire	14	**Tyne & Wear**	
Haringey	10	Leicestershire	*	Gateshead	4
Harrow	1	Lincolnshire	36	Newcastle u T	30
Havering	0	Norfolk	1	North Tyneside	48
Hillingdon	7	Northamptonshire	48	South Tyneside	5
Hounslow	20	Northumberland	79	Sunderland	0
Kingston u Thames	27	North Yorkshire	34	**West Midlands**	
Merton	16	Nottinghamshire	10	Birmingham	5
Newham	3	Oxfordshire	22	Coventry	20
Redbridge	34	Shropshire	15	Dudley	41
Richmond u Thames	27	Somerset	50	Sandwell	1
Sutton	6	Staffordshire	20	Solihull	31
Waltham Forest	24	Suffolk	27	Walsall	3
		Surrey	55	Wolverhampton	3
		Warwickshire	26	**West Yorkshire**	
		West Sussex	14	Bradford	25
		Wiltshire	30	Calderdale	2
				Kirklees	38
				Leeds	17
				Wakefield	15
				Welsh Counties	
				Clwyd	30
				Dyfed	67
				Gwent	17
				Gwynedd	88
				Mid Glamorgan	48
				Powys	80
				South Glamorgan	45
				West Glamorgan	4

Note: * missing or doubtful information
Source: adapted from *The Times* 30 March 1995, p. 32

of which represents an item of data which is linked to the stem. Thus, the 0 to the right of the 0 refers to the lowest value in the distribution, namely the percentage figure of 0. We can see that three authorities failed to issue any reports within six months and four issued only 1 per cent of reports within six months. When we come to the row starting with 1, we can see that five managed to issue 10 per cent of reports within six months. It is important to ensure that all of the leaves – the digits to the right of the stem – are vertically aligned. It is not necessary for the leaves to be ordered in magnitude, i.e. from 0 to 9, but it is easier to read. We can see that the distribution is very bunched at the lower end of the distribution. The appearance of the diagram has been controlled by requesting that incremental jumps are in tens, i.e. first teens, then twenties, then thirties, and so on. The output can also be controlled by requesting that any outliers are separately positioned. Practitioners of exploratory data analysis use a specific criterion for the identification of outliers. Outliers at the low end of the range are identified by the formula

first quartile – (1.5 × the inter-quartile range)

and at the high end of the range by the formula

third quartile – (1.5 × the inter-quartile range)

The first quartile for 'needs' is 8.0 and the third quartile is 36.0. Substituting in these two simple equations means that outliers will need to be below −36.0 or above 78.0. Using this criterion, four outliers at the high (HI) end of the range are identified.

This output can be generated in the prompt system thus:

MTB > stem-and-leaf 'needs';
SUBC> trim;
SUBC> increment 10.

With the menu system, the following sequence will produce the same end:

→**Graph** →**Character Graphs** →**Stem-and-Leaf...** →**needs** →**Select** [this will bring **needs** into the **Variables:** box] → the box by **Trim outliers** [if a mark in the box is not already there] → the box with the heading **Increment:** and then **10** →**OK**

The output is in Figure 5.5. The figures in the column to the left of the starting parts represent cumulative frequencies moving toward the median, which is 20 and is found in the row in which a frequency appears in brackets (19). These are a useful, but not strictly necessary, adjunct to a stem and leaf display. It is always important to stipulate the unit in which the leaves are presented which in this case is simply 1 – for a single percentage point. We can also see that there are missing data for two authorities.

Character Stem-and-Leaf Display

Stem-and-leaf of needs	N = 114
Leaf Unit = 1.0	N* = 2

```
 30   0 000111122333333444445566778889
 56   1 0000011223444445555566666777
(19)  2 00011223344555677779
 39   3 00012344555667778
 23   4 014558888
 14   5 0055
 10   6 01379
  5   7 2
```

HI   79, 80, 88,   95,

Figure 5.5 Stem-and-leaf display for the percentage of special needs reports issued within 6 months in local authorities in England and Wales (Minitab for Windows *Release 10* output)

The stem and leaf display provides a similar presentation to a histogram, in that it gives a sense of the shape of the distribution (such as whether values tend to be bunched at one end), the degree of dispersion, and whether there are outlying values. However, unlike the histogram it retains all the information, so that values can be directly examined to see whether particular ones tend to predominate.

The boxplot

Figure 5.6 provides the skeletal outline of a basic boxplot. The box comprises the middle 50 per cent of observations. Thus the lower end of the box, in terms of the measure to which it refers, is the first quartile and the upper end is the third quartile. In other words, the box comprises the inter-quartile range. The line in the box is the median. The broken lines (the whiskers) extend downwards to the lowest value in the distribution and upwards to the largest value *excluding outliers*, i.e. extreme values, which are separately indicated. It has a number of advantages. Like the stem and leaf display, the boxplot provides information about the shape and dispersion of a distribution. For example, is the box closer to one end or is it near the middle? The former would denote that values tend to bunch at one end. In this case, the bulk of the observations are at the lower end of the distribution, as is the median. This provides further information about the shape of the distribution, since it raises the question of whether the median is closer to one end of the box, as it is in this case. On the other hand, the

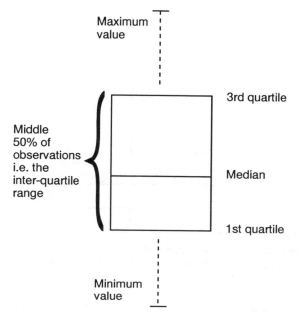

Maximum value

3rd quartile

Middle 50% of observations i.e. the inter-quartile range

Median

1st quartile

Minimum value

Figure 5.6   Boxplot

boxplot does not retain information like the stem and leaf display. Figure 5.7 provides a boxplot of the data from Table 5.7 using Professional Graphics in Minitab for Windows. The four outliers are signalled, using the previously-discussed criterion, with asterisks. It is clear that in half the authorities (all those below the line representing the median) 20 per cent or fewer reports are issued within six months. If Standard Graphics are enabled, the boxplot will be rather different.

In order to generate a boxplot for **'needs'** with the prompt system, the following command will produce a basic boxplot:

MTB > boxplot 'needs'

With the menu system, the following sequence will produce the same end:

→**Stat** →**EDA** →**Boxplot...** →**needs** →**Select** [this will bring **needs** into the **Graph Variables:** box beneath the **Y** and to the right of the figure **1**] →if **IQ Range Box** and **Outlier S**≫ do not appear in the **Data display:** box, click on the downward pointing arrow to the right of **Display** and enable each of these by choosing first **IQ Range Box**, then click again on the downward pointing arrow and then choose **Outlier S>> →OK**

Both of these exploratory data analysis techniques can be recommended as providing useful first steps in gaining a feel for data when you first start to

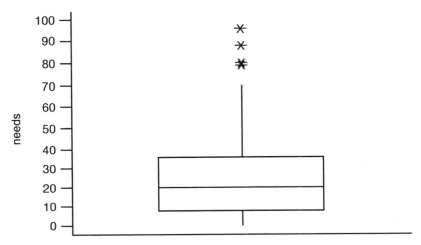

Figure 5.7 Boxplot of the percentage of special needs reports issued within 6 months in local authorities in England and Wales (professional graphics)

analyse them. Should they be used as alternatives to histograms and other more common diagrammatic approaches? Here they suffer from the disadvantage of not being well known. The stem and leaf diagram is probably the easier of the two to assimilate, since the boxplot diagram requires an understanding of quartiles and the median. If used in relation to audiences who are likely to be unfamiliar with these techniques, they may generate some discomfort even if a full explanation is provided. On the other hand, for audiences who are (or should be) familiar with these ideas, they have much to recommend them.

THE SHAPE OF A DISTRIBUTION

On a number of occasions, reference has been made to the shape of a distribution. For example, values in a distribution may tend to cluster at one end of the distribution or in the middle. In this section, we will be more specific about the idea of shape and introduce some ideas that are central to some aspects of data analysis to be encountered in later chapters.

Statisticians recognise a host of different possible distribution curves. By far the most important is the *normal distribution*. The normal distribution is a bell-shaped curve. It can take a number of different forms depending upon the degree to which the data are dispersed. Two examples of normal distribution curves are presented in Figure 5.8. The term 'normal' is potentially very misleading, because perfectly normal distributions are very rarely found in reality. However, the values of a variable may approximate to a normal distribution and when they do, we tend to think of them as

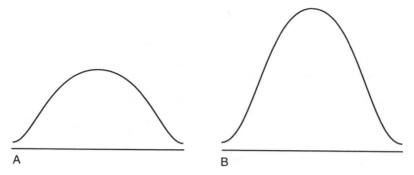

Figure 5.8 Two normal distributions

having the properties of a normal distribution. Many of the most common statistical techniques used by social scientists presume that the variables being analysed are nearly normally distributed (see the discussion of parametric and non-parametric tests in Chapter 7).

The normal distribution should be thought of as subsuming all of the cases which it describes beneath its curve. Fifty per cent will lie on one side of the arithmetic mean; the other 50 per cent on the other side (see Figure 5.9). The median value will be identical to the mean. As the curve implies, most values will be close to the mean. This is why the curve peaks at the mean. But the tapering off at either side indicates that as we move in either direction away from the mean, fewer and fewer cases are found. Only a small proportion will be found at its outer reaches. People's heights illustrate this fairly well. The mean height for an adult woman in the UK is 5ft 3ins (160.9 cm). If women's heights are normally distributed, we would expect that most women would cluster around this mean. Very few will be very short or very tall. We know that women's heights have these

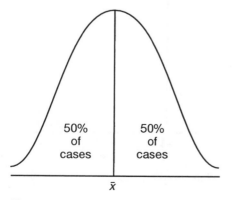

Figure 5.9 The normal distribution and the mean

properties, though whether they are perfectly normally distributed is another matter.

The normal distribution displays some interesting properties that have been determined by statisticians. These properties are illustrated in Figure 5.10. In a perfectly normal distribution

68.26 per cent of cases will be within one standard deviation of the mean
95.44 per cent of cases will be within two standard deviations of the mean
99.7 per cent of cases will be within three standard deviations of the mean.

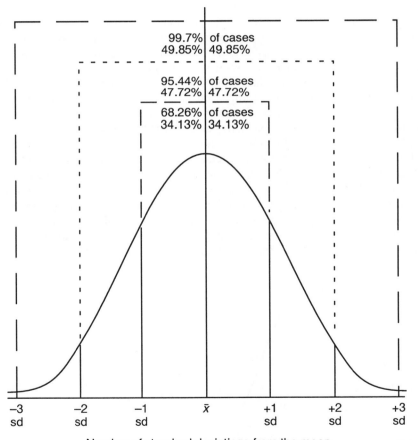

Figure 5.10 Properties of the normal distribution

Thus, if we have a variable which is very close to being normally distributed, we can say that if the mean is 20 and the standard deviation is 1.5, 95.44 per cent of cases will lie between 17 and 23 (i.e. $20 \pm 2 \times 1.5$). Turning this point around slightly, we can assert that there is a 95.44 per cent probability that a case will lie between 17 and 23. Likewise, 99.7 per cent of cases will lie between 15.5 and 24.5 (i.e. $20 \pm 3 \times 1.5$). Thus, we can be 99.7 per cent certain that the value relating to a particular case will lie between 15.5 and 24.5.

The data in Table 5.5 can be used to illustrate these ideas further. Ignoring the fact that we have all of the Mathematics scores for the students of these two teachers for a moment, if we know the mean and standard deviation for each of the two distributions, assuming normality we can work out the likelihood of cases falling within particular regions of the mean. With teacher A's students, 68.26 per cent of cases will fall within ±4.91 (the standard deviation) of 65.55 (the mean). In other words, we can be 68.26 per cent certain that a student will have gained a mark of between 60.64 and 70.46. The range of probable marks for Teacher B's students is much wider, largely because the standard deviation of 12.37 is much larger. For teacher B's class, there is a 68 per cent probability of gaining a mark of between 50.83 and 75.77. Table 5.8 presents the ranges of marks for one, two and three standard deviations from the mean for each teacher. The larger standard deviation for Teacher B's class means that for each standard deviation from the mean we must tolerate a wider range of probable marks.

It should be noted that as we try to attain greater certainty about the likely value of a particular case, the range of possible error increases from 1 × the standard deviation to 3 × the standard deviation. For teacher A, we can be 68.26 per cent certain that a score will lie between 70.46 and 60.64; but if we aimed for 99.7 per cent certainty, we must accept a wider band of possible scores, i.e. between 80.28 and 50.82. As we shall see in the context of the discussion of statistical significance in Chapter 6, these properties of the normal distribution are extremely useful and important when the researcher wants to make inferences about populations from data relating to samples.

Table 5.8 Probable mathematics marks (from data in Table 5.5)

	One standard deviation from the mean	Two standard deviations from the mean	Three standard deviations from the mean
	68.26% of cases will fall between:	*95.44% of cases will fall between:*	*99.7% of cases will fall between:*
Teacher A	70.46 and 60.64	75.37 and 55.73	80.28 and 50.82
Teacher B	75.57 and 50.83	87.94 and 48.46	100.31 and 26.09

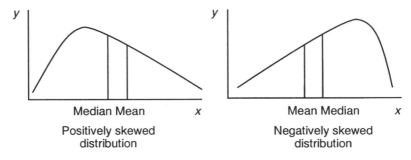

Figure 5.11   Positively and negatively skewed distributions

It is important to realize that some variables will not follow the shape of the normal distribution curve. In some cases, they may depart very strikingly from it. This tendency is most clearly evident when the values in a distribution are *skewed* – that is, they tend to cluster at either end. When this occurs, the mean and median no longer coincide. These ideas are illustrated in Figure 5.11. The left-hand diagram shows a curve that is *positively skewed* in that cases tend to cluster to the left and there is a long 'tail' to the right. The variable **'needs'** is an illustration of a positively skewed distribution, as the boxplot in Figure 5.7 suggests (the mean is 24.75 and the median is 20.00). In the right-hand diagram, the curve is *negatively skewed*. Another kind of distribution is one which possesses more than one peak.

Although there is a recognition that some variables in the social sciences do not exhibit the characteristics of a normal curve and that therefore we often have to treat variables as though they were normally distributed, when there is a very marked discrepancy from a normal distribution, such as in the two cases in Figure 5.11, some caution is required. For example, many writers would argue that it would not be appropriate to apply certain kinds of statistical test to variables which are profoundly skewed when that test presumes normally distributed data. Very often, skewness or other pronounced departures from a normal distribution can be established from the examination of a frequency table or of a histogram.

EXERCISES

1. Using Minitab how would you generate a frequency table for **'prody'** (Job Survey data), along with percentages and median?

2. Run the job for the commands from Question 1. What is the percentage of respondents in the 'poor' category?

3. Which of the following should *not* be used to represent an interval variable: (a) a boxplot; (b) a stem and leaf display; (c) a bar chart; or (d) a histogram?

4. Using Minitab how would you calculate the inter-quartile range for **'income'** (Job Survey data)?

5. What is the inter-quartile range for **'satis'**?

6. Why might the standard deviation be a superior measure of dispersion to the inter-quartile range?

7. Taking **'satis'** again, what is the likely range of **'satis'** scores that lie within two standard deviations of the mean? What percentage of cases is likely to lie within this range?

Chapter 6

Sampling and statistical significance

In this chapter, we will be encountering some issues which are fundamental to an appreciation of how people (or whatever is the unit of analysis) should be selected for inclusion in a study and of how it is possible to generalize to the population from which people are selected. These two related issues are concerned with sampling and the statistical significance of results. In examining sampling we will be examining the procedures for selecting people so that they are representative of the population from which they are selected. The topic of statistical significance raises the issue of how confident we can be that findings relating to a sample of individuals will also be found in the population from which the sample was selected.

SAMPLING

The issue of sampling is important because it is rarely the case that we have sufficient time and resources to conduct research on all of those individuals who could potentially be included in a study. Two points of clarification are relevant at this early stage. We talk about sampling from a population in the introduction to this chapter. It should be recognized that when we sample, it is not necessarily people who are being sampled. We can just as legitimately sample other units of analysis such as organizations, schools, local authorities, and so on. Second, by a 'population' is meant a discrete group of units of analysis and not just populations in the conventional sense, such as the population of England and Wales. Populations can be populations of towns, of particular groups (e.g. all accountants in the United Kingdom), of individuals in a firm, or of firms themselves. When we sample, we are selecting units of analysis from a clearly defined population.

Clearly, some populations can be very large and it is unlikely that all of the units in a population can be included because of the considerable time and cost that such an exercise would entail. Sometimes, they can be sufficiently small for all units to be contacted; or if they are not too large, it may be possible to carry out postal questionnaire or telephone interview surveys on a whole population. On the other hand, researchers are very often faced with the need to sample. By and large, researchers will want to form a representative sample, that is, a sample that can be treated as though it were the population. It is rare that perfectly representative samples can be created, but the chances of forming a representative sample can be considerably enhanced by probability sampling. The distinction between probability and non-probability sampling is a basic distinction in discussions of sampling. With probability sampling, each unit of a population has a specifiable probability of inclusion in a sample. In the basic forms of probability sampling, such as simple random samples (see below), each unit will have an equal probability of inclusion.

As an example of a non-probability sampling procedure, consider the following scenario. An interviewer is asked to obtain answers to interview questions for fifty people – twenty-five of each gender. She positions herself in a shopping area in a town at 9.00 a.m. on a Monday and starts interviewing people one by one. Will a representative sample be acquired? While it is not impossible that the sample is representative, there are too many doubts about its representativeness. For example, most people who work will not be shopping, she may have chosen people to be interviewed who were well-dressed and some people may be more likely to use the shops by which she positions herself than others. In other words, there is a strong chance that the sample is not representative of the people of the town. If the sample is unrepresentative, then our ability to generalize our findings to the population from which it was selected is sharply curtailed. If we do generalize, our inferences may be incorrect. If the sample is heavily biased towards people who do not work, who appeal to the interviewer because of their appearance and who only shop in certain retail outlets, it is likely to be a poor representation of the wider population.

By contrast, probability sampling permits the selection of a sample that should be representative. The following is a discussion of the main types of probability sample that are likely to be encountered.

Simple random sample

The simple random sample is the most basic type of probability sample. Each unit in the population has an equal probability of inclusion in the sample. Like all forms of probability sample, it requires a sampling frame, which provides a complete listing of all the units in a population. Let us say that we want a representative sample of 200 non-manual employees from a firm which has 600 non-manual employees. The sample is often denoted as n and the population as N. A sampling frame is constructed which lists the 600 non-manual employees. Each employee is allocated a number between 1 and N (i.e. 600). Each employee has a probability of n/N of being included in the sample, i.e. 1 in 3. Individuals will be selected for inclusion on a random basis to ensure that human choice is eliminated from decisions about who should be included and who excluded.

Each individual in the sampling frame is allocated a number 1 to N. The idea is to select n from this list. To ensure that the process is random, a table of random numbers should be consulted. These tables are usually in columns of five-digit numbers. For example, the figures might be

26938
37025
00352

Since we need to select a number of individuals which is in three digits (i.e. 200), only three digits in each five-digit random number should be considered. Let us say that we take the last three digits in each random number, that is we exclude the first two from consideration. The first case for inclusion would be that numbered 938. However, since the population is only 600, we cannot have a case numbered 938, so this figure is ignored and we proceed to the next random number. The figure 37025 implies that the case numbered 025 will be the first case for inclusion. The person numbered 025 will be the first sampled case. The next will be the person numbered 352, and so on. The process continues until n (i.e. 200) units have been selected.

By relying on a random process for the selection of individuals, the possibility of bias in the selection procedure is largely eliminated and the chances of generating a representative sample is enhanced. Sometimes, a systematic sample is selected rather than a simple random sample. With a systematic sample, the selection of individuals is undertaken directly from the sampling frame and without the need to connect random numbers and cases. In the previous example, a random start between 1 and 3 would be made. Let us say that the number is 1. The first case on the sampling frame would be included. Then, every third case would be selected, since 1 in 3 must be sampled. Thus, the fourth, seventh, tenth, thirteenth and so on would be selected. The chief advantage of the systematic sample over the simple random sample is that it obviates the need to plough through a table of random numbers and to tie in each number with a corresponding case. This procedure can be particularly time-consuming when a large sample must be selected. However, in order to select a systematic sample, the researcher must ensure that there is no inherent ordering to the list of cases in the sampling frame, since this would distort the ensuing sample and would probably mean that it was not representative.

Stratified sampling

Stratified sampling is commonly used by social scientists because it can lend an extra ingredient of precision to a simple random or systematic sample. When selecting a stratified sample, the researcher divides the population into strata. The strata must be categories of a criterion. For example, the population may be stratified according to the criterion of gender, in which case two strata – male and female – will be generated. Alternatively, the criterion may be department in the firm, resulting in possibly five strata: production, marketing, personnel, accounting, and research and development. Provided that the information is readily available, people are grouped into the strata. A simple random or systematic sample is then taken from the listing in each stratum. It is important for the stratifying criterion to be relevant to the issues in which the researcher is interested; it should not be undertaken for its own sake. The researcher may be interested in how the attitudes of non-manual employees is affected by the department to which they are attached in the firm. The advantage of stratified sampling is that it offers the possibility of greater accuracy, by ensuring that the groups that are created by a stratifying criterion are represented in the same proportions as in the population.

Table 6.1 provides an illustration of the idea of a stratified sample. The table provides the numbers of non-manual personnel in each department in the first column and the number of each department (i.e. stratum) that would be selected on a 1 in 3 basis. The important point to note is that the proportions of personnel from each department in the sample are the same as in the population. The largest department – production – has 35 per cent of all non-manual employees in the firm and 35 per cent of non-manual employees in the sample. A simple random or systematic sample without stratification might have achieved the same result, but a stratified sample greatly enhances the likelihood of the proper representation of strata in the sample. Two or more stratifying criteria can be employed in tandem. For example, if the researcher were interested in the effects of gender on job attitudes, as well as belonging to different departments, we would then have ten strata (five departments × two sexes), that is, men and women in production, men and women in marketing, and so on. From each of the ten strata a 1 in 3 sample would then be taken.

If the numbers in some strata are likely to be small, it may be necessary to sample disproportionately. For example, we may sample 2 in 3 of those

Table 6.1 Devising a stratified random sample: non-manual employees in a firm

Department	Population N	Sample n
Production	210	70
Marketing	120	40
Personnel	63	21
Accounting	162	54
Research and development	45	15
Total	600	200

in Research and Development. This would mean that 30, rather than 15, would be sampled from this department. However, to compensate the extra 15 individuals that are sampled in Research and Development, slightly less than 1 in 3 for Production and Accounting may need to be sampled. When this occurs, it has to be recognized that the sample is differentially weighted relative to the population, so that estimates of the sample mean will have to be corrected to reflect this weighting.

Multistage cluster sampling

One disadvantage of the probability samples covered so far is that they do not deal very well with geographically dispersed populations. If we took a simple random sample of all chartered accountants in the UK or indeed of the population of the UK itself, the resulting sample will be highly scattered. If the aim was to conduct an interview survey, interviewers would spend a great deal of time and money travelling to their respondents. A multistage cluster sample is a probability sampling procedure that allows such geographically dispersed populations to be adequately covered, while simultaneously saving interviewer time and travel costs.

Initially, the researcher samples clusters, that is areas of the geographical region being covered. The case of seeking to sample households in a very large city can be taken as an example of the procedure. At the first stage, all of the electoral wards in the city would be ascribed a number 1 to N and a simple random sample of wards selected. At the second stage, a simple random sample of streets in each ward might be taken. At the third stage, a simple random sample of households in the sampled streets would be selected from the list of addresses in the electoral rolls for the relevant wards. By concentrating interviewers in small regions of the city, much time and travel costs can be saved. Very often, stratification accompanies the sampling of clusters. For example, wards might be categorized in terms of an indicator of economic prosperity (e.g. high, medium and low) like the percentage of heads of household in professional and managerial jobs. Stratification will ensure that clusters are properly represented in terms of this criterion.

SAMPLING PROBLEMS

One of the most frequently asked questions in the context of sampling is 'how large should a sample be?'. In reality, there can only be a few guidelines to answering this question, rather than a single definitive response.

First, the researcher almost always works within time and resource constraints, so that decisions about sample size must always recognize these boundaries. There is no point in working out an ideal sample size for a project if you have nowhere near the amount of resources required to bring it into effect. Second, the larger the sample the greater the accuracy. Contrary to expectations, the size of the sample relative to the size of the population (in other words n/N) is rarely relevant to the issue of a sample's accuracy. This means that sampling error – differences between the sample and the population which are due to sampling – can be reduced by increasing sample size. However, after a certain level, increases in accuracy tend to tail off as sample size increases, so that greater accuracy becomes economically unacceptable.

Third, the problem of non-response should be borne in mind. Most sample surveys attract a certain amount of non-response. Thus, it is likely that only some of the 200 non-manual employees we sample will agree to participate in the research. If it is our aim to ensure as far as possible that 200 employees are interviewed and if we think that there may be a 20 per cent rate of non-response, it may be advisable to select 250 individuals, on the grounds that approximately 50 will be non-respondents. Finally, the researcher should bear in mind the kind of analysis he or she intends to undertake. For example, if the researcher intends to examine the relationship between department in the firm and attitudes to white-collar unions, a table in which department is cross-tabulated against attitude can be envisaged. If 'attitude to white-collar unions' comprises four answers and since 'department' comprises five categories, a table of twenty 'cells' would be engendered (see discussion of contingency tables and cross-tabulation in Chapter 8). In order for there to be an adequate number of cases in each cell a fairly large sample will be required. Consequently, considerations of sample size should be sensitive to the kinds of analysis that will be subsequently required.

The issue of non-response draws attention to the fact that a well-crafted sample can be jeopardized by the failure of individuals to participate. The problem is that respondents and non-respondents may differ from each other in certain respects, so that respondents may not be representative of the population. Sometimes, researchers try to discern whether respondents are disproportionately drawn from particular groups, such as whether men are clearly more inclined not to participate than women. However, such tests can only be conducted in relation to fairly superficial characteristics like gender; deeper differences, such as attitudinal ones, cannot be readily tested. In addition, some members of a sample may not be contactable, because they have moved or are on holiday. Moreover, even when a questionnaire is answered, there may still be questions which, by design or error, are not answered. Each of these three elements – non-response, inability to contact and missing information for certain variables – may be sources of bias, since we do not know how representative those who do respond to each variable are of the population.

Finally, although social scientists are well aware of the advantages of probability sampling procedures, a great deal of research does not derive from probability samples. In a review of 126 articles in the field of organization studies which were based on correlational research, Mitchell (1985) found that only twenty-one were based on probability samples. The rest used convenience samples, that is, samples which are either 'chosen' by the investigator or which choose themselves (e.g. volunteers). However, when it is borne in mind that response rates to sample surveys are often quite low and are declining (Goyder, 1988), the difference between research based on random samples and convenience samples in terms of their relative representativeness is not always as great as is sometimes implied. None the less, many of the statistical tests and procedures to be encountered later in this book assume that the data derive from a random sample. The point being made here is that this requirement is often not fulfilled and that even when a random sample has been used, factors like non-response may adversely affect its random qualities.

STATISTICAL SIGNIFICANCE

How do we know if a sample is typical or representative of the population from which it has been drawn? To find this out we need to be able to describe the nature of the sample and the population. This is done in terms of the distributions of their values. Thus, for example, if we wanted to find out whether the proportion of men to women in our sample was similar to that in some specified population, we would compare the two proportions. The main tests for tackling such problems are described in Chapters 7 and 9. It should be noted that the same principle lies behind all statistical tests including those concerned with describing the relationship between two or more variables. Here, the basic idea underlying them will be outlined.

To do this we will take the simple case of wanting to discover whether a coin was unbiased in the sense that it lands heads and tails an equal number of times. The number of times we tossed the coin would constitute the sample while the population would be the outcomes we would theoretically expect if the coin was unbiased. If we flipped the coin just once, then the probability of it turning up heads is once every two throws or 0.5. In other words, we would have to toss it at least twice to determine if both possibilities occur. If we were to do this, however, there would be four possible theoretical outcomes as shown in Table 6.2: (1) a tail followed by a head; (2) a head followed by a tail; (3) two tails; and (4) two heads. What happens on each throw is *independent* of, or not affected by, the outcome of any other throw. If the coin was unbiased, then each of the four outcomes would be equally probable. In other words, the probability of obtaining either two tails or two heads (but not both possibilities) is one in four or 0.25, while that of obtaining a head and a tail is two in four, or 0.5. The probability of obtaining a head and a tail (0.5) is greater than that of two tails (0.25) or two heads (0.25) but is the same as that for two tails and two

Table 6.2 Four possible outcomes of tossing a coin twice

Possible outcomes		Probability (p)
1	Head	Tail	0.25
2	Tail	Head	0.25
3	Head	Head	0.25
4	Tail	Tail	0.25

1 Head Tail 0.25 ⎱ = 0.5
2 Tail Head 0.25 ⎰

heads combined (0.25 + 0.25). From this it should be clear that it is not possible to draw conclusions about a coin being unbiased from so few throws or such a small sample. This is because the frequency of improbable events is much greater with smaller samples. Consequently, it is much more difficult with such samples to determine whether they come from a certain population.

If we plot or draw the distribution of the probability of obtaining the same proportion of heads to tails as shown in Figure 6.1, then it will take the shape of an inverted 'V'. This shape will contain all the possible outcomes which will add up to 1 (0.25 + 0.25 + 0.25 + 0.25 = 1).

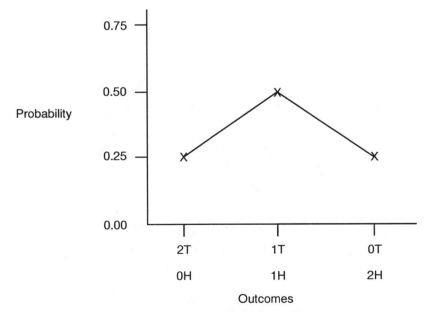

Figure 6.1 The distribution of similar theoretical outcomes of tossing a coin twice

Theoretically, the more often we throw the coin, the more similar the distribution of the possible outcomes will be to an inverted 'U' or normal distribution. Suppose, for example, we threw the same coin six times (or, what amounts to the same thing, six coins once). If we did this, there would be sixty-four possible outcomes. These are shown in Table 6.3. The total number of outcomes can be calculated by multiplying the number of possible outcomes on each occasion (2) by those of the other occasions ($2 \times 2 \times 2 \times 2 \times 2 \times 2 = 64$). The probability of obtaining six heads or six tails in a row (but not both) would be one in sixty-four or about 0.016. Since there are six possible ways in which one head and five tails can be had, the probability of achieving this is six out of sixty-four or about 0.10 (i.e., 0.016×6). The distribution of the probability of obtaining different sequences of the same number of tails and heads grouped together (for example, the six sequences of finding five tails and a head) is presented in Figure 6.2.

It should be clear from this discussion that we can never be 100 per cent certain that the coin is unbiased, because even if we threw it 1,000 times, there is a very small chance that it will turn up all heads or all tails on every one of those throws. So what we do is to set a criterion or cut-off point at or beyond which we assume the coin will be judged to be biased. This point is

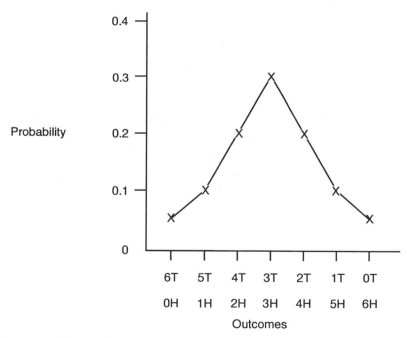

Figure 6.2 The distribution of similar theoretical outcomes of tossing a coin six times

Table 6.3 Theoretical outcomes of tossing a coin six times and the probabilities of similar outcomes

	Theoretical outcomes	probability		Theoretical outcomes	probability
1	TTTTTT	0.016	64	HHHHHH	0.016
2	TTTTTH ⎫		63	HHHHHT ⎫	
3	TTTTHT ⎪		62	HHHHTH ⎪	
4	TTTHTT ⎪	0.094	61	HHHTHH ⎪	0.094
5	TTHTTT ⎬		60	HHTHHH ⎬	
6	THTTTT ⎪		59	HTHHHH ⎪	
7	HTTTTT ⎭		58	THHHHH ⎭	
8	TTTTHH ⎫		57	HHHHTT ⎫	
9	TTTHHT ⎪		56	HHHTTH ⎪	
10	TTHHTT ⎪		55	HHTTHH ⎪	
11	TTTHTH ⎪		54	HHHTHT ⎪	
12	TTHTHT ⎪		53	HHTHTH ⎪	
13	TTHTTH ⎪		52	HHTHHT ⎪	
14	THTHTT ⎪		51	HTHTHH ⎪	
15	THHTTT ⎬	0.234	50	HTTHHH ⎬	0.234
16	THTTTH ⎪		49	HTHHHT ⎪	
17	THTTHT ⎪		48	HTHHTH ⎪	
18	HTTHTT ⎪		47	THHTHH ⎪	
19	HTTTHT ⎪		46	THHHTH ⎪	
20	HTHTTT ⎪		45	THTHHH ⎪	
21	HTTTTH ⎪		44	THHHHT ⎪	
22	HHTTTT ⎭		43	TTHHHH ⎭	
23	TTTHHH		42	HHHTTT ⎫	
24	TTHHHT		41	HHTTTH ⎪	
25	TTHHTH		40	HHTTHT ⎪	
26	TTHTHH		39	HHTHTT ⎪	
27	THTHTH		38	HTHTHT ⎪	
28	THTHHT		37	HTHTTH ⎬	0.312
29	THHTTH		36	HTTHHT ⎪	
30	THHTHT		35	HTTHTH ⎪	
31	THTTHH		34	HTHHTT ⎪	
32	THHHTT		33	HTTTHH ⎭	

arbitrary and is referred to as the *significance level*. It is usually set at a probability or *p* level of 0.05 or five times out of a hundred. Since the coin can be biased in one of two ways, i.e. in favour of either heads or tails, this 5 per cent is shared equally between these two possibilities. This means, in effect, that the probability of the coin being biased towards heads will be 0.025 and that the probability of its bias towards tails will also be 0.025. In other words, if it turns up heads or tails six times in a row, then the probability of both these outcomes occurring would be about 0.032 (i.e., 0.016 + 0.016) which is below the probability of 0.05. If either of these two events happened we would accept that the coin was biased. If, however, it landed tails once and heads five times, or heads once and tails five times, there are six ways in which either of these two outcomes could happen. Consequently, the probability of either one happening is six out of sixty-four or about 0.10. The probability of both outcomes occurring is about 0.2 (i.e., 0.10 + 0.10). In this case, we would have to accept that the coin was unbiased since this probability level is above the criterion of 0.05.

Because we can never be 100 per cent certain that the coin is either biased or unbiased, we can make one of two kinds of error. The first kind is to decide that the coin is biased when it is not. This is known as a *Type I error* and is sometimes referred to as α (alpha). For example, as we have seen, an unbiased coin may land heads six times in a row. The second kind of error is to judge the coin to be unbiased when it is biased. This is called a *Type II error* and is represented by β (beta). It is possible, for instance, for a biased coin to come up tails once and heads five times. We can reduce the possibility of making a Type I error by accepting a lower level of significance, say 0.01 instead of 0.05. But doing this increases the probability of making a Type II error. In other words, the probability of a Type I error is inversely related to that of a Type II one. The more likely we are to make a Type I error, the less likely we are to commit a Type II error.

At this stage, it is useful to discuss briefly three kinds of probability distribution. The first is known as a *binomial* distribution and is based on the idea that if only either of two outcomes can occur on any one occasion (for example, heads or tails if a coin is thrown), then we can work out the theoretical distribution of the different combinations of outcomes which could occur if we knew the number of occasions that had taken place. One characteristic of this distribution is that it consists of a limited or finite number of events. If, however, we threw an infinite number of coins an infinite number of times, then we would have a distribution which would consist of an infinite possibility of events. This distribution is known variously as a DeMoivre's, Gaussian, normal, standard normal or z curve or distribution. If random samples of these probabilities are taken and plotted, then the shape of those distributions will depend on the size of the samples. Smaller samples will produce flatter distributions with thicker tails than the normal distribution, while larger ones will be very similar to it. These distributions are known as t distributions. What this means is that when we want to know the likelihood that a particular series of events could have occurred by chance, we need to take into account the size of the sample on which those events are based.

So far, in order to convey the idea that certain events may occur just by chance, we have used the example of tossing a coin. Although this may seem a bit remote from the kinds of data we collect in the social sciences, we use this underlying principle to determine issues such as whether a sample is representative of its population and whether two or more samples or treatments differ from each other. Suppose we drew a small sample of six people and wanted to determine if the proportion of males to females in it was similar to that of the population in which the number of men and women are equal. Each person can only be male or female. Since there are six people, there are sixty-four possible outcomes (i.e., $2 \times 2 \times 2 \times 2 \times 2 \times 2$). These, of course, are the same as those displayed in Table 6.3 except that we now substitute males for tails and females for heads. The joint probability of all six people being either male or female would be about 0.03 (i.e. $0.016 + 0.016$), so that if this were the result we would reject the notion that the sample was representative of the population. However, if one was male and the other five female, or there was one female and five males, then the probability of this occurring by chance would be about 0.2 (i.e. $0.096 + 0.096$). This would mean that at the 0.05 significance level we would accept either of these two outcomes or samples as being typical of the population because the probability of obtaining these outcomes is greater than the 0.05 level. This shows that sample values can diverge quite widely from those of their populations and still be drawn from them, although it should be emphasized that this outcome would be less frequent the larger the sample. Statistical tests which compare a sample with a population are known as *one-sample tests* and can be found in the next chapter.

The same principle underlies tests which have been developed to find out if two or more samples or treatments come from the same population or different ones, although this is a little more difficult to grasp. For example, we may be interested in finding out whether women are more perceptive than men, or whether alcohol impairs performance. In the first case, the two samples are women and men while in the second they are alcohol and no alcohol. Once again, in order to explain the idea that underlies these tests, it may be useful to think about it initially in terms of throwing a coin, except that this time we throw two coins. The two coins represent the two samples. We want to know whether the two coins differ in their tendency to be unbiased. If the two coins were unbiased and if we were to throw them six times each, then we should expect the two sets of theoretical outcomes obtained to be the same as that in Table 6.3. In other words, the two distributions should overlap each other exactly.

Now if we threw the two coins six times each, it is unlikely that the empirical outcomes will be precisely the same, even if the coins were unbiased. In fact, we can work out the theoretical probability of the two distributions being different in the same way as we did earlier for the coin turning up heads or tails. It may be easier in the first instance if we begin by comparing the outcomes of tossing two coins just once. If we do this, there are four possible outcomes: (1) two tails; (2) two heads; (3) one tail and one head; and (4) one head and one tail. If we look at these outcomes in terms of whether they are the same or different, then two of them are the same (two tails and two heads) while two of them are different (one tail and one head, and vice versa). In other words, the probability of finding a difference is two out of four or 0.5, which is the same as that for discovering no difference. We stand an equal chance of finding no difference as we do of a difference if we throw two unbiased coins once.

Thinking solely in terms of the outcomes of the two coins being the same or different, if we threw the two coins twice, then there would be four possible outcomes: (1) two the same; (2) two different; (3) the first the same and the second different; and (4) the first different and the second the same. In other words, the probability of obtaining the same outcome when two unbiased coins are thrown twice is 0.25. The probability of the outcomes being mixed is greater with the value being 0.5. The probability of the outcomes being the same on all six throws would be about 0.016 ($0.5 \times 0.5 \times 0.5 \times 0.5 \times 0.5 \times 0.5 = 0.016$). Hence, if the two coins were unbiased, we would not expect them to give the same outcome on each occasion they were tossed. The distribution of the outcomes of the two coins represents, in effect, what we would expect to happen if the differences between two samples or two treatments were due to chance.

Applying this idea to the kind of question that may be asked in the social sciences, we may wish to find out if women and men differ in their perceptiveness. There are three possible answers to this question: (1) women may be more perceptive than men; (2) they may be no different from them; or (3) they may be less perceptive than them. In other words, we can have three different expectations or hypotheses about what the answer might be. Not expecting any difference is known as the *null hypothesis*. Anticipating a difference but not being able to predict what it is likely to be is called a *non-directional hypothesis*. However, it is unlikely that we would ask this sort of question if we did not expect a difference of a particular nature, since there is an infinite number of such questions which can be posed. In carrying out research we are often concerned with showing that a particular relationship either holds or does not hold between two or more variables. In other words, we are examining the direction as well as the existence of a relationship. In this case, we may be testing the idea that women are more perceptive than men. This would be an example of a *directional hypothesis*. As we shall see, specifying the direction of the hypothesis means that we can adopt a slightly higher and more lenient level of significance.

Since there are three possible outcomes (i.e. a probability of 0.33 for any one outcome) for each paired comparison, if we tested this hypothesis on a small sample of five men and five women, then the probability of all five women being more perceptive than men just by chance would be about 0.004 (i.e. $0.33 \times 0.33 \times 0.33 \times 0.33 \times 0.33$). If we obtained this result, and if we adopted the usual 0.05 or 5 per cent as the significance level at or below which this finding is unlikely to be due to chance, then we would accept the hypothesis since 0.004 is less than 0.05. In other words, we would state that women were significantly more perceptive than men below the 5 per cent level – see Figure 6.3(a). As we shall see, Minitab provides the exact level of significance for each test when this level is given. It has been customary in the social sciences to provide the significance level only for results which fall at or below the 0.05 level and to do so for certain cut-off points below that such as 0.01, 0.001, and 0.0001. However, with the advent of computer programs such as Minitab which give exact significance levels, it could be argued that this tradition does not maximize the information that could be supplied without any obvious disadvantages.

If, however, we found that only four of the women were more perceptive than the men, then the probability of this happening by chance would be about 0.04, since there are ten ways or sequences in which this result could occur $(0.004 \times 10 = 0.04)$. This finding is still significant. However, if we had adopted a non-directional hypothesis and had simply expected a

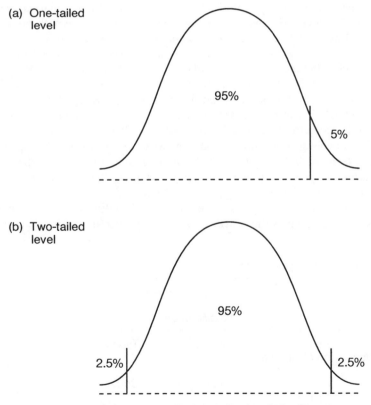

Figure 6.3 One-tailed and two-tailed 0.05 levels of significance

difference between men and women without specifying its direction, then this result would not be significant at the 0.05 level since this 0.05 would have to be shared between both tails of the distribution of possible outcomes as in Figure 6.3(b). In other words, it would become 0.025 at either end of the distribution. This result would require a probability level of 0.025 or less to be significant when stated as a non-directional hypothesis. As it is, the probability of either four women being more perceptive than men or four men being more perceptive than women is the sum of these two probabilities, namely 0.08, which is above the 0.05 level. The important point to note is that non-directional hypotheses require *two-tailed* significance levels while directional hypotheses only need *one-tailed* ones. If we find a difference between two samples or treatments we did not expect, then to test the significance of this result we need to use a two-tailed test.

It may be worth reiterating at this stage that a finding that four out of the five women being more perceptive than the five men may still be obtained by chance even at the 0.04 one-tailed level. In other words, this means that there remains a four in a hundred possibility that this result could be due to chance. In accepting this level of significance for rejecting the null hypothesis that there is no difference between men and women, we may be committing a Type I error, namely thinking that there is a difference between them when in fact there is no such difference. In other words, a Type I error is rejecting the null hypothesis when it is true as shown in Table 6.4. We may reduce the probability of making this kind of error by lowering the significance level from 0.05 to 0.01, but this increases the probability of committing a Type II error, which is accepting that there is no difference when there is one. A Type II error is accepting the null hypothesis when it is false. Setting the significance level at 0.01 means that the finding that four out of the five women were more perceptive than the men is assuming that this result is due to chance when it may be indicating a real difference.

The probability of correctly assuming that there is a difference when there actually is one is known as the *power* of a test. A powerful test is one that is

Table 6.4 Type I and Type II errors

		Reality	
		No difference	A difference
Interpretation of reality	Accept no difference	Correct	Type II error β
	Accept a difference	Type I error α	Correct

more likely to indicate a significant difference when such a difference exists. Statistical power is inversely related to the probability of making a Type II error and is calculated by subtracting beta from one, (i.e. $1 - \beta$).

Finally, it is important to realize that the level of significance has nothing to do with the size or importance of a difference. It is simply concerned with the probability of that difference arising by chance. In other words, a difference between two samples or two treatments which is significant at the 0.05 level is not necessarily bigger than one which is significant at the 0.0001 level. The latter difference is only less probable than the former one.

EXERCISES

1. What is the difference between a random sample and a representative sample?

2. Why might a stratified sample be superior to a simple random sample?

3. In what context might multistage cluster sampling be particularly useful?

4. If a sample of grocery shops was selected randomly from the *Yellow Pages* in your town, would you necessarily have a representative sample?

5. Flip a coin four times. What is the probability of finding the particular sequence of outcomes you did?

6. If the coin were unbiased, would you obtain two heads and two tails if you threw it four times?

7. What is the probability of obtaining any sequence of two heads and two tails?

8. You have developed a test of general knowledge, which consists of a hundred statements, half of which are false and half of which are true. Each person is given one point for a correct answer. How many points is someone who has no general knowledge most likely to achieve on this test?

9. Fifty people are tested to see if they can tell margarine from butter. Half of them are given butter and the other half are given margarine. They have to say which of these two products they were given (i.e. there were no 'don't knows'). If people cannot discriminate between them, how many people on average are likely to guess correctly?

10. If we wanted to see if women were more talkative than men, what would the null hypothesis be?

11. What would the non-directional hypothesis be?

Chapter 7

Bivariate analysis

Exploring differences between scores on two variables

In this chapter we will be looking at ways of determining whether the differences between the distributions of two variables are statistically significant. Thus, for example, when analysing data we may wish to know the answers to some of the following kinds of questions: Is the proportion of black to white workers the same among men as it is among women? Do women workers earn less than their male counterparts? Does job satisfaction change from one month to the next? Do the scores in one treatment group differ from those in another?

In looking at differences between two variables, the variable which we use to form our comparison groups usually has a small number of values or levels, say between two and six. We shall call this the comparison-group variable to distinguish it from the other one which we shall refer to as the criterion variable. The comparison-group variable is sometimes known as the *independent* variable, and the criterion variable as the *dependent* one. An example of a comparison-group variable would be gender if we wanted to compare men with women. This typically has two levels (i.e. men and women) which go to make up two comparison groups. Race or ethnic origin, on the other hand, may take on two or more levels (e.g., Caucasian, Negroid, Asian and Mongolian), thereby creating two or more comparison groups. Other examples of comparison-group variables include different experimental treatments (for example, drugs versus psychotherapy in treating depression), different points in time (for example, two consecutive months), and the categorization of participants into various levels on some variable (such as high, intermediate and low job satisfaction). The other variable is the one that we shall use to make our comparison (for example, income or job satisfaction).

CRITERIA FOR SELECTING BIVARIATE TESTS OF DIFFERENCES

There is a relatively large number of statistical tests to determine whether a difference between two or more groups is significant. In deciding which is the most appropriate statistical test to use to analyse your data, it is necessary to bear the following considerations in mind.

Categorical data

If the data are of a categorical or nominal nature, where the values refer to the number or frequency of cases that fall within particular categories, such as the number of black female workers, it is only possible to use what is referred to as a *non-parametric* test (see below for an explanation). Thus, for example, in trying to determine whether there are significantly more white than black female employees, it would be necessary to use a non-parametric test.

Ordinal and interval/ratio data

If the data are of a non-categorical nature, such as the rating of how skilled workers are or how much they earn, then it is necessary to decide whether it is more appropriate to use a *parametric* or non-parametric test. Since this issue is a complex and controversial one, it will be discussed later in some detail.

Means or variances?

Most investigators who use parametric tests are primarily interested in checking for differences between means. Differences in *variances* are also normally carried out but only to determine the appropriateness of using such a test to check for differences in the means. Variance is an expression showing the spread or dispersion of data around the mean and is the square of the standard deviation. If the variances are found to differ markedly, then it may be more appropriate to use a non-parametric test. However, differences in variance (i.e. variability) may be of interest in their own right and so these tests have been listed separately. Thus, for example, it may be reasonable to suppose that the variability of job satisfaction of women will be greater than that of men, but that there will be no difference in their mean scores. In this case, it would also be necessary to pay attention to the differences between the variances to determine if this is so.

Related or unrelated comparison groups?

Which test you use also depends on whether the values that you want to compare come from different cases or from the same or similar ones. If, for example, you are comparing different groups of people such as men and women or people who have been assigned to different experimental treatments, then you are dealing with unrelated samples of subjects. It is worth noting that this kind of situation or design is also referred to in some of the following ways: *independent* or *uncorrelated* groups or samples; and *between-subjects* design. If, on the other hand, you are comparing the way that the same people have responded on separate occasions or under different conditions, then you are dealing with *related* samples of observations. This is also true of groups of people who are or have been *matched* or *paired* on one or more important characteristic such as, for example, husbands and wives, which may also make them more similar in terms of the criterion variable under study. Once again, there is a number of other terms used to describe related scores such as the following: *dependent* or *correlated* groups or samples; *repeated measures*; and *within-subjects* design.

Two or more comparison groups?

Different tests are generally used to compare two rather than three or more comparison groups.

The tests to be used given these criteria are listed in Table 7.1. Readers may wish to use this table as a guide to the selection of tests appropriate to their needs. Page numbers have been inserted in the table to facilitate finding further information on the tests.

PARAMETRIC VERSUS NON-PARAMETRIC TESTS

One of the unresolved issues in data analysis is the question of when parametric rather than non-parametric tests should be used. Some writers have argued that it is only appropriate to use parametric tests when the data fulfil the following three conditions: (1) the level or scale of measurement is of equal interval or ratio scaling i.e. more than ordinal; (2) the distribution of the population scores is normal; and (3) the variances of both variables are equal or *homogeneous*. The term *parameter* refers to a measure which describes the distribution of the population such as its mean or variance. Since parametric tests are based on the assumption that we know certain characteristics of the population from which the sample is drawn, they are called *parametric tests*. *Non-parametric* or *distribution-free* tests are so named because they do not depend on assumptions about the precise form of the distribution of the sampled populations.

However, the need to meet these three conditions for using parametric tests has been strongly questioned. Some of the arguments will be mentioned here and these will be simply stated, with sources provided where further details can be found. As far as the first condition is concerned, level of measurement, it has been suggested that parametric tests can also be used with ordinal variables since tests apply to numbers and not to what those numbers signify (for example, Lord, 1953). Thus, for

Table 7.1 Tests of differences

Nature of criterion variable	Type of test	Type of data	Number of comparison groups	Name of test	Page numbers
Categorical: nominal or frequency	Non-parametric	Unrelated	1	Binomial	114–16
			2+	Chi-square	116–19
Non-categorical:	Non-parametric	Unrelated	2	Mann-Whitney U	119–21
		Related	3+	Kruskal-Wallis H	121–4
			2	Sign	124–6
			2	Wilcoxon	126–7
			3+	Friedman	127–30
	Parametric: Means	Unrelated	1–2	t	130–6
			2+	One-way and two-way analysis of variance	137–41
					197–201
		Related	2	t	141–3
			3+	Repeated measures analysis of variance	144–7
		Related and Unrelated	2+	Two-way analysis of variance with repeated measures on one factor	206–10
				Two-way analysis of covariance	201–4
	Parametric: Variances	Unrelated	2	F	134–8
				Levene's test	136–7
		Related	2	t	143–4

example, we apply these tests to determine if two scores differ. We know what these scores indicate, but the test obviously does not. Therefore, the data are treated as if they are of interval or ratio scaling. Furthermore, it can be argued that since many psychological and sociological variables such as attitudes are basically ordinal in nature (see p. 57), parametric tests should not be used to analyse them if this first condition is valid. However, it should be noted that parametric tests are routinely applied to such variables.

With respect to the second and third conditions, the populations being normally distributed and of equal variances, a number of studies have been carried out (for example, Boneau, 1960; Games and Lucas, 1966) where the values of the statistics used to analyse samples drawn from populations which have been artificially set up to violate these conditions have been found not to differ greatly from those for samples which have been drawn from populations which do not violate these conditions. Tests which are able to withstand such violations are described as being *robust*.

One exception to this general finding was where both the size of the samples and the variances were unequal although some have argued that this exception applies even with equal sample sizes (Wilcox, 1987). Another exception was where both distributions of scores were non-normal. In such circumstances, it may be prudent to compare the results of a non-parametric test with those of a parametric test. Where the distributions of scores are not normal, it may also be worth running a parametric test on the scores as they are and after they have been transformed closer to normality. For more details on transforming scores to normality, see Mosteller and Tukey (1977). It may also be more desirable to use non-parametric tests when the size of the samples is small, say under fifteen, since under these circumstances it is more difficult to determine the extent to which these conditions have been met. A fuller description of non-parametric tests may be found in Siegel and Castellan (1988) or Conover (1980).

CATEGORICAL VARIABLES AND NON-PARAMETRIC TESTS

Binomial test for one dichotomous variable

The binomial test is used to compare the frequency of cases actually found in the two categories of a dichotomous variable with those which are expected on some basis. Suppose, for example, that we wanted to find out whether the ratio of female to male workers in the industry covered by our Job Survey was the same as that in the industry in general, which we knew to be 1:3. We could do this by carrying out a binomial test in which the proportion of women in our survey was compared with that of an expected proportion of 1 : 4 or one out of every four workers. In our survey there are 31 women and 39 men.

With the Minitab prompt system, a one-tailed binomial test can be calculated with the **pdf** (which stands for **p**robability **d**istribution **f**unction) command and the **binomial** subcommand. On the **pdf** command specify the smaller of the two frequencies, which is **31**, followed by a semi-colon.

MTB > pdf 31;

On the **binomial** subcommand, type **binomial** followed by the total number of cases in the sample (which is **70**), the expected probability of obtaining the less frequent value (which is **.25**) and a full stop.

SUBC> binomial 70 .25.

The menu action for doing this is

→**Calc** →**Probability Distributions** →**Binomial...** →**Probability** [as this is the default it is already selected] →box beside **Number of trials:** and type in the sample size [e.g. **70**] →box beside **Probability of success:** and type in probability of obtaining the less frequent category [e.g. **.25**] →**Input constant:** →box beside it and in it type the frequency of that category [e.g. **31**] →**OK**

The output displays the value of the smaller frequency (**K**) and the probability of obtaining that outcome (**P**) as follows:

K	P(X = K)
31.00	0.0002

The one-tailed probability of the sample containing 31 women is **0.0002** when the expected probability of obtaining a woman is 0.25. This means that the probability of obtaining this result by chance is highly unlikely with p equal to **0.0002** or less. In other words, the likelihood of this result happening by chance is 1 out of 10,000 times. Therefore, we would conclude that the ratio of female to male workers is not 1 : 3.

If we wanted to find out if the number of white workers (which is 36) in our sample does not differ significantly from the number of non-white workers (which is 34), we would use the **cdf** command (which stands for **c**umulative **d**istribution **f**unction) and the **binomial** subcommand. On the **cdf** command we specify the smaller of the two frequencies, which is **34**, followed by a semi-colon.

MTB > cdf 34;
SUBC> binomial 70 .5.

The menu procedure for doing this is

→<u>C</u>alc →Probability <u>D</u>istributions
→<u>B</u>inomial... →<u>C</u>umulative probability →box beside <u>N</u>umber of
trials: and type in the sample size [e.g. 70] →box beside Proba<u>b</u>ility
of success: and type in probability of obtaining the less frequent
category [e.g. .5] →Input co<u>n</u>stant: →box beside it and in it type the
frequency of that category [e.g. 34] →<u>O</u>K

The output for this procedure is

K	P(X LESS OR = K)
34.00	0.4525

The one-tailed probability of the sample comprising 34 non-white workers
is **0.4525** when the expected probability of having a non-white worker is
0.5. This means that the probability of finding this result is high. Consequently, we would conclude that there is no significant difference in the
number of non-white and white workers.

Incidentally, the similarity of these examples to those used to illustrate
the notion of significance testing in the previous chapter should be noted,
except that there we were comparing the frequency of finding one tail (or
one male) to every five heads (or five females) against an expected
frequency or probability of 0.5.

Chi-square test for two or more unrelated samples

If we wanted to compare the frequency of cases found in one variable in
two or more unrelated samples or categories of another variable, we would
use the chi-square test. We will illustrate this test with the relatively simple
example in which we have two dichotomous variables, gender (male and
female) and ethnic group (white and non-white), although it can also be
applied to two variables which have three or more categories. Suppose, for
instance, we wished to find out whether the proportion of male to female
workers was the same in both white and black workers.

We would begin by recoding **'ethnicgp'** as follows

MTB > code (3 : 5) 2 'ethnicgp' c31

We could name **c31** as **'rethncgp'**.

MTB > name c31 'rethncgp'

The menu procedure for doing this is

→<u>M</u>anip →Code Data <u>V</u>alues... →ethnicgp →Select [this puts
ethnicgp in the box under <u>C</u>ode data from columns:] →type
rethncgp in the box under <u>I</u>nto columns: →first box under Or<u>i</u>ginal

values [eg, 1 : 4 12]: and in it type **3 : 5** →first corresponding box under **New:** and in it type **2** →**OK**

Next we need to count the number of male and female white and non-white workers using the following **table** command and **count** subcommand

MTB > table 'gender' 'rethncgp';
SUBC> count.

The menu action for doing this is

→**Stat** →**Tables** →**Cross Tabulation...** →**gender** →**Select** [this puts **gender** in the box under **Classification Variables**] →**rethncgp** →**Select** →box beside **Counts** [this puts a cross in this box] →**OK**

The variable listed first will form the rows of the table while that listed second will form the columns.

The output from this procedure is shown in Table 7.2. The rows in Table 7.2 represent **'gender'** with **1** signifying men and **2** women while the columns reflect **'rethncgp'** with **1** denoting white workers and **2** non-white workers.

We then create two new columns which contain the frequency of male and female white and non-white workers

MTB > set c32
DATA> 22 14
DATA> end
MTB > set c33
DATA> 17 17
DATA> end

We are now ready to conduct a chi-square test on these two new columns with the following **chisquare** command

MTB > chisquare c32 c33

Table 7.2   Table showing frequency of male and female white and non-white workers in the Job Survey

ROWS:	gender	COLUMNS:	rethncgp
	1	2	ALL
1	22	17	39
2	14	17	31
ALL	36	34	70

CELL CONTENTS –

COUNT

The output from this command is presented in Table 7.3. The expected frequencies or **counts** are displayed below the observed frequencies. Thus, the expected frequency of male white workers is **20.06** which is slightly lower than the observed frequency of **22**. In other words, there are slightly fewer white male workers than expected. The chi-square value for this analysis is **0.875** with **1 df** or *degree of freedom*. The term *degrees of freedom (df)*, associated with any statistic, refers to the number of components which are free to vary. It is a difficult concept which is well explained elsewhere (Walker, 1940). In chi-square, degrees of freedom are calculated by subtracting 1 from the number of categories in each of the two variables and multiplying the remaining values which in this case gives 1 [i.e. $(2 - 1) \times (2 - 1) = 1$].

To work out the statistical significance of obtaining a chi-square of **0.875** at the 0.05 two-tailed level, we use the **invcdf** (**inv**erse **c**umulative **d**istribution **f**unction) command followed by the **chisquare** subcommand.

On the **invcdf** command the level of statistical significance is specified by subtracting that level from 1.00. So, for the 0.05 probability level the appropriate figure is 0.95 $(1.00 - 0.05 = 0.95)$.

MTB > invcdf .95;

On the **chisquare** subcommand, which gives critical values for the chi-square distribution, the appropriate degrees of freedom are listed after the keyword **chisquare**. Therefore, the subcommand for finding the 0.05 two-tailed critical value of chisquare with 1 degree of freedom is

SUBC> chisquare 1.

The following output is provided

0.9500   3.8415

Table 7.3 **Chisquare** output comparing number of white and non-white men and women in the Job Survey

Expected counts are printed below observed counts

	C32	C33	Total
1	22	17	39
	20.06	18.94	
2	14	17	31
	15.94	15.06	
Total	36	34	70
ChiSq =	0.188 +	0.199 +	
	0.237 +	0.251 = 0.875	
df = 1			

The first figure refers to the inverse cumulative distribution function of **0.9500** while the second is the critical chi-square value of **3.8415**. As the chi-square value we obtained, which was **0.875**, is smaller than the critical value of **3.8415**, we would conclude that the frequencies did not differ significantly from those expected by chance at less than the two-tailed 0.05 level. Since the value of chi-square is not significant, this means that the proportion of male to female workers is the same for both whites and nonwhites.

To obtain chi-square with the menu system, we carry out the following sequence

→**Stat** →**Tables** →**Chisquare Test...** →**c32** →**Select** [this puts **c32** in the box under **Columns containing the table:**] →**c33** →**Select** →**OK**

In *Release 10* the probability of obtaining chi-square is given, which for our example is displayed as **p = 0.350.**

In *Releases 8* and *9*, the critical value of chi-square is found by

→**Calc** →**Probability Distribution** →**Chisquare...** →**Inverse cumulative probability** →box beside **Degrees of freedom** and type degrees of freedom [e.g. **1**] in it →box beside **Input constant:** and in it type the cumulative probability level [e.g. **.95**] →**OK**

There is a restriction on using chi-square when the expected frequencies are small. With only two categories (or one degree of freedom), the number of cases expected to fall in these categories should be at least 5 before this test can be applied. If the expected frequencies are less than 5, then the binomial test should be used instead. With three or more categories (or more than one degree of freedom), chi-square should not be used when any expected frequency is smaller than 1 or when more than 20 per cent of the expected frequencies are smaller than 5. In these situations, it may be possible to increase the expected frequencies in a category by combining it with those of another.

NON-CATEGORICAL VARIABLES AND NON-PARAMETRIC TESTS

Mann-Whitney *U* test for two unrelated samples

The Mann-Whitney test compares the number of times a score from one of the samples is ranked higher than a score from the other sample. If the two groups are similar, then the number of times this happens should also be similar for the two groups.

To find out if rated quality of work is similar for men and women, we first have to separate rated quality of work (**'qual'**) for men and women using the following **unstack** command and **subscripts** subcommand:

MTB > unstack ('id' 'gender' 'qual') (c31 c32 c33)(c34-c36);
SUBC> subscripts 'gender'.

The menu system for doing this is

→**Manip** →**Unstack...** →**id** →**Select** [this puts **id** in the box below **Unstack:**] →**gender** →**Select** →**qual** →**Select**→box beside **Using subscripts:** →**gender** →**Select** →**Store results in blocks:** [this is automatically selected] →type **c31 c32 c33** in the first box [which is automatically selected] →second box and in it type **c34-c36** →**OK**

The **Unstack** dialog box is pictured in Figure 7.1.

To enable you to check that this procedure has worked correctly, we have also included the identification number (**'id'**) of the participants although it is not necessary to do this once you have learned how to use this command.

The original variables we want to re-arrange are **'id'**, **'gender'** and **'qual'**. We want to put these variables in new columns according to the values of **'gender'** which only takes the two values **1** and **2**. We do this with the **subscripts** subcommand since it is as if we are putting the subscript **1** against all male values and the subscript **2** against all female values. Consequently, we need three extra columns for the male data (**c31**, **c32** and **c33**) and three for the female data (**c34**, **c35** and **c36**) for the identification number, gender and rated quality of work respectively.

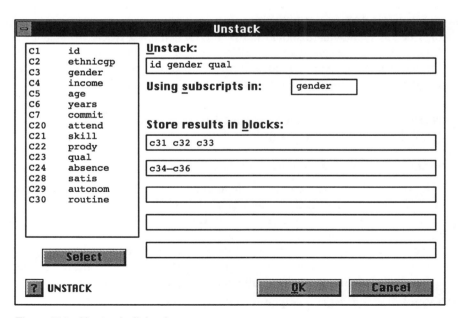

Figure 7.1 **Unstack** dialog box

To remind us that **c33** contains rated quality of work for men and **c36** rated quality of work for women we will name these two new columns **'mqual'** and **'fqual'** respectively.

MTB > name c33 'mqual' c36 'fqual'

To check that this procedure has worked, we will print **'id'**, **'gender'**, **'qual'** and **c31** to **c36**.

MTB > print 'id' 'gender' 'qual' c31-c36

The menu sequence for doing this is

→**File** →**Display Data...** →**id** →**Select** [this puts **id** in the box beneath **Columns, constants, and matrices to display:**] →**gender** →**Select** →**qual** →**Select** →**c31-c36** →**Select** →**OK**

The output for this procedure is displayed in Table 7.4. For case 70 who is male we can see that the rating of 4 has been placed in **'mqual'** while for case 66 who is female the rating of 3 has been put in **'fqual'**.

To carry out a Mann-Whitney test comparing rated quality of work for men and women, we used the **mann-whitney** command with the variables **'mqual'** and **'fqual'**:

MTB > mann-whitney 'mqual' 'fqual'

The menu sequence for doing this is

→**Stat** →**Nonparametrics** →**Mann-Whitney...** →**mqual** →**Select** [this puts **mqual** in the box beside **First Sample:**] →**fqual** →**Select** [this puts **fqual** in the box beside **Second Sample:**] →**OK**

The output from this sequence is shown in Table 7.5. We can see that the value of the Mann-Whitney statistic, the Wilcoxon **W** (which is the sum of the ranks of the smaller group) is **1440.5**. The probability of obtaining this value is **0.5003** when an adjustment is made for the number of scores which receive or tie for the same rank. As this probability is greater than 0.05 and so is not significant, we can conclude that there is no statistically significant difference between men and women in the mean ranking of the rated quality of their work.

Kruskal-Wallis H test for three or more unrelated samples

The Kruskal-Wallis H test is similar to the Mann-Whitney U test in that the cases in the different samples are ranked together in one series. However, unlike the Mann-Whitney U test, it can be used to compare scores in more than two groups. To compare the rated quality of work for people in the four ethnic groups, we use the following command:

MTB > kruskal-wallis 'qual' 'ethnicgp'

Table 7.4 **'Qual'** unstacked for men and women as **'mqual'** and **'fqual'**

ROW	id	gender	qual	C30	C31	mqual	C33	C34	fqual
1	1	1	1	1	1	1	5	2	3
2	2	1	4	2	1	4	9	2	1
3	3	1	4	3	1	4	10	2	4
4	4	1	4	4	1	4	14	2	2
5	5	2	3	6	1	4	18	2	3
6	6	1	4	7	1	2	19	2	4
7	7	1	2	8	1	4	20	2	1
8	8	1	4	11	1	3	24	2	3
9	9	2	1	12	1	3	25	2	2
10	10	2	4	13	1	5	28	2	5
11	11	1	3	15	1	5	30	2	3
12	12	1	3	16	1	3	32	2	4
13	13	1	5	17	1	3	33	2	5
14	14	2	2	21	1	2	34	2	5
15	15	1	5	22	1	5	35	2	3
16	16	1	3	23	1	5	39	2	4
17	17	1	3	26	1	5	41	2	2
18	18	2	3	27	1	4	43	2	1
19	19	2	4	29	1	4	47	2	3
20	20	2	1	31	1	2	48	2	4
21	21	1	2	36	1	2	49	2	4
22	22	1	5	37	1	4	52	2	1
23	23	1	5	38	1	4	54	2	3
24	24	2	3	40	1	2	55	2	5
25	25	2	2	42	1	2	58	2	3
26	26	1	5	44	1	3	59	2	5
27	27	1	4	45	1	3	61	2	3
28	28	2	5	46	1	4	63	2	1
29	29	1	4	50	1	4	64	2	4
30	30	2	3	51	1	2	65	2	1
31	31	1	2	53	1	3	66	2	3
32	32	2	4	56	1	1			
33	33	2	5	57	1	2			
34	34	2	5	60	1	1			
35	35	2	3	62	1	2			
36	36	1	2	67	1	5			
37	37	1	4	68	1	4			
38	38	1	4	69	1	4			
39	39	2	4	70	1	4			
40	40	1	2						
41	41	2	2						
42	42	1	2						
43	43	2	1						
44	44	1	3						
45	45	1	3						
46	46	1	4						
47	47	2	3						
48	48	2	4						
49	49	2	4						

Table 7.4   Continued

ROW	id	gender	qual	C30	C31	mqual	C33	C34	fqual
50	50	1	4						
51	51	1	2						
52	52	2	1						
53	53	1	3						
54	54	2	3						
55	55	2	5						
56	56	1	1						
57	57	1	2						
58	58	2	3						
59	59	2	5						
60	60	1	1						
61	61	2	3						
62	62	1	2						
63	63	2	1						
64	64	2	4						
65	65	2	1						
66	66	2	3						
67	67	1	5						
68	68	1	4						
69	69	1	4						
70	70	1	4						

Note that the variable to be compared (**'qual'**) is listed first followed by the variable which provides the categories (**'ethnicgp'**).

The menu action for doing this is

→**Stat** →**Nonparametrics** →**Kruskal-Wallis…** →**qual** →**Select** [this puts **qual** in the box beside **Response:**] →**ethnicgp** →**Select** [this puts **ethnicgp** in the box beside **Factor:**] →**OK**

Table 7.5 **Mann-Whitney** output comparing rated quality of work for men (**'mqual'**) and women ('**fqual**')

Mann-Whitney Confidence Interval and Test

mqual	N = 39	Median =	4.000
fqual	N = 31	Median =	3.000

Point estimate for ETA1-ETA2 is   −0.000
95.0 pct c.i. for ETA1-ETA2 is (0.000,1.000)
W = 1440.5
Test of ETA1 = ETA2 vs. ETA1 n.e. ETA2 is significant at 0.5117

The test is significant at 0.5003 (adjusted for ties)

Cannot reject at alpha = 0.05

The output from this procedure is presented in Table 7.6. The number of observations or cases (**NOBS**) for the four ethnic groups or **LEVEL**s is displayed in the second column and their average rank (**AVE. RANK**) in the fifth column. The H and its significance level is shown both unadjusted (**p = 0.786**) and adjusted for ties [**p = 0.772 (adj. for ties)**]. Since the significance level is greater than 0.05 on both tests, this indicates there is no difference between workers of the four ethnic groups in the mean ranking of the rated quality of their work.

Sign test for two related samples

The sign test compares the number of positive and negative differences between two scores from the same cases at two points in time, in two treatments, or from two samples which have been matched to be similar in certain respects such as having the same distributions of age, gender, and socio-economic status. The sign test ignores the size of any differences. If the two samples are similar, then these differences should be normally distributed. Suppose, for example, we wanted to find out if there had been any changes in the rated quality of work during two consecutive months. If the number of positive differences (i.e. decreases in ratings) was similar to the number of negative ones (i.e. increases in ratings), this would mean that there was no change in one particular direction between the two occasions.

The use of tests to analyse information from two or more related samples will be illustrated with the small set of data in Table 7.7. This consists of one example of the three kinds of variables (categorical, ordinal and interval/ratio) measured at three consecutive monthly intervals on twelve workers. The categorical variable is the attendance at the firm's monthly meeting (**attend1** to **attend3**), the ordinal one is the quality of the work as rated by the supervisor (**qual1** to **qual3**), while the interval/ratio one is self-expressed job satisfaction (**satis1** to **satis3**). A study in which data are

Table 7.6   **Kruskal-Wallis** output comparing rated quality of work for four ethnic groups

LEVEL	NOBS	MEDIAN	AVE. RANK	Z VALUE
1	36	3.000	35.0	−0.22
2	18	3.000	33.5	−0.49
3	14	4.000	37.7	0.46
4	2	4.000	47.5	0.85
OVERALL	70		35.5	

$H = 1.06$ d.f. $= 3$ $p = 0.786$
$H = 1.12$ d.f. $= 3$ $p = 0.772$ (adj. for ties)

* NOTE * One or more small samples

Table 7.7 The Panel Study data

id	attend1	qual1	satis1	attend2	qual2	satis2	attend3	qual3	satis3
01	1	5	17	1	4	18	1	5	16
02	1	4	12	2	3	9	2	2	7
03	2	3	13	1	4	15	2	3	14
04	2	4	11	2	5	14	2	3	8
05	2	2	7	2	3	10	1	3	9
06	1	4	14	1	4	15	2	3	10
07	1	3	15	2	1	6	1	4	12
08	2	4	12	1	3	9	1	4	13
09	1	4	13	2	5	14	1	3	15
10	1	1	5	2	2	4	2	3	9
11	1	3	8	2	3	7	1	3	6
12	1	4	11	2	4	13	1	3	10

collected from the same individuals at two or more points is known as a *prospective*, *longitudinal*, or *panel* design. Consequently, this example will be referred to as the Panel Study.

To compare rated quality of work in the first and second month, we first have to subtract one variable from the other using the following **let** command:

MTB > let c11 = 'qual1'-'qual2'

The menu procedure for doing this is

→**C**alc →**Mathematical E**xpressions... →c11 →**Select** [this puts **c11** in the box beside **V**ariable **[new or modified]:**] →box under **E**xpression: and in it type **'qual1'-'qual2'** →**O**K

We can display the data for these three variables with the **print** command

MTB > print 'qual1' 'qual2' c11

The menu action for doing this is

→**F**ile →**Display Data...** →qual1 →**Select** [this puts **qual1** in the box beneath **Columns, constants, and matrices to display:**] →qual2 →**Select** →c11 →**Select** →**O**K

We can see from the output displayed in Table 7.8 that five of the differences are positive, four are negative and three are zero.

To determine if the number of positive differences differs from the number of negative differences, we carry out the sign test on the differences stored in **c11** with the following **stest** command

MTB > stest c11

Table 7.8 The difference (**C11**) between **qual1** and **qual2**

ROW	qual1	qual2	C11
1	5	4	1
2	4	3	1
3	3	4	−1
4	4	5	−1
5	2	3	−1
6	4	4	0
7	3	1	2
8	4	3	1
9	4	5	−1
10	1	2	−1
11	3	3	0
12	4	4	0

The menu procedure for doing this is

→**Stat** →**Nonparametrics** →**1-Sample Sign...** →**c11** →**Select** [this puts **c11** in the box under **Variables:**] →**OK**

The output from this procedure is displayed in Table 7.9. With almost equal numbers of positive and negative differences, it is not surprising that the test is non-significant. In other words, there is no change in rated quality of work over the two months.

Wilcoxon matched-pairs signed-ranks test for two related samples

This test, like the Mann-Whitney, takes account of the size of the differences between two sets of related scores by ranking and then summing those with the same sign. If there are no differences between the two samples, then the number of positive signs should be similar to the number of negative ones. This test would be used, for example, to determine if the rated quality of work in the Panel Study was the same in the first and second month (**qual1** and **qual2**). To do this we would use the following **wtest** command on the difference between **qual1** and **qual2** stored in **c11**:

MTB > wtest c11

The menu procedure for doing this is

→**Stat** →**Nonparametrics** →**1-Sample Wilcoxon...** →**c11** →**Select** [this puts **c11** in the box under **Variables:**] →**OK**

The output from this procedure is presented in Table 7.10. The Wilcoxon statistic reported is the sum of the ranks for the positive differences. Once

Table 7.9 **Stest** output comparing the number of positive and negative differences between **qual1** and **qual2**

SIGN TEST OF MEDIAN = 0.00000 VERSUS N.E. 0.00000

	N	BELOW	EQUAL	ABOVE	P-VALUE	MEDIAN
C11	12	5	3	4	1.0000	0.0000

Table 7.10 **Wtest** output comparing the sum of the ranked positive and negative differences in size between **qual1** and **qual2**

TEST OF MEDIAN = 0.000000 VERSUS MEDIAN N.E. 0.000000

	N	N FOR TEST	WILCOXON STATISTIC	P-VALUE	ESTIMATED MEDIAN
C11	12	9	22.5	1.000	0.000E + 00

again we see that there is no significant difference in the rated quality of work between the first and second month.

Friedman test for three or more related samples

If we wanted to compare the scores of three or more related samples, such as the rated quality of work across all three months rather than just two of them, we would use the Friedman two-way analysis of variance test. It ranks the scores for each of the cases and then calculates the mean rank score for each sample. If there are no differences between the samples, their mean ranks should be similar.

To compare the rated quality of work over the three months in the Panel Study, we first need to create three new columns. The first column contains rated quality of work on the three occasions and can be set up with the following **stack** command:

MTB > stack 'qual1' 'qual2' 'qual3' c12

The column containing **'qual1'** is placed on top of the column holding **'qual2'** which in turn is put on top of the column storing **'qual3'**. These three columns are stacked in this way in **c12** which we could name **'qual'**:

MTB > name c12 'qual'

The menu action for stacking is

→**Manip** →**Stack...** →**qual1** →**Select** [this puts **qual1** in the first box below **Stack the following blocks:**] →second box under **Stack the following blocks:** →**qual2** →**Select** [this puts **qual2** in this box] →third box under **Stack the following blocks:** →**qual3** →**Select** →box under **Store results in blocks:** and in it type **c12** or **qual** →**OK**

The second column we have to make consists of a code telling us to which of the three months the rated quality of work refers. The first month we will code as **1**, the second month as **2** and the third month as **3**. So, the first 12 values in **c14** refer to the first month, the second 12 values to the second month and the third 12 values to the third month. We form this second column with the **set** command:

MTB > set c13
DATA> 1 1 1 1 1 1 1 1 1 1 1 1 2 2 2 2 2 2 2 2 2 2 2 2 3 3 3 3 3 3 3 3 3 3 3 3
DATA> end

We could call **c13 'month'**.

MTB > name c13 'month'

The third column we have to make simply contains the number of the participants at each of the three times and can be created by stacking **'id'** three times in the new column **c14**:

MTB > stack 'id' 'id' 'id' c14

We could call **c14 'subjects'**:

MTB > name c14 'subjects'

The menu procedure for doing this is

→**Manip** →**Stack...** →**id** →**Select** [this puts **id** in the first box below **Stack the following blocks:**] →second box under **Stack the following blocks:** →**id** →**Select** [this puts **id** in this box] →third box under **Stack the following blocks:** →**id** →**Select** →box under **Store results in blocks:** and in it type **subjects** →**OK**

The values of these three new columns can be displayed with the **print** command

MTB > print 'subjects' 'month' 'qual'

The menu action for doing this is

→**File** →**Display Data...** →**subjects** →**Select** [this puts **subjects** in the box beneath **Columns, constants, and matrices to display:**] →**month** →**Select** →**qual** →**Select** →**OK**

These three columns are reproduced in Table 7.11.
To carry out a Friedman test on the data in Table 7.11, we use the following command

MTB > friedman 'qual' 'month' 'subjects'

where the variable to be compared (**'qual'**) is listed first followed by the variable forming the category (**'month'**) followed by the variable which orders or blocks the participants (**'subjects'**).

Table 7.11 Panel Study rated quality of work data rearranged for the **Friedman** command

ROW	subjects	month	qual
1	1	1	5
2	2	1	4
3	3	1	3
4	4	1	4
5	5	1	2
6	6	1	4
7	7	1	3
8	8	1	4
9	9	1	4
10	10	1	1
11	11	1	3
12	12	1	4
13	1	2	4
14	2	2	3
15	3	2	4
16	4	2	5
17	5	2	3
18	6	2	4
19	7	2	1
20	8	2	3
21	9	2	5
22	10	2	2
23	11	2	3
24	12	2	4
25	1	3	5
26	2	3	2
27	3	3	3
28	4	3	3
29	5	3	3
30	6	3	3
31	7	3	4
32	8	3	4
33	9	3	3
34	10	3	3
35	11	3	3
36	12	3	3

The menu procedure for doing this is

→**Stat** →**Nonparametrics** →**Friedman...** →**qual** →**Select** [this puts **qual** in the box beside **Response:**] →**month** →**Select** [this puts **month** in the box beside **Treatment:**] →**subjects** →**Select** [this puts **subjects** in the box beside **Blocks:**] →**OK**

The output for this procedure is shown in Table 7.12 which includes the S statistic adjusted and unadjusted for ties, the degrees of freedom and the

Table 7.12 **Friedman** output comparing the mean rank of rated quality of work across the three months

Friedman test of qual by month blocked by subjects

S = 0.54   d.f. = 2   p = 0.763
S = 0.68   d.f. = 2   p = 0.710 (adjusted for ties)

month	N	Est. Median	Sum of RANKS
1	12	3.5000	24.5
2	12	3.6667	25.5
3	12	3.3333	22.0

Grand median = 3.5000

sum of ranks. Since there is the same number of participants across the three months, it makes no difference whether the sum or the mean of ranks is used. The mean is simply the sum divided by the number of cases. The degrees of freedom is the number of samples minus 1. The non-significant *S* value means there is no difference in the mean ranks of rated quality of work across the three months.

NON-CATEGORICAL VARIABLES AND PARAMETRIC TESTS

t test for one sample

This test is used to determine if the mean of a sample is similar to that of the population. If, for example, we knew what the mean score for job satisfaction was for workers in the industry covered in the Job Survey and we wanted to find out if the mean of our sample was similar to it, we would carry out a *t* test. Suppose the population mean was 10. To compare this population mean with our sample mean, we would use the following **ttest** command in which the population mean is listed before the column number or name of the variable concerned:

MTB > ttest 10 'satis'

The menu action for doing this is

→**S̲tat** →**B̲asic Statistics** →**1̲-Sample t...** →**satis** →**Select** [this puts satis in the box beside **V̲ariables:**] →**T̲est mean:** →box beside it and in it type **10** →**O̲K**

The output for this procedure is presented in Table 7.13. The mean for the total job satisfaction score for our sample of 68 cases is **10.838**. We see that there is a significant difference between the population mean of 10 and the sample mean of **10.838** at the two-tailed probability level of 0.04.

A one-tailed probability can be computed by adding the following **alternative** subcommand.

MTB > ttest 10 'satis';
SUBC> alternative=1.

The menu sequence for doing this is

→**S**tat →**B**asic Statistics →**1**-Sample t... →satis →Select →**T**est mean: →box beside it and in it type 10 →the down button on the box beside **A**lternative: →greater than →**O**K

The output from this procedure is displayed in Table 7.14. The one-tailed probability value (**0.020**) is half that of the two-tailed level (**0.040**).

Standard error of the mean

It is important to outline more fully what the *standard error of the mean* is since this important idea also constitutes the basis of other parametric tests such as the analysis of variance. One of the assumptions of many parametric tests is that the population of the variable to be analysed should be normally distributed. The errors of most distributions are known to take this form. For example, if a large group of people were asked to guess today's temperature, the distribution of their guesses would approximate that of a normal distribution, even if the temperature does not itself represent a normal distribution. In addition, it has been observed that the distribution of certain characteristics also takes this form. If, for example,

Table 7.13 Two-tailed **ttest** output comparing a sample and population mean

TEST OF MU = 10.000 VS MU N.E. 10.000

	N	MEAN	STDEV	SE MEAN	T	P VALUE
satis	68	10.838	3.304	0.401	2.09	0.040

Table 7.14 One-tailed **ttest** output comparing a sample and population mean

TEST OF MU = 10.000 VS MU G.T. 10.000

	N	MEAN	STDEV	SE MEAN	T	P VALUE
satis	68	10.838	3.304	0.401	2.09	0.020

you plot the distribution of the heights of a large group of adult human beings, it will be similar to that of a normal distribution.

If we draw samples from a population of values which is normally distributed, then the means of those samples will also be normally distributed. In other words, most of the means will be very similar to that of the population, although some of them will vary quite considerably. The standard error of the mean represents the standard deviation of the sample means. The one-sample t test compares the mean of a sample with that of the population in terms of how likely that difference has arisen by chance. The smaller this difference is, the more likely it is to have resulted from chance.

t test for two unrelated means

This test is used to determine if the means of two unrelated samples differ. It does this by comparing the difference between the two means with the standard error of the difference in the means of different samples:

$$t = \frac{\text{sample one mean} - \text{sample two mean}}{\text{standard error of the difference in means}}$$

The *standard error of the difference in means*, like the standard error of the mean, is also normally distributed. If we draw a large number of samples from a population whose values are normally distributed and plot the differences in the means of each of these samples, the shape of this distribution will be normal. Since the means of most of the samples will be close to the mean of the population and therefore similar to one another, if we subtract them from each other the differences between them will be close to zero. In other words, the nearer the difference in the means of two samples is to zero, the more likely it is that this difference is due to chance.

To compare the means of two samples, such as the mean job satisfaction of male and female workers in the Job Survey, we could first unstack **'satis'** according to **'gender'** using the following command:

MTB > unstack ('gender' 'satis')(c31 c32)(c33 c34);
SUBC> subscripts 'gender'.

The menu procedure for doing this is

→**Manip** →**Unstack...** →**gender** →**Select** [this puts **gender** in the box below **Unstack:**] →**satis** →**Select** →box beside **Using subscripts:** →**gender** →**Select** →**Store results in blocks:** [this is automatically selected] →type **c31 c32** in the first box which is automatically selected →second box and type **c33 c34** →**OK**

We would then compare job satisfaction for men in **c31** with that for women in **c33** with the **twosample** command:

MTB > twosample c31 c33

The menu procedure for doing this is

→ **S**tat → **B**asic Statistics → **2**-Sample t... → Samples in **d**ifferent columns → box beside **F**irst: → **c31** → Select [this puts **c31** in this box] → **c32** → Select [this puts **c32** in the box beside **S**econd:] → **O**K

Alternatively, we could avoid having to unstack **'satis'** by using the following **twot** command:

MTB > twot 'satis' 'gender'

The variable to be compared (**'satis'**) is listed before the variable forming the two groups (**'gender'**).

The menu action for doing this is

→ **S**tat → **B**asic Statistics → **2**-Sample t... → Samples in **o**ne column [this is automatically selected] → box beside **S**amples: → satis [this puts **x1** in this box] → Select → gender → Select [this puts **gender** in the box beside **S**ubscripts:] → **O**K

The output from both the **twosample** and **twot** procedures is the same apart from the names of the variables. Output from the **twot** command is shown in Table 7.15. To obtain the one-tailed probability we would simply add the following **alternative** subcommand

SUBC> alternative=1.

The menu system for doing this is

→ the down button on the box beside **A**lternative: → greater than → **O**K

Table 7.15 **Twot** output comparing the means of total job satisfaction in men and women in the Job Survey (two-tailed test with separate variance estimates)

TWOSAMPLE T FOR satis

gender	N	MEAN	STDEV	SE MEAN
1	37	10.95	3.32	0.55
2	31	10.71	3.33	0.60

95 PCT CI FOR MU 1 – MU 2: (–1.38, 1.86)

TTEST MU 1 = MU 2 (VS NE): T = 0.29   P = 0.77   DF = 63

In this case the one-tailed probability would be given as **P = 0.39** which is almost half that of **P = 0.77**.

There is one further complication we need to consider when interpreting the result of an unrelated t test. Since we do not know what the standard error of the difference in means is of the population in question, we have to estimate it. How this is done depends on whether the difference in the variances of the two samples are statistically significant. We use the F test or ratio to determine if the variances of the two groups differ.

F test for two unrelated variances

To calculate the F test, we first square the standard deviations which gives 11.0224 (**3.32 × 3.32** = 11.0224) for men and 11.0889 (**3.33 × 3.33** = 11.0889) for women. We then divide the larger variance by the smaller variance, which produces 1.01 (11.0889/11.0224 = 1.0060). Next we find the critical value of the F distribution with the requisite degrees of freedom by using the **invcdf** (**in**verse **c**umulative **d**istribution **f**unction) command and the **f** subcommand. On the **invcdf** command the level of statistical significance is specified by subtracting that level from 1.00. So, for the 0.05 probability level the appropriate figure is 0.95 (1.00 − 0.05 = 0.95).

MTB > invcdf .95;

On the **f** subcommand, which provides critical values for the F distribution, the degrees of freedom for the numerator and denominator need to be respectively listed after the **f**. Therefore, the subcommand for finding the 0.05 two-tailed critical value of F with 1 and 1 degree of freedom in the numerator and denominator respectively is

SUBC> f 1 1.

The menu sequence for doing this is

→**Calc** →**Probability Distributions** →**F...** →**Inverse cumulative probability** →box beside **Numerator degrees of freedom:** and type **1** →box beside **Denominator degrees of freedom:** and type **1** →**Input constant:** →box beside it and in it type **.95** →**OK**

The output from this procedure first gives the inverse cumulative distribution function of **0.9500** followed by the critical F value of **161.4475**.

0.9500   161.4475

As our F value of 1.01 is smaller than the critical value of **161.4475**, the variances of the two groups do not differ significantly and we need to pool the two variances to estimate the standard error of the difference in means. If the variances had been significantly different, we would have used the separate variances to calculate the standard error of the difference in means. The values of the *t* test and its probability level shown in Table 7.15 is based on treating the variances separately.

It should be pointed out that the variance, the standard deviation and the standard error of a sample are related. The *variance* or mean squared deviation is calculated by subtracting the mean of the sample from each of its scores (to provide a measure of their deviation from the mean), squaring them, adding these squares together and dividing them by one less than the number of cases. Since the deviations would sum to zero, they are squared to make the negative deviations positive. The *standard deviation* is simply the square root of the variance. The advantage of the standard deviation over the variance is that it is expressed in the original values of the data. For example, the standard deviation of job satisfaction is described in terms of the 20 points on this scale. The *standard error* is the standard deviation divided by the square root of the number of cases. The relationships between these three measures can be checked out on the statistics shown in Table 7.15.

t test with pooled variances

To calculate a *t* test where the variances have been pooled, simply add the **pooled** subcommand to either the **twosample** or **twot** command:

MTB > twosample c31 c33;
SUBC> pooled.

The menu procedure for doing this is

→**Stat** →**Basic Statistics** →**2-Sample t...** →**Samples in one column** [this is automatically selected] →box beside **Samples:** →satis →**Select** →**gender** →**Select** [this puts **gender** in the box beside **Subscripts:**] →box beside **Assume equal variances** →**OK**

The output for the **twosample** procedure comparing job satisfaction in men and women is shown in Table 7.16. In this case, there is no difference in the *t* and *p* values in terms of whether pooled or separate variances are used in calculating the standard error of the difference in means. Note, however, the degrees of freedom differ (**DF**), being **66** and **63** for the pooled and separate variance tests respectively. In both cases, the difference in job satisfaction between men and women is not significant.

Unrelated *t* test and ordinal data

Some people have argued that parametric tests should only be used on interval/ratio data (for example, Stevens, 1946). Others, as we have mentioned earlier, have reasoned that such a restriction is unnecessary. In

Table 7.16 **Twosample** output comparing the means of total job satisfaction in men and women in the Job Survey (two-tailed test with pooled variance estimates)

TWOSAMPLE T FOR C31 VS C33

	N	MEAN	STDEV	SE MEAN
C31	37	10.95	3.32	0.55
C33	31	10.71	3.33	0.60

95 PCT CI FOR MU C31 − MU C33: (−1.38, 1.85)

TTEST MU C31 = MU C33 (VS NE): T = 0.29 P = 0.77 DF = 66

POOLED STDEV =   3.33

view of this controversy, it may be interesting to see whether the use of an unrelated t test on an ordinal variable such as rated quality of work gives very dissimilar results to that of the Mann-Whitney previously used. According to Siegel (1956), the Mann-Whitney test is about 95 per cent as powerful as the t test. What this means is that the t test requires 5 per cent fewer subjects than the Mann-Whitney test to reject the null hypothesis when it is false. The following procedure was used to generate the output in Table 7.17:

MTB > twot 'qual' 'gender';
SUBC> pooled.

The menu action for doing this is

→**Stat** →**Basic Statistics** →**2-Sample t...** →**Samples in one column** [this is automatically selected] →box beside **Samples:** →**qual** →**Select** →**gender** →**Select** [this puts **gender** in the box beside **Subscripts:**] →box beside **Assume equal variances** →**OK**

As can be seen, this test also indicates that there is no significant difference between men and women in the mean of their rated quality of work.

Levene's test for two unrelated variances

Levene's test rather than the F ratio should be used when the data are not normally distributed. This test is available on *Release 10* using the following **%vartest** command

MTB > %vartest 'satis' 'gender'

The dependent variable **'satis'** is listed first followed by the independent variable **'gender'**.

Table 7.17 **Twot** output comparing rated quality of work for men and women in the Job Survey (two-tailed test with pooled variance estimates)

TWOSAMPLE T FOR qual

gender	N	MEAN	STDEV	SE MEAN
1	39	3.28	1.21	0.19
2	31	3.06	1.34	0.24

95 PCT CI FOR MU 1 – MU 2: (–0.39, 0.83)

TTEST MU 1 = MU 2 (VS NE): T = 0.71 P = 0.48 DF = 68

POOLED STDEV =   **1.27**

The menu action for doing this is

→**S**tat →**B**asic Statistics →**H**omogeneity of Variance... →satis
→**S**elect [this puts **satis** in the box beside **R**esponse:] →gender
→**S**elect [this puts **gender** in the box beside **F**actors:] →**O**K

The output from this procedure is shown in Table 7.18. The value of Levene's test is **0.074** which is not significant since it has a *p* of **0.786** or less of occurring. In other words, the variances of **'satis'** for men and women do not differ significantly.

One-way analysis of variance for three or more unrelated means

To compare the means of three or more unrelated samples, such as the mean job satisfaction of the four ethnic groups in the Job Survey, it is necessary to compute a one-way analysis of variance. This is essentially an *F* test in which an estimate of the *between-groups* variance (or *mean-square* as the estimate of the variance is referred to in analysis of variance) is compared with an estimate of the *within-groups* variance by dividing the former by the latter:

$$F = \frac{\text{between-groups estimated variance or mean-square}}{\text{within-groups estimated variance or mean-square}}$$

The total amount of variance in the dependent variable (i.e. job satisfaction) can be thought of as comprising two elements: that which is due to the independent variable (i.e. ethnic group) and that which is due to other factors. This latter component is often referred to as *error* or *residual* variance. The variance that is due to the independent variable is frequently described as *explained* variance. If the between-groups (i.e. explained)

Table 7.18 **% variance** output showing the results of Levene's test comparing the variance of **satis** across **gender** (*Release 10*)

Homogeneity of Variance

Response	satis
Factors	gender
ConfLvl	95.0000

Bonferroni confidence intervals for standard deviations

Lower	Sigma	Upper	n	Factor Levels
2.62755	3.32454	4.49340	37	1
2.57917	3.32860	4.65093	31	2

Bartlett's Test (normal distribution)

Test Statistic: 0.000
p value: 0.996

Levene's Test (any continuous distribution)

Test Statistic: 0.074
p value : 0.786

estimated variance is considerably larger than that within-groups (i.e. error or residual), then the value of the F ratio will be higher which implies that the differences between the means is unlikely to be due to chance.

The within-groups mean-square or estimated variance is its sum-of-squares divided by its degrees of freedom. These degrees of freedom are the sum of the number of cases minus one in each group [i.e. (the number of cases in group one − 1) + (the number of cases in group two − 1) and so on]. The sum-of-squares is the sum of squared differences between each score in a group and its mean, summed across all groups. The between-groups sum-of-squares, on the other hand, is obtained by subtracting each group's mean from the overall (total or grand) mean, squaring them, multiplying them by the number of cases in each group, and summing the result. It can also be calculated by subtracting the within-groups sum-of-squares from the total sum-of-squares since the total sum-of-squares is the sum of the between- and within-groups sum-of-squares:

$$\begin{array}{lll} \text{total} & \text{between-groups} & \text{within-groups} \\ \text{sum-of-squares} = & \text{(i.e. explained)} + & \text{(i.e. error)} \\ & \text{sum-of-squares} & \text{sum-of-squares} \end{array}$$

The between-groups mean-square or estimated variance is its sum-of-squares divided by its degrees of freedom. These degrees of freedom are the number of groups minus one. The degrees of freedom for the total sum-of-squares are the sum of those for the within- and between-groups sum-of-squares or the total number of subjects minus one. Although this test may sound complicated, the essential reasoning behind it is that if the groups or samples come from the same population, then the between-groups estimate of the population's variance should be similar to the within-groups estimated variance.

To compare the mean job satisfaction of the four ethnic groups in the Job Survey, we would use the following command:

MTB > oneway 'satis' 'ethnicgp'

The variable to be compared is listed first (**'satis'**) followed by the grouping variable (**'ethnicgp'**).

The menu sequence for doing this is

→**S̲tat** →**A̲NOVA** →**O̲neway...** →**satis** →**Select** [this puts **satis** in the box beside **R̲esponse:**] →**ethnicgp** →**Select** [this puts **ethnicgp** in the box beside **F̲actors:**] →**O̲K**

The output for this procedure is displayed in Table 7.19. The F ratio, which is the between-group mean square (**ethnicgp**) divided by the within-group one (**ERROR**) is **0.26** ($2.9/11.3 = 0.256$), which is non-significant (**0.855**). Consequently, there is no statistically significant difference in job satisfaction between the four ethnic groups.

The F test or ratio only tells us whether there is a significant difference between one or more of the groups. It does not inform us where this difference lies. To determine this, we need to carry out further statistical tests. Which tests we use depends on whether or not we predicted where the differences

Table 7.19 **Oneway** output comparing job satisfaction across four ethnic groups in the Job Survey

ANALYSIS OF VARIANCE ON satis

SOURCE	DF	SS	MS	F	p
ethnicgp	3	8.7	2.9	0.26	0.855
ERROR	64	722.5	11.3		
TOTAL	67	731.2			

INDIVIDUAL 95 PCT CI'S FOR MEAN
BASED ON POOLED STDEV

LEVEL	N	MEAN	STDEV	
				------+---------+---------+---------+
1	35	10.543	3.284	(---*---)
2	17	10.941	3.596	(----*-----)
3	14	11.286	3.292	(-----*-----)
4	2	12.000	2.828	(----------------*----------------)
				------+---------+---------+---------+

POOLED STDEV = 3.360   9.0   12.0   15.0   18.0

would be. If, for example, we *predicted* that whites would be less satisfied than Asians and the F test had been significant, then we would carry out an unrelated t test as described above using a one-tailed level of significance.

If, however, we had not expected any differences but found that the F test was significant, then we would need to take into account the fact that if we carried out a large number of comparisons some of these would be significant just by chance. Indeed, at the 5 per cent level of significance, 5 per cent or one in twenty comparisons could be expected to be significant by definition. A number of tests which take account of this fact have been developed and are available on the Minitab **oneway** command. Because these tests are carried out after the data have been initially analysed, they are referred to as *post hoc* or *a posteriori* tests. One of these, the Tukey test, will be briefly outlined. To conduct a Tukey test to compare job satisfaction between every possible pair of ethnic group, add the following **tukey** subcommand to the **oneway** command:

SUBC> tukey.

The menu procedure for doing this is

→**C̲omparisons…** →box beside T̲ukey's, family error rate:
→O̲K

The output for this procedure is shown in Table 7.20. The pairs of numbers in the table give the confidence intervals for the mean of one group minus the mean of another group for all possible comparisons. So, for

Table 7.20 **Tukey** output comparing job satisfaction across the four ethnic groups in the Job Survey

Tukey's pairwise comparisons

   Family error rate = 0.0500
Individual error rate = 0.0104

Critical value = 3.73

Intervals for (column level mean) – (row level mean)

	1	2	3
2	−3.018		
	2.221		
3	−3.545	−3.543	
	2.059	2.854	
4	−7.900	−7.683	−7.413
	4.986	5.566	5.985

example, the first pair of numbers (−**3.018**, **2.221**) provides the confidence interval for the mean of group 1 (whites) minus the mean of group 2 (Asians). Comparisons where the confidence limits exclude zero (e.g. 0.56, 3.24 or −1.21, −4.07) indicate a significant difference. Since none of the comparisons have confidence limits which omit zero, there are no significant differences between any of the groups, taken two at a time.

t test for two related means

To compare the means of the same subjects in two conditions or at two points in time, we would use a related *t* test. We would also use this test to compare subjects who had been matched to be similar in certain respects. The advantage of using the same subjects or matched subjects is that the amount of error deriving from differences between subjects is reduced. The unrelated *t* test compares the mean difference between pairs of scores within the sample with that of the population in terms of the standard error of the difference in means:

$$t = \frac{\substack{\text{sample mean} - \text{population mean} \\ \text{differences} \qquad \text{differences}}}{\text{standard error of the difference in means}}$$

Since the population mean difference is zero, the closer the sample mean difference is to zero, the less likely it is that the two sets of scores differ significantly from one another.

The difference between a related and an unrelated *t* test lies essentially in the fact that two scores from the same person are likely to vary less than two scores from two different people. For example, if we weigh the same person on two occasions, the difference between those two weights is likely to be less than the weights of two separate individuals. This fact is reflected in the different way in which the standard error of the difference in means is calculated for the two tests which we do not have space to go into here. The variability of the standard error for the related *t* test is less than that for the unrelated one, as illustrated in Figure 7.2. In fact, the variability of the standard error of the difference in means for the related *t* test will depend on the extent to which the pairs of scores are similar or related. The more similar they are, the less the variability will be of their estimated standard error.

To compare two related sets of scores such as job satisfaction in the first two months (**'satis1'** and **'satis2'**) in the Panel Study, we first have to subtract one of the scores from the other for each case and to put these differences in a new column with the **let** command:

MTB > let c12 = 'satis1' − 'satis2'

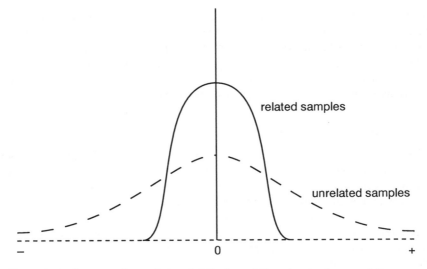

Figure 7.2   A comparison of the distribution of the standard error of the differences in means for related and unrelated samples

The menu system for doing this is

→**Calc** →**Mathematical Expressions...** →**c12** →**Select** [this puts **c12** in the box beside **Variable [new or modified]:**] →box under **Expression:** and in it type **'satis1'-'satis2'** →**OK**

To carry out the related *t* test, we simply specify this new column (**c12**) on the **ttest** command

MTB > ttest c12

The menu sequence for doing this is

→**Stat** →**Basic Statistics** →**1-Sample t...** →**c12** →**Select** [this puts **c12** in the box beside **Variables**] →**OK**

The output from this procedure is shown in Table 7.21. Since the **P VALUE** is greater than 0.05, we would conclude that job satisfaction does not differ significantly between the first and second month. If we wanted the

Table 7.21   Two-tailed **ttest** output comparing job satisfaction in the first and second month in the Panel Study

TEST OF MU = 0.000 VS MU N.E. 0.000

	N	MEAN	STDEV	SE MEAN	T	P VALUE
C12	12	0.333	3.420	0.987	0.34	0.74

one-tailed *p* value, we would add the following **alternative** subcommand to the **ttest** command

SUBC> alternative=1.

which would give a **P VALUE** of **0.37.**

The menu procedure for doing this is

→the down button on the box beside **Alternative:** →**greater than** →**OK**

t test for two related variances

If we want to determine whether the variances of two related samples are significantly different from one another, we have to calculate it using the following formula (McNemar, 1969) since it is not available on Minitab:

$$t = \frac{(\text{larger variance} - \text{smaller variance}) \times \sqrt{(\text{number of cases} - 2)}}{\sqrt{\begin{array}{l}(1 - \text{correlation of 2 sets of scores squared}) \\ \times (4 \times \text{larger variance} \times \text{smaller variance})\end{array}}}$$

To apply this formula to the job satisfaction variances in the above example, we would first have to calculate their variances and the correlation between the two variables.

We could calculate the standard deviation of the two variables using the **stdev** command for the first and then the second variable

MTB > stdev 'satis1'
ST.DEV. = 3.4245
MTB > stdev 'satis2'
ST.DEV. = 4.2817

The menu sequence for doing this is

→**Calc** →**Column Statistics...** →**Standard deviation** →box beside **Input variables:** →satis1 →**Select** →**OK**
→**Calc** →**Column Statistics...** →**Standard deviation** →box beside **Input variables:** →satis2 →**Select** →**OK**

To convert these standard deviations into variances we simply square them which makes them 11.73 and 18.33 respectively.

In *Release 10*, we could obtain the variances directly with the following **stats** command

MTB > stats 'satis1' 'satis2';
SUBC> variance c12 c13.

The variances will be stored in the worksheet where they can be read.

To calculate the correlation between the two variables we use the following **correlation** command

MTB > correlation 'satis1' 'satis2'

The menu action for doing this is

→**S**tat →**B**asic Statistics →Correlation... →satis1 →Select [this puts satis1 in the box under **V**ariables:] →satis2 →Select →**O**K

The following output is displayed

Correlation of satis1 and satis2 = 0.626

Substituting the appropriate values in the above equation, we arrive at a t value of 0.91, which with 10 degrees of freedom is not significant with a two-tailed test. To have been significant at this level, we would have needed a t value of 2.228 or greater.

A single-factor repeated-measures analysis of variance for three or more related means

To compare three or more means from the same or matched subjects, such as job satisfaction during three consecutive months, we would need to carry out a repeated-measures analysis of variance (ANOVA) test which has one within-subjects or *repeated-measures* variable. The categorizing or independent variables in analysis of variance are called *factors* and the categories or treatments are termed *levels*. In this analysis there is one factor consisting of the time or month of assessment and this factor has three *levels* since it is repeated three times. This design is referred to variously as a single group (or factor) repeated-measures and treatments-by-subjects design. To conduct it on the present example, we first have to create three new columns.

The first column contains job satisfaction on the three occasions and can be set up with the following **stack** command:

MTB > stack 'satis1' 'satis2' 'satis3' c11

The column containing **'satis1'** is placed on top of the column holding **'satis2'** which in turn is put on top of the column storing **'satis3'**. These three columns are stacked in this way in **c11** which we could name **'satis'**:

MTB > name c11 'satis'

The menu procedure for doing this is

→**M**anip →**S**tack... →satis1 →Select [this puts **satis1** in the first box below **Stack the following b**locks:] →second box under **Stack the following b**locks: →satis2 →Select [this puts **satis2** in this box] →third box under **Stack the following b**locks: →satis3 →Select →box under **Store results in b**locks: and in it type **satis** →**O**K

The second column we have to make consists of a code telling us to which of the three months the rated quality of work refers. The first month we will code as **1**, the second month as **2** and the third month as **3**. So, the first 12 values in **c12** refer to the first month, the second 12 values to the second month and the third 12 values to the third month. We form this second column with the **set** command:

MTB > set c12
DATA> 1 1 1 1 1 1 1 1 1 1 1 1 2 2 2 2 2 2 2 2 2 2 2 2 3 3 3 3 3 3 3 3 3 3 3 3
DATA> end

Alternatively, we could use the following abbreviation to set this pattern of values

DATA> (1:3)12

The numbers to be repeated are placed within parentheses. The colon represents consecutive numbers between **1** and **3** (i.e. 1,2,3). The number **12** after the closing parenthesis means the first number **1** is repeated 12 times, the second number **2** is repeated 12 times and so on. There must be no space between this number and the closing bracket.

We could call **c12 'month'**.

MTB > name c12 'month'

The third column we have to make consecutively numbers the participants at each of the three times in the same order and can be created by stacking **'id'** three times in the new column **c13**:
We could call **c13 'subjects'**:

MTB > name c13 'subjects'
MTB > stack 'id' 'id' 'id' c13

The menu sequence for doing this is

→**Manip** →**Stack...** →**id** →**Select** →second box under **Stack the following blocks:** →**id** →**Select** →third box under **Stack the following blocks:** →**id** →**Select** →box under **Store results in blocks:** and in it type **subjects** →**OK**

The values of these three new columns can be displayed with the **print** command

MTB > print 'subjects' 'month' 'satis'

The menu action for doing this is

→**File** →**Display Data...** →**subjects** →**Select** →**month** →**Select** →**satis** →**Select** →**OK**

To carry out this single factor repeated-measures analysis of variance we would use the following **anova** command

MTB > anova satis = month subjects;
SUBC> means month.

The dependent variable **satis** is listed first followed by an equals sign =, the factor **month** and the variable **subjects** which orders subjects. Note that the quotation marks around the variable names can be omitted in the **anova** command. If, as usual, we want to display the mean of the dependent variable across the levels of the categorizing variable we add the **means** subcommand which lists the name of the categorizing variable **month**.

The menu procedure for doing this is

→Stat →ANOVA →Balanced ANOVA... →satis →Select [this puts
satis in the box beside **Response:**] →box under **Model:** →month
→Select [this puts **month** in this box] →subjects →Select →box
under **Display means for (list of terms):** →month →Select →OK

The output from this procedure is shown in Table 7.22. The **F** ratio for **month** tells us whether job satisfaction differs significantly across the three months. It is calculated by dividing the mean square (**MS**) of **month** (**1.694**) by the **Error** mean square (**5.604**) which gives an **F** ratio of **0.30** (**1.694/5.604** = 0.302). This **F** ratio is not significant since its p value is greater (**0.742**) than 0.05. Note that the factors in this model are described as being **fixed** as opposed to being **random**. This means that the levels of

Table 7.22 A single-factor repeated-measures **anova** output comparing job satisfaction across three months in the Job Survey

Factor	Type	Levels	Values								
month	fixed	3	1	2	3						
subjects	fixed	12	1	2	3	4	5	6	7	8	9
			10	11	12						

Analysis of Variance for satis

Source	DF	SS	MS	F	P
month	2	3.389	1.694	0.30	0.742
subjects	11	321.639	29.240	5.22	0.000
Error	22	123.278	5.604		
Total	35	448.306			

MEANS

month	N	satis
1	12	11.500
2	12	11.167
3	12	10.750

the factors have not been chosen at random so that the results cannot be generalized to the factors as a whole.

As was the case for the one-way analysis of variance test, the F test only tells us whether there is a significant difference between the three related scores but does not inform us where this difference lies. If a significant overall difference had been found, we would need to carry out some supplementary analyses. If we had predicted a difference between two scores, then we can determine if this prediction was confirmed by conducting a related t test as described above. If we had found but had not predicted a difference, then we need to use a *post hoc* test, of which there are a number (Maxwell, 1980). Since these are not available on Minitab, they have to be calculated separately. If the scores are significantly correlated, the Bonferroni inequality test is recommended, whereas if they are not, the Tukey test is advocated.

The Bonferroni test is based on the related t test but modifies the significance level to take account of the fact that more than one comparison is being made. To calculate this, work out the total number of possible comparisons between any two groups, divide the chosen significance level (which is usually 0.05) by this number, and treat the result as the appropriate significance level for comparing more than three groups. In the case of three groups, the total number of possible comparisons is 3 which means the appropriate significance level is 0.017 (0.05/3).

The calculation for the Tukey test is more complicated (Stevens, 1992). The difference between any two means is compared against the value calculated by multiplying the square root of the repeated measures within-cells mean-square error term (divided by the number of cases) with the studentized range statistic, a table of which can be found in Stevens (1992). If the difference between any two means is greater than this value, then this difference is significant. The within-cells mean-square error term is presented in the output in Table 7.21 and is about 5.6. The square root of this divided by the number of cases is 0.68 ($\sqrt{5.6/12}$). The appropriate studentized range value with 3 groups and 22 degrees of freedom for the error term is 3.58. This multiplied by 0.68 gives 2.43. If any two means differed by more than this, they would be significant at the 0.05 level.

EXERCISES

1. Suppose you wanted to find out whether there had been a statistically significant change in three types of books (classified as romance, crime and science fiction) sold by two shops. What test would you use?

2. What would the null hypothesis be?

3. The data for the two shops are in the columns of the table while the data for the three categories of books are in its rows. The first column is called

shop1 and the second **shop2.** What would be the Minitab procedure for running this test?

4. Would you use a one- or a two-tailed level of significance?

5. If the probability level of the result of this test were 0.25, what would you conclude about the number of books sold?

6. Would a finding with a probability level of 0.0001 mean that there was a greater change in the number of books sold than one with a probability level of 0.037?

7. If the value of this test were statistically significant, how would you determine if there had been a significant change between any two cells, say romance books for the two shops?

8. Would you use a one- or a two-tailed level of significance to test the expectation that the first shop should sell more romance books than the second?

9. How would you determine a one-tailed level of significance from a two-tailed one of, say, 0.084?

10. If you wanted to find out if more men than women said that they had fallen in love at first sight, would it be appropriate to test for this difference using a binomial test in which the number of men and women reporting this experience was compared?

11. What test would you use to determine if women reported having a greater number of close friends than men?

12. When would you use the pooled rather than the separate variance estimates in interpreting the results of a t test?

13. What test would you use if you wanted to find out if the average number of books sold by the same ten shops had changed significantly in the three months of October, November, and December?

Chapter 8

Bivariate analysis
Exploring relationships between two variables

This chapter focuses on relationships between pairs of variables. Having examined the distribution of values for particular variables through the use of frequency tables, histograms, and associated statistics as discussed in Chapter 5, a major strand in the analysis of a set of data is likely to be bivariate analysis – how two variables are related to each other. The analyst is unlikely to be satisfied with the examination of single variables alone, but will probably be concerned to demonstrate whether variables are related. The investigation of relationships is an important step in explanation and consequently contributes to the building of theories about the nature of the phenomena in which we are interested. The emphasis on relationships can be contrasted with the material covered in the previous chapter, in which the ways in which cases or subjects may differ in respect to a variable were described. The topics covered in the present chapter bear some resemblance to those examined in Chapter 7, since the researcher in both contexts is interested in exploring variance and its connections with other variables. Moreover, if we find that members of different ethnic groups differ in regard to a variable, such as income, this may be taken to indicate that there is a relationship between ethnic group and income. Thus, as will be seen, there is no hard-and-fast distinction between the exploration of differences and of relationships.

What does it mean to say that two variables are related? We say that there is a relationship between two variables when the distribution of values for one variable is associated with the distribution exhibited by another variable. In other words, the variation exhibited by one variable is patterned in such a way that its variance is not randomly distributed in relation to the other variable. Examples of relationships that are frequently encountered are: middle class individuals are more likely to vote Conservative than members of the working class; infant mortality is higher among countries with a low per capita income than those with a high per capita income; work alienation is greater in routine, repetitive work than in varied work. In each case, a relationship between two variables is indicated: between social class and voting behaviour; between the infant mortality rate and one measure of a nation's prosperity (per capita income); and between work alienation and job characteristics. Each of these examples implies that the variation in one variable is patterned, rather than randomly distributed, in relation to the other variable. Thus, in saying that there is a relationship between social class and voting behaviour from the above example, we are saying that people's tendency to vote Conservative is not randomly distributed across categories of social class. Middle class individuals are more likely to vote for this party; if there was no relationship we would not be able to detect such a tendency since there would be no evidence that the middle and working classes differed in their propensity to vote Conservative.

CROSSTABULATION

In order to provide some more flesh to these ideas the idea of *crosstabulation* will be introduced in conjunction with an example. Crosstabulation is one of the simplest and most frequently used ways of demonstrating the presence or absence of a relationship. To illustrate its use, consider the hypothetical data on thirty individuals that are presented in Table 8.1. We have data on two variables: whether each person exhibits job satisfaction and whether they have been absent from work in the past six months. For ease of presentation, each variable can assume either of two values – yes or no. In order to examine the relationship between the two variables, individuals will be allocated to one of the four possible combinations that the two variables in conjunction can assume. Table 8.2 presents these four possible combinations, along with the frequency of their occurrence (as indicated from the data in Table 8.1). This procedure is very similar to that associated with frequency tables for one or more variables. We are trying to summarize and reduce the amount of information with which we are confronted to make it readable and analysable. Detecting a pattern in the relationship between two variables as in Table 8.1 is fairly easy when there are only thirty subjects and the variables are dichotomous; with larger data sets and more complex variables the task of seeing patterns without the employment of techniques for examining relationships would be difficult and probably lead to misleading conclusions.

The crosstabulation of the two variables is presented in Table 8.3. This kind of table is often referred to as a *contingency table*. Since there are four possible combinations of the two variables, the table requires four cells, in which the frequencies listed in Table 8.2 are placed. The following additional information is also presented. First, the figures to the right of the table are called the *row marginals* and those at the bottom of the table are the *column marginals*. These two items of information help us to interpret frequencies in the cells. Also, if the frequencies for each of the two variables have not been presented previously in a report or publication, the row and column marginals provide this information. Second, a percentage in

Table 8.1   Data for thirty individuals on job satisfaction
and absenteeism

Subject	Job satisfaction	Absent
1	Yes	No
2	Yes	Yes
3	No	Yes
4	Yes	Yes
5	No	Yes
6	No	Yes
7	Yes	No
8	Yes	No
9	No	No
10	Yes	No
11	No	No
12	No	Yes
13	No	Yes
14	No	No
15	No	Yes
16	Yes	No
17	Yes	Yes
18	No	No
19	Yes	No
20	No	Yes
21	No	No
22	Yes	No
23	No	Yes
24	No	Yes
25	Yes	No
26	Yes	Yes
27	Yes	No
28	No	Yes
29	Yes	No
30	Yes	No

Table 8.2   Four possible combinations

Job satisfaction	Absenteeism	N
Yes	Yes	4
Yes	No	10
No	Yes	11
No	No	5

each cell is presented. This allows any patterning to be easily detectable, a
facility that becomes especially helpful and important when tables with
large numbers of cells are being examined. The percentages presented in
Table 8.3 are *column percentages*, that is, the frequency in each cell is

Table 8.3   The relationship between job satisfaction and absenteeism

| | Job satisfaction | | |
	Yes	No	Row marginals
	1	2	
Yes	4 (7) 29%	11 (8) 69%	15
Absenteeism			
	3	4	
No	10 (7) 71%	5 (8) 31%	15
Column marginals	14	16	30

Note: The top figure in each cell is the frequency, i.e. the number of cases to which that cell applies. The figure in brackets is the expected frequency – that is, the frequency that would be obtained on the basis of chance alone (see discussion of χ^2). The percentages are column percentages.

treated as a percentage of the column marginal for that cell. Thus, for cell 1 the frequency is 4 and the column marginal is 14; the column percentage is $4/14 \times 100$, i.e. 28.6 (rounded up to 29 per cent).

What then does the contingency table show? Table 8.3 suggests that there is a relationship between job satisfaction and absence. People who express job satisfaction tend not to have been absent from work (cell 3), since the majority (71 per cent) of the fourteen individuals who express satisfaction have not been absent; on the other hand, of the sixteen people who are not satisfied, a majority of 69 per cent have been absent from work (cell 2). Thus, a relationship is implied; satisfied individuals are considerably less likely to be absent from work than those who are not satisfied.

In saying that a relationship exists between job satisfaction and absence, we are not suggesting that the relationship is perfect; some satisfied individuals are absent from work (cell 1) and some who are not satisfied have not been absent (cell 4). A relationship does not imply a perfect correspondence between the two variables. Such relationships are not specific to the social sciences – everyone has heard of the relationship between lung cancer and smoking, but no one believes that it implies that everyone who smokes will contract lung cancer or that lung cancer only afflicts those who smoke. If there had been a perfect relationship between satisfaction and absence, the contingency table presented in Table 8.4a would be in evidence; if there was no relationship, the crosstabulation in Table 8.4b would be expected. In the case of Table 8.4a, all individuals who express satisfaction would be in the 'No' category, and all who are not

Table 8.4 Two types of relationship

(a) A perfect relationship

	Job satisfaction		
	Yes	No	
Absenteeism Yes	0	16 100%	16
No	14 100%	0	14
	14	16	30

(b) No relationship

	Job satisfaction		
	Yes	No	
Absenteeism Yes	7 50%	8 50%	15
No	7 50%	8 50%	15
	14	16	30

satisfied would be in the absence category. With Table 8.4b, those who are not satisfied are equally likely to have been absent as not absent.

As noted above, the percentages in Tables 8.2 to 8.4 are column percentages. Another kind of percentage that might have been preferred is a *row percentage*. With this calculation, the frequency in each cell is calculated in terms of the row totals, so that the percentage for cell 1 would be $4/15 \times 100$ i.e. 27 per cent. The row percentages for cells 2, 3 and 4 respectively would be 73 per cent, 67 per cent and 33 per cent. In taking row percentages, we would be emphasizing a different aspect of the table, for example, the percentage of those who have been absent who are satisfied (27 per cent in cell 1) and the percentage who are not satisfied with their jobs (73 per cent in cell 2). The question of whether to use row or column percentages in part depends on what aspects of the data you want to highlight. It is sometimes suggested that the decision depends on whether the independent variable is across the top or along the side of the table: if the former, column percentages should be used; if the latter, row percentages should be employed. Typically, the independent variable will go across the table, in which case column percentages should be used. However, this suggestion implies that there is a straightforward means of identifying the independent and dependent variables, but this is not always the case and great caution should be exercised in making such an inference for reasons that will be explored below. It may appear that job satisfaction is the independent and absence the dependent variable, but it is hazardous to make such an attribution.

Minitab can produce tables without percentages, though such tables are unlikely to be very helpful, and can produce output with either row or column percentages or both.

Crosstabulation with Minitab

Crosstabulations can easily be created with Minitab. Let us turn now to the Job Survey data. Let us say that we want to examine the relationship between **'skill'** and **'gender'** and that we want the following information in the table: counts (i.e. the frequency for each cell); the row percentages; the column percentages; and a chi-square test. This last piece of information will be dealt with in detail below. The following sequence would be used when employing the prompt system in the Minitab for Windows session window or in the mainframe or PC versions of Minitab:

MTB > table 'skill' 'gender';
SUBC> counts;
SUBC> rowpercents;
SUBC> colpercents;
SUBC> chisquare.

Note that the dependent variable, **'skill'**, comes first and the independent variable, **'gender'**, comes second. This will create a contingency table in which **'gender'** goes across and **'skill'** down. In the Minitab for Windows menu system the following sequence would be used with the menu system:

→**S̲tat** →**T̲ables** →**C̲ross Tabulation...** →skill →**Select** →gender →**Select** [this will have brought **skill** and then **gender** into the **Classification V̲ariables** box] →[If you want frequencies, row percentages, and column percentages in each cell, ensure that there is a mark in the small boxes by **Cou̲nts**, **R̲ow percents**, and **C̲olumn percents**. If no mark is present, click once in the relevant boxes. Also, click on the box by **Chisquare a̲nalysis**, a topic that will be dealt with shortly. A cross will appear in each box that has been chosen.] →**O̲K**

If column percentages only were required, you need only click on that box or when using the prompt system only use the subcommand for column percentages. In fact, it is likely that only column percentages would be used since **'gender'** has been identified as the independent variable and goes across the table; the row percentages are requested and presented here for illustrative purposes. Table 8.5 provides the output deriving from these instructions along with some additional features that will be explained below.

Table 8.5 Contingency table for **skill** by **gender** (Minitab for Windows *Release 10* output from Job Survey data)

Tabulated Statistics

ROWS: skill   COLUMNS: gender

	1	2	ALL
1	5	9	14
	35.71	64.29	100.00
	12.82	29.03	20.00
	5	9	14
2	11	7	18
	61.11	38.89	100.00
	28.21	22.58	25.71
	11	7	18
3	11	10	21
	52.38	47.62	100.00
	28.21	32.26	30.00
	11	10	21
4	12	5	17
	70.59	29.41	100.00
	30.77	16.13	24.29
	12	5	17
ALL	39	31	70
	55.71	44.29	100.00
	100.00	100.00	100.00
	39	31	70

CHI-SQUARE =   4.101   WITH D.F. = 3

CELL CONTENTS –
> COUNT
> % OF ROW
> % OF COL
> COUNT

CROSSTABULATION AND STATISTICAL SIGNIFICANCE: THE CHI-SQUARE (χ^2) TEST

As the discussion of statistical significance in Chapter 6 implies, a problem that is likely to be of considerable concern is the question of whether there really is a relationship between the two variables or whether the relationship has arisen by chance, for example as a result of sampling error having engendered an idiosyncratic sample. If the latter were the case, concluding that there is a relationship would mean that an erroneous inference was being made: if we find a relationship between two variables from an idiosyncratic sample, we would infer a relationship even though the two variables are independent (i.e. not related) in the population from which the sample was taken. Even though the sample may have been selected randomly, sampling error may have engendered an idiosyncratic sample, in which case the findings cannot be generalized to the population from which the sample was selected. What we need to know is the probability that there *is* a relationship between the two variables in the population from which a random sample was derived. In order to establish this probability, the chi-square (χ^2) test is widely used in conjunction with contingency tables. This is a test of statistical significance, meaning that it allows the researcher to ascertain the probability that the observed relationship between two variables may have arisen by chance. In the case of Table 8.3, it might be that there is no relationship between job satisfaction and absence in the company as a whole, and that the relationship observed in our sample is a product of sampling error (i.e. the sample is in fact unrepresentative).

The starting point for the administration of a chi-square test, as with tests of statistical significance in general, is a null hypothesis of no relationship between the two variables being examined. In seeking to discern whether a relationship exists between two variables in the population from which a random sample was selected, the procedure entails needing to reject the null hypothesis. If the null hypothesis is confirmed, the proposition that there is a relationship must be rejected. The chi-square statistic is then calculated. This statistic is calculated by comparing the observed frequencies in each cell in a contingency table with those that would occur if there were no relationship between the two variables. These are the frequencies that would occur if the values associated with each of the two variables were randomly distributed in relation to each other. In other words, the chi-square test entails a comparison of actual frequencies with those which would be expected to occur on the basis of chance alone (often referred to as the *expected frequencies*). The greater the difference between the observed and the expected frequencies, the larger the ensuing chi-square value will be; if the observed frequencies are very close to the expected frequencies, a small value is likely to occur.

The next step is for the researcher to decide what significance level to employ. This means that the researcher must decide what is an acceptable risk that the null hypothesis may be incorrectly rejected (i.e. a Type I error). The null hypothesis would be incorrectly rejected if, for example, there was in fact no relationship between job satisfaction and absence in the population, but our sample data (see Table 8.3) suggested that there was such a relationship. The significance level relates to the probability that we might be making such a false inference. If we say that the computed chi-square value is significant at the 0.05 level of statistical significance, we are saying that we would expect that a maximum of 5 in every 100 possible samples that could be drawn from a population might appear to yield a relationship between two variables when in fact there is no relationship between them in that population. In other words, there is a 1 in 20 chance that we are rejecting the null hypothesis of no relationship when we should in fact be confirming it. If we set a more stringent qualification for rejection, the 0.01 level of significance, we are saying that we are only prepared to accept a chi-square value that implies a maximum of 1 sample in every 100 showing a relationship where none exists in the population. The probability estimate here is important – the probability of your having a deviant sample (i.e. one suggesting a relationship where none exists in the population) is greater if the 0.05 level is preferred to the 0.01 level. With the former, there is a 1 in 20 chance, but with the latter a 1 in 100 chance, that the null hypothesis will be erroneously rejected. An even more stringent test is to take the 0.001 level which implies that a maximum of 1 in 1000 samples might constitute a deviant sample. These three significance levels – 0.05, 0.01, 0.001 – are the ones most frequently encountered in reports of research results.

The calculated chi-square value must therefore be related to a significance level, but how is this done? It is *not* the case that a larger value implies a higher significance level. For one thing, the larger a table is, i.e. the more cells it has, the larger a chi-square value is likely to be. This is because the value is computed by taking the difference between the observed and the expected frequencies for each cell in a contingency table and then adding all the differences. It would hardly be surprising if a contingency table comprising four cells exhibited a lower chi-square value than one with twenty cells. This would be a ridiculous state of affairs, since larger tables would always be more likely to yield statistically significant results than smaller ones. In order to relate the chi-square value to the significance level it is necessary to establish the number of degrees of freedom associated with a crosstabulation. This is calculated as follows:

(number of columns − 1)(number of rows − 1)

In Table 8.3, there are two columns and two rows (excluding the column and row marginals which are of no importance in calculating the degrees of freedom), implying that there is one degree of freedom, i.e. $(2 − 1)(2 − 1)$. In addition to calculating the chi-square value, Minitab will calculate the degrees of freedom associated with each crosstabulation. In order to generate such output with the Minitab for Windows menu system, simply click on the box next to **Chisquare analysis** when setting up a cross-tabulation. When using the prompt system in the mainframe and PC version or the session window in Minitab for Windows, simply add chi-square as a sub-command as on page 154.

The chi-square value is 4.101 with 3 degrees of freedom. In order to determine whether this is statistically significant within Minitab the following procedure can be activated in the mainframe and PC versions of Minitab or in the Minitab for Windows session window. In order to establish whether this chi-square value is significant at the $p < 0.05$ level we type in:

MTB > invcdf .95;
SUBC> chisquare 3.

The first line stipulates the 95 per cent confidence level, which is in effect the obverse of $p < 0.05$. If the chi-square value was found to be statistically significant, we would be 95 per cent confident that the relationship had not occurred by chance, which is the same as saying that there is only a 5 per cent possibility that the relationship could have arisen by chance. The subcommand stipulates the number of degrees of freedom − in this case 3. With the menu system, the following steps should be followed:

→**Calc** →**Probability Distribution** →**Chisquare...** →**Inverse cumulative probability** →box beside **Degrees of freedom** →type **3** →box beside **Input constant:** →type **.95** →**OK**

When we enter this command and subcommand, the output informs us that the chi-square value that we would need is 7.8147. Thus, with three degrees of freedom, we would need a chi-square value of 7.817 to be 95 per cent confident that the relationship has not arisen by chance and hence for p to be less than 0.05. In fact, the chi-square value of 4.101 is less than this, so that there is unlikely to be a relationship between the two variables: although, for example, men (1) are more likely than women (2) to work on higher skill jobs (4), the respective column percentages being 30.8 per cent and 16.1 per cent, the chi-square value is not sufficiently large for us to be confident that the relationship could not have arisen by chance since as many as 25 per cent of samples could fail to yield a relationship. In other words, the null hypothesis of independence between the two variables is confirmed. By contrast, the contingency table presented in Table 8.3 generates a chi-square value of 4.82 which is significant at the 0.05 level, implying that we could have confidence in a relationship between the two variables in the population.

It is also possible to calculate the chi-square value for an existing table. Table 8.6 presents a slightly adapted table taken from Marshall *et al.* (1988) showing the relationship between sex and class according to one particular categorization of social class. We can establish the chi-square value with Minitab, using the prompt system either in the Minitab for Windows session window or with the mainframe or PC versions of Minitab, by 'reading' the

Table 8.6   Social class by gender (percentages in brackets)

Social class	Gender	
	Male	*Female*
Bourgeoisie	23 (3.0)	3 (0.6)
Small employers	50 (6.5)	9 (1.7)
Petit bourgeoisie	54 (7.0)	25 (4.6)
Managers	117 (15.2)	46 (8.5)
Advisory managers	44 (5.7)	15 (2.8)
Supervisors	78 (10.1)	46 (8.5)
Semi-autonomous employees	70 (9.1)	83 (15.3)
Workers	335 (43.5)	317 (58.3)
Total	771	544

Source: Adapted from: G. Marshall *et al.* (1988, Table 4.13)

data into columns as follows:

MTB > read C1-C2
DATA> 22 3
DATA> 50 9
DATA> 54 25
DATA> 117 46
DATA> 44 15
DATA> 78 46
DATA> 70 83
DATA> 335 317
DATA> END
      8 rows read.
MTB > chisquare C1-C2

With the menu system in Minitab for Windows, the data would need to be entered into a new Minitab worksheet. We will then have created two columns – **c1** and **c2**. We then follow the following sequence:

→<u>S</u>tat →<u>T</u>ables... →<u>C</u>hisquare Test →c1 →Select →c2 →Select [**c1** and **c2** should now be in the box under <u>C</u>**olumns containing the table:**] →<u>O</u>**K**

The output from this exercise is presented in Table 8.7. The figure under the frequency in each cell is the expected frequency. These expected frequencies provide a stronger 'feel' for the degree to which the observed frequencies differ from the distribution that would occur if chance alone was operating. This additional information can aid the understanding and

Table 8.7 Chi-square analysis of data in Table 8.6 (Minitab for Windows *Release 10*)

Chi-Square Test

Expected counts are printed below observed counts

	C1	C2	Total
1	22	3	25
	14.65	10.35	
2	50	9	59
	34.57	24.43	
3	54	25	79
	46.29	32.71	
4	117	46	163
	95.52	67.48	
5	44	15	59
	34.57	24.43	
6	78	46	124
	72.66	51.34	
7	70	83	153
	89.66	63.34	
8	335	317	652
	382.07	269.93	
Total	770	544	1314

ChiSq = 3.688 + 5.220 +
         6.883 + 9.742 +
         1.283 + 1.816 +
         4.832 + 6.839 +
         2.570 + 3.638 +
         0.392 + 0.555 +
         4.310 + 6.100 +
         5.799 + 8.208 = 71.873
df = 7, p = 0.000

interpretation of a relationship, but is rarely provided in tables when they are presented to the reader. In Minitab for Windows 10, the actual chi-square level *and* the p level are presented. Earlier versions of Minitab do not provide the p level. The chi-square value is 72.538, there are 7 degrees of freedom and the p level is 0.000, which means that the chi-square value is very significant and is better than $p < 0.001$. If an earlier version of

Minitab is being used the *p* level would need to be worked out. Since 72.538 is a large value, we might want to check whether $p < 0.01$. We can proceed as follows:

MTB > invcdf .99;
SUBC> chisquare 7.

With the menu system, the following steps would be taken:

→**Calc** →**Probability Distribution** →**Chisquare...** →**Inverse cumulative probability** →box beside **Degrees of freedom** →type **7** →box beside **Input constant:** →type **.99** →**OK**

Can we be 99 per cent confident that the relationship has not arisen by chance? The output informs us that the chi-square value for 7 degrees of freedom and 99 per cent confidence is 18.4753. The chi-square value of 72.538 for the table exceeds this by a wide margin, so we can be very confident that the relationship has not arisen by chance and therefore that $p < 0.01$.

When presenting a contingency table and its associated chi-square test for a report or publication, some attention is needed to its appearance and to what is conveyed. Table 8.8 presents a 'cleaned' table of the output provided in Table 8.5. A number of points should be noted. First, only column marginals have been presented. Second, observed and expected frequencies are not included. Some writers prefer to include observed frequencies as well as column percentages, but if as in Table 8.8 the column marginals are included, observed frequencies can be omitted. Percentages have been rounded. Strictly speaking, this should only be done for large samples (e.g. in excess of 200), but rounding is often undertaken on smaller samples since it simplifies the understanding of relationships. The chi-square value is inserted at the bottom with the associated level of

Table 8.8 Rated skill by gender (Job Survey data)

Rated skill	Gender	
	Male percentage	Female percentage
Unskilled	13	29
Semi-skilled	28	23
Fairly skilled	28	32
Skilled	31	16
Total	N = 39	N = 31

$\chi^2 = 4.10$ NS, $p > .05$

significance. In this case, the value is not significant at the 0.05 level, the usual minimum level for rejecting the null hypothesis. This is often indicated by NS (i.e. *non*-significant) and an indication of the significance level employed. Thus, $p > 0.05$ means that the chi-square value is below that necessary for achieving the 0.05 level, meaning that there is more than a 5 per cent chance that there is no relationship in the population. If the chi-square value exceeds that necessary for achieving the 0.05 level, one would write $p < 0.05$.

A number of points about chi-square should be registered in order to facilitate an understanding of its strengths and limitations, as well as some further points about its operation. First, chi-square is not a strong statistic in that it does not convey information about the strength of a relationship. This notion of strength of relationship will be examined in greater detail below when correlation is examined. By strength is meant that a large chi-square value and a correspondingly strong significance level (e.g. $p < 0.001$) cannot be taken to mean a closer relationship between two variables than when chi-square is considerably smaller but moderately significant (e.g. $p < 0.05$). What it is telling us is how confident we can be that there is a relationship between two variables. Second, the combination of a contingency table and chi-square is most likely to occur when either both variables are nominal (categorical) or when one is nominal and the other is ordinal. When both variables are ordinal or interval/ratio other approaches to the elucidation of relationships, such as correlation which allows strength of relationships to be examined and which therefore conveys more information, are likely to be preferred. When one variable is nominal and the other interval, such as the relationship between voting preference and age, the latter variable will need to be 'collapsed' into ordinal groupings (i.e. 20–29, 30–39, 40–49, etc.) in order to allow a contingency table and its associated chi-square value to be provided.

Third, chi-square should be adapted for use in relation to a 2×2 table, such as Table 8.3. A different formula is employed, using something called 'Yates' Correction for Continuity'. It is not necessary to go into the technical reasons for this correction, save to say that some writers take the view that the conventional formula results in an overestimate of the chi-square value when applied to a 2×2 table. Minitab does not provide Yates' correction for 2×2 tables, but accounts of the formula can be found in Cohen and Holliday (1982) and Cramer (1994b). If Yates' correction has been used in the computation of the chi-square statistic, this should be clearly stated when the data are presented for publication.

Fourth, chi-square can be unreliable if expected cell frequencies are less than five, although like Yates' correction for 2×2 tables, this is a source of some controversy. Minitab output alerts the user to the number of cells with expected frequencies (counts) fewer than five.

Some writers suggest that the phi coefficient can be preferable to chi-square as a test of association between two dichotomous variables. This statistic, which is similar to the correlation coefficient (see below) in that it varies between 0 and 1 to provide an indication of the strength of a relationship, is not available in Minitab but can easily be generated by the formula

$$\text{phi} = \sqrt{\frac{\text{chi-square}}{\text{number of cases}(N)}}$$

Thus, if chi-square equals 28.8 and there are 80 cases, chi-square is equal to $\sqrt{(28.8/80)}$, i.e. $\sqrt{0.36}$. Thus, the phi coefficient will be 0.6. The significance of phi can then be examined by checking the chi-square values for one degree of freedom (since a 2 by 2 table will always yield one degree of freedom) in a table of chi-square values. For $p < 0.05$ the chi-square value will need to be at or equal to 3.8414; at $p < 0.01$ the relevant value is 6.6349; and for $p < 0.001$ it is 10.828. Thus, in our example, the phi value of 0.6 with 80 cases would imply that there is very likely to be a relationship in the population.

A statistic related to phi is Cramer's V. This can be used to estimate the degree of association between pairs of nominal variables and can also be used in relation to calculate the degree of association between a nominal variable and an ordinal variable with few categories. It varies between 0 and $+1$. It is not directly available in Minitab but can easily be calculated once chi-square has been computed. The formula is:

$$\text{Cramer's } V = \sqrt{\frac{\text{chi-square } (\chi^2)}{\text{no. of cases}(N) \times (\text{smaller no. of rows/columns} - 1)}}$$

Thus, chi-square is divided by the number of cases multiplied by the number of rows minus 1 or the number of columns minus 1, whichever is the smaller. In the case of Table 8.6, the chi-square value was found to be 71.873. The number of cases is 1315 and there are fewer columns than rows, so the calculation becomes:

$$\text{Cramer's } V = \sqrt{\frac{71.873}{1315 \times (2 - 1)}}$$
$$= 0.23$$

Thus, there is a rather weak association between the two variables in Table 8.6. In the case of 2×2 tables, Cramer's V and phi will always be the same.

CORRELATION

The idea of correlation is one of the most important and basic in the elaboration of bivariate relationships. Unlike chi-square, measures of correlation indicate both the strength and the direction of the relationship between a pair of variables. Two types of measure can be distinguished: measures of linear correlation using interval variables and measures of rank correlation using ordinal variables. While these two types of measure of correlation share some common properties, they also differ in some important respects which will be examined after the elucidation of measures of linear correlation.

Linear correlation: relationships between interval variables

Correlation entails the provision of a yard-stick whereby the intensity or strength of a relationship can be gauged. To provide such estimates, correlation coefficients are calculated. These provide succinct assessments of the closeness of a relationship among pairs of variables. Their widespread use in the social sciences has meant that the results of tests of correlation have become easy to recognise and interpret. When variables are interval, by far the most common measure of correlation is Pearson's Product Moment Correlation Coefficient, often referred to as Pearson's r. This measure of correlation presumes that interval variables are being used, so that even ordinal variables are not supposed to be employed, although this is a matter of some debate (e.g. O'Brien, 1979).

In order to illustrate some of the fundamental features of correlation, scatter diagrams (often called 'scattergrams') will be employed. A scatter diagram plots each individual case on a graph, thereby representing for each case the points at which the two variables intersect. Thus, if we are examining the relationship between income and political liberalism in the imaginary data presented in Table 8.9, each point on the scatter diagram represents each respondent's position in relation to each of these two variables. Let us say that political liberalism is measured by a scale of five statements to which individuals have to indicate their degree of agreement on a five-point array ('Strongly Agree' to 'Strongly Disagree'). The maximum score is 25, the minimum 5. Table 8.9 presents data on eighteen individuals for each of the two variables. The term 'cases' is employed in the table, rather than subjects, as a reminder that the objects to which data may refer can be entities such as firms, schools, cities, and the like. In Figure 8.1, the data on income and political liberalism from Table 8.9 are plotted to form a scatter diagram. Thus, case number 1, which has an income of £9,000 and a liberalism score of 18, is positioned at the intersection of these two values on the graph. This case has been encircled to allow it to stand out.

Initially, the nature of the relationship between two variables can be focused upon. It should be apparent that the pattern of the points moves downwards from left to right. This pattern implies a negative relationship, meaning that as one variable increases the other decreases: higher incomes are associated with lower levels of political liberalism; lower incomes with

Table 8.9   Data on age, income and political liberalism

Case no.	Income	Age	Political-liberalism score
1	9,000	23	18
2	11,000	33	11
3	7,000	21	23
4	12,500	39	13
5	10,000	27	17
6	11,500	43	19
7	8,500	21	22
8	8,500	27	20
9	15,000	43	9
10	13,000	38	14
11	7,500	30	21
12	14,500	54	11
13	16,000	63	8
14	15,500	58	10
15	8,000	25	22
16	10,500	51	12
17	10,000	36	15
18	12,000	34	16

Character Plot

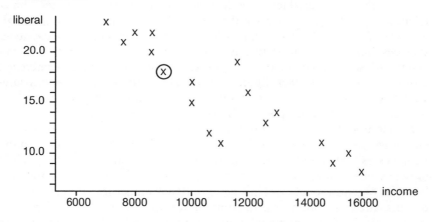

Figure 8.1   Scatter diagram: political liberalism by income (Minitab **plot** with Standard Graphics)

higher levels of liberalism. In Figure 8.2 a different kind of relationship between two variables is exhibited. Here, there is a positive relationship, with higher values on one variable (income) being associated with higher values on the other (age). These data derive from Table 8.9. In Figure 8.2,

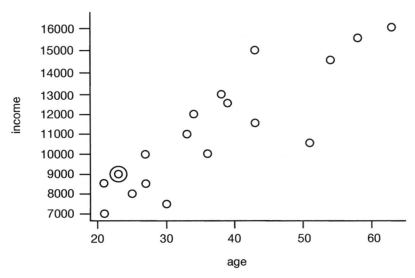

Figure 8.2 Scatter diagram: income by age (Minitab **plot** with Professional Graphics)

case number 1 is again circled. Notice how in neither case is the relationship between the two variables a perfect one. If there was a perfect linear relationship, all of the points in the scatter diagram would be on a straight line (see Figure 8.3), a situation which almost never occurs in the social sciences. Instead, we tend to have, as in Figures 8.1 and 8.2, a certain amount of scatter, though a pattern is often visible, such as the negative and positive relationships each figure respectively exhibits. If there is a large amount of scatter, so that no patterning is visible, we can say that there is no or virtually no relationship between two variables (see Figure 8.4).

In addition to positive and negative relationships we sometimes find curvilinear relationships, in which the shape of the relationship between two variables is not straight, but curves at one or more points. Figure 8.5 provides three different types of curvilinear relationship. The relationship between organizational size and organizational properties, like the amount of specialization, often takes a form similar to diagram (c) in Figure 8.5 (Child, 1973). When patterns similar to those exhibited in Figure 8.5 are found, the relationship is non-linear, that is it is not straight, and it is not appropriate to employ a measure of linear correlation like Pearson's r. When scatter diagrams are similar to the patterns depicted in Figure 8.5 (b) and (c), researchers often transform the independent variable into a logarithmic scale, which will usually engender a linear relationship and hence will allow the employment of Pearson's r. Here we see an important reason for investigating scatter diagrams before computing r – if there is a

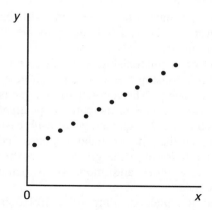

Figure 8.3 A perfect relationship

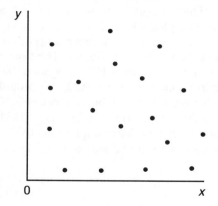

Figure 8.4 No relationship (or virtually no relationship)

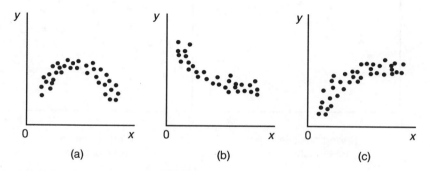

Figure 8.5 Three curvilinear relationships

non-linear relationship the computed estimate of correlation will be meaningless, but unless a scatter diagram is checked it is not possible to determine whether the relationship is not linear.

Scatter diagrams allow three aspects of a relationship to be discerned: whether it is linear; the direction of the relationship (i.e. whether positive or negative); and the strength of the relationship. The amount of scatter is indicative of the strength of the relationship. Compare the pairs of positive and negative relationships in Figures 8.6 and 8.7 respectively. In each case the right-hand diagram exhibits more scatter than the left-hand diagram. The left-hand diagram exhibits the stronger relationship: the greater the scatter (with the points on the graph departing more and more from being positioned on a straight line as in Figure 8.4).

Scatter diagrams are useful aids to the understanding of correlation. Pearson's r allows the strength and direction of linear relationships between variables to be gauged. Pearson's r varies between -1 and $+1$. A relationship of -1 or $+1$ would indicate a perfect relationship, negative or positive respectively, between two variables. Thus, Figure 8.4 would denote a perfect positive relationship of $+1$. The complete absence of a relationship would engender a computed r of zero. The closer r is to 1 (whether positive or negative), the stronger the relationship between two variables. The nearer r is to zero (and hence the further it is from $+$ or -1), the weaker the relationship. These ideas are expressed in Figure 8.8. If r is 0.82, this would indicate a strong positive relationship between two variables, whereas 0.24 would denote a weak positive relationship. Similarly, -0.79 and -0.31 would be indicative of strong and weak negative relationships respectively. In Figures 8.6 and 8.7, the left-hand diagrams would be indicative of larger computed rs than those on the right.

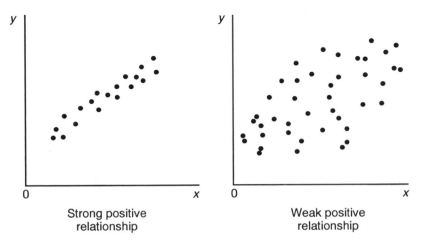

Strong positive
relationship

Weak positive
relationship

Figure 8.6 Two positive relationships

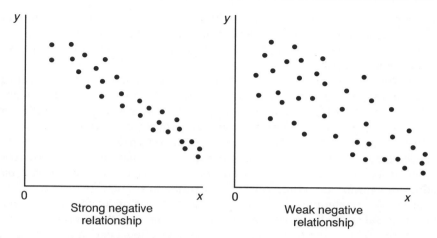

Figure 8.7 Two negative relationships

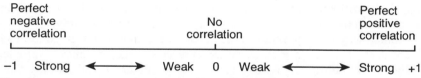

Figure 8.8 The strength and direction of correlation coefficients

What is a large correlation? Cohen and Holliday (1982) suggest the following: 0.19 and below is very low; 0.20 to 0.39 is low; 0.40 to 0.69 is modest; 0.70 to 0.89 is high; and 0.90 to 1 is very high. However, these are rules-of-thumb and should not be regarded as definitive indications, since there are hardly any guidelines for interpretation over which there is substantial consensus.

Further, caution is required when comparing computed coefficients. We can certainly say that an r of -0.60 is larger than one of -0.30, but we cannot say that the relationship is twice as strong. In order to see why not, a useful aid to the interpretation of r will be introduced – the coefficient of determination (r^2). This is simply the square of r multiplied by 100. It provides us with an indication of how far variation in one variable is accounted for by the other. Thus, if $r = -0.6$, then $r^2 = 36$ per cent. This means that 36 per cent of the variance in one variable is due to the other. When $r = -0.3$, then r^2 will be 9 per cent. Thus, although an r of -0.6 is twice as large as one of -0.3, it cannot indicate that the former is twice as strong as the latter, because *four* times more variance is being accounted for by an r of -0.6 than one of -0.3. Thinking about the coefficient of determination can have a salutary effect on one's interpretation of r. For example, when correlating two variables, x and y, an r of 0.7 sounds quite high, but it would mean that less than half of the variance in y can be attributed to x (i.e. 49 per cent). In other words, 51 per cent of the variance in y is due to variables other than x.

A word of caution is relevant at this point. In saying that 49 per cent of the variation in y is attributable to x, we must recognize that this also means that 49 per cent of the variation in x is due to y. Correlation is not the same as cause. We cannot determine from an estimate of correlation that one variable causes the other, since correlation provides estimates of covariance, i.e. that two variables are related. We may find a large correlation of 0.8 between job satisfaction and organizational commitment, but does this mean that 64 per cent of the variation in job satisfaction can be attributed to commitment? This would suggest that organizational commitment is substantially caused by job satisfaction. But the reverse can also hold true: 64 per cent of the variation in organizational commitment may be due to job satisfaction. It is not possible from a simple correlation between these two variables to arbitrate between the two possibilities. Indeed, as Chapter 10 will reveal, there may be reasons other than not knowing which causes which for needing to be cautious about presuming causality.

Another way of expressing these ideas is through Venn diagrams (see Figure 8.9). If we treat each circle as representing the amount of variance exhibited by each of two variables, x and y, Figure 8.9 illustrates three conditions: in the top diagram we have independence in which the two variables do not overlap, i.e. a correlation of zero as represented by Figure 8.4 or in terms of a contingency table by Table 8.4(b); in the middle diagram there is a perfect relationship in which the variance of x and y coincides perfectly, i.e. a correlation of 1 as represented by Figure 8.3 or the contingency table in Table 8.4(a); and the bottom diagram which points to a less than perfect, though strong, relationship between x and y, i.e. as represented by the left-hand diagrams in Figures 8.6 and 8.7. Here only part of the two circles intersect, i.e. the shaded area, which represents just over 67 per cent of the variance shared by the two variables; the unshaded area of each circle denotes a sphere of variance for each variable that is unrelated to the other variable.

It is possible to provide an indication of the statistical significance of r. This is described in the next section. The way in which its significance is calculated is strongly affected by the number of cases for which there are pairs of data. For example, if you have approximately 500 cases, r only needs to be 0.088 or 0.115 to be significant at the 0.05 and 0.01 levels respectively. If you have just eighteen cases (as in Table 8.6), the rs will need to be at least 0.468 or 0.590 respectively. Some investigators only provide information about the significance of relationships. However, this is a grave error since what is and is not significant is profoundly affected by the number of cases. What statistical significance does tell us is the likelihood

(a) Independence: the two variables are totally unrelated

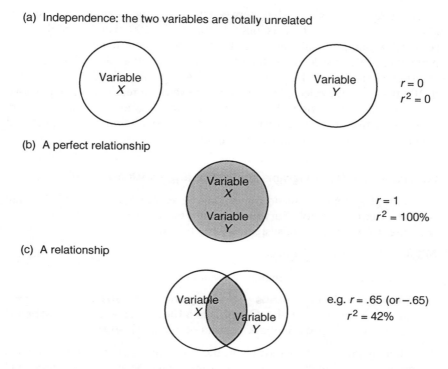

(b) A perfect relationship

(c) A relationship

Figure 8.9 Types of relationship

that a relationship of at least this size could have arisen by chance. It is necessary to interpret both r and the significance level when computing correlation coefficients. For example, a correlation of 0.17 in connection with a random sample of 1,000 individuals would be significant at the 0.001 level, but would indicate that this weak relationship is unlikely to have arisen by chance and that we can be confident that a relationship of at least this size holds in the population. Consider an alternative scenario of a correlation of 0.43 based on a sample of 42. The significance level would be 0.01, but it would be absurd to say that the former correlation was more important than the latter simply because the correlation of 0.17 is more significant. The second coefficient is larger, though we have to be somewhat more circumspect in this second case than in the first in inferring that the relationship could not have arisen by chance. Thus, the size of r and the significance level must by considered in tandem. The test of statistical significance tells us whether a correlation could have arisen by chance (e.g. by sampling error) or whether it is likely to exist in the population from which the sample was selected. It tells us how likely it is that we might conclude from sample data that there is a relationship between two variables when there is no relationship between them in the population. Thus, if $r = 0.7$ and $p < 0.01$, there is only 1 chance in 100 that we could have selected a sample that shows a relationship when none exists in the population. We would almost certainly conclude that the relationship is statistically significant. However, if $r = 0.7$ and $p < 0.1$, there are 10 chances in 100 that we have selected a sample which shows a relationship when none exists in the population. We would probably decide that the risk of concluding that there is a relationship in the population is too great and conclude that the relationship is non-significant.

Generating Scatter Diagrams and computing r with Minitab

The prompt system command for generating scatter diagrams with Minitab is **plot**. Taking the Job Survey data, if you wanted to plot **'satis'** and **'routine'** using the prompt system, simply type in:

MTB > plot 'satis' * 'routine'

With the menu system, the sequence would be:

→**Graph** →**P**lot... →satis →**Select** [notice that **satis** will now appear in the **Y** column in the **Graph variables** box] →routine →**Select** [**routine** will appear in the **X** column of the box] →**O**K

A scatter diagram with **'routine'** on the horizontal axis will be generated. Examples of Minitab output from **plot** using Standard Graphics and Professional Graphics are provided in Figures 8.1 and 8.2 respectively.

In order to generate correlation coefficients for the variables **'routine'**, **'autonom'** and **'satis'**, using the prompt system in the mainframe and PC versions of Minitab (or if using the session window in Minitab for Windows), use the following simple command:

MTB > correlation 'routine' 'autonom' 'satis'

The following sequence should be followed for the menu system:

→**S**tat →**B**asic Statistics →**C**orrelation... →routine →**Select** [**routine** will now appear in the **V**ariables: box] →autonom →**Select** [**autonom** will now appear in the **V**ariables: box] →satis →**Select** [**satis** will now appear in the **V**ariables: box] →**O**K

A matrix of correlation coefficients will be generated, as in Table 8.10. This table shows the size of the correlation for each variable entered into the analysis. In order to find out whether the correlations are statistically significant, the table in Appendix I needs to be consulted. This gives the critical values at the $p < 0.10$, $p < 0.05$, and $p < 0.02$ levels for a two-tailed test. These are equivalent to $p < 0.05$, $p < 0.025$, and $p < 0.01$ respectively for a one-tailed test. We must look up the values associated with the

Table 8.10   Pearson product-moment correlation coefficients (Minitab for Windows *Release 10* output from Job Survey data)

Correlations (Pearson)

	routine	autonom
autonom	−0.487	
satis	−0.580	0.733

appropriate row using the simple formula – Number of cases (*N*) −2. This represents the number of degrees of freedom in the analysis. We have 70 cases suggesting that the appropriate row is 68. The nearest row below this figure is in fact 60 at which point the correlation coefficients need to exceed 0.2108, 0.2500, and 0.2948 for the $p < 0.10$, $p < 0.05$, or $p < 0.02$ levels respectively (0.05, 0.025, or 0.01 if the test is one-tailed). All three correlations exceed these levels substantially.

Rank correlation: relationships between ordinal variables

In order to employ Pearson's *r*, variables must be interval and the relationship must be linear. When variables are at the ordinal level, an alternative measure of correlation can be used called rank correlation. The most prominent method for examining the relationship between pairs of ordinal variables is Spearman's rho (ρ). The interpretation of the results of this method is identical to Pearson's *r*, in that the computed coefficient will vary between −1 and +1. Thus, it provides information on the strength *and* direction of relationships. Moreover, unlike Pearson's *r*, rho is a non-parametric method which means that it can be used in a wide variety of contexts since it makes fewer assumptions about variables.

Let us say that we want to correlate **'skill'**, **'prody'** and **'qual'**, each of which is an ordinal measure. Even though these are ordinal variables, they have to be rank ordered. The reason for this apparent paradox is that many respondents will exhibit *tied ranks*. This means that, for example, many respondents will have a **'skill'** score of 4 (in fact, 17 respondents have this score). The **rank** procedure in Minitab will adjust for such tied ranks. With the prompt system, the following would produce ranked variables:

MTB > rank 'skill' c40
MTB > rank 'prody' c41
MTB > rank 'qual' c42
MTB > name c40 'rskill' c41 'rprody' c42 'rqual'

The first three commands create new variables – **c40**, **c41** and **c42** – which are **'skill'**, **'prody'** and **'qual'** respectively in ranked form. The fourth command names these new variables **'rskill'**, **'rprody'**, and **'rqual'**. With the menu system, the following steps would need to be followed:

→**Manip** →**Rank...** →**skill** →**Select** [this brings **skill** into the **Rank data in:** box] → [the cursor will be flashing in the **Store ranks in:** box, into which you should type **rskill**] →**OK**
→**Manip** →**Rank...** →**prody** →**Select** [this brings **prody** into the **Rank data in:** box] → [the cursor will be flashing in the **Store ranks in:** box, into which you should type **rprody**] →**OK**
→**Manip** →**Rank...** →**qual** →**Select** [this brings **qual** into the **Rank data in:** box] → [the cursor will be flashing in the **Store ranks in:** box, into which you should type **rqual**] →**OK**

The ranked variables then need to be correlated. With the prompt system, the following simple command will yield the appropriate analysis:

MTB > correlation 'rskill' 'rprody' 'rqual'

If you are using the menu system, the following sequence should be employed:

→**Stat** →**Basic Statistics** →**Correlation...** →**rskill** →**Select** →**rprody** →**Select** →**rqual** →**Select** [**rskill**, **rprody** and **rqual** should now be in the **Variables:** box] →**OK**

The resulting output is provided in Table 8.11. All of the correlations reported in Table 8.11 are low, the largest being the correlation between **rprody** and **rskill** (0.24 rounded up) for rho. In order to establish the statistical significance of the resulting correlations, the table in Appendix II should be consulted. We must search out the row which corresponds best to the number of cases (N), not $N - 2$. The levels specified are $p < 0.10$, $p < 0.05$, $p < 0.02$ for two-tailed tests (and hence 0.05, 0.25, and 0.01 for one-tailed tests). Taking $N = 30$ as the closest point to our sample of 70, we can see that none of the correlation coefficients achieves statistical significance at $p < 0.05$.

If you need to correlate an ordinal variable with interval/ratio variable, both variables must be rank-ordered. Spearman's rho would then be

Table 8.11 Spearman rho correlation coefficients (Minitab for Windows *Release 10* output from Job Survey data)

Correlations (Pearson)

	rskill	rprody
rprody	0.239	
rqual	0.013	0.171

computed to establish the level of correlation. If we want to know whether more skilled workers earn more, we will need to correlate **'skill'** and **'income'**. The former is ordinal and the latter is interval/ratio. We have already ranked **'skill'** (**'rskill'**). In order to rank **'income'**, the product of which we will call **'rankinc'**, we would do the following in the prompt system:

MTB > rank 'income' c43
MTB > name c43 'rankinc'

The following sequence would be used for the menu system:

→**Manip** →**Rank…** →**income** →**Select** [this brings **income** into the **Rank data in:** box] → [the cursor will be flashing in the **Store ranks in:** box, into which you should type **'rankinc'**] →**OK**

Once **'income'** has been rank-ordered, the rank correlation (ρ) between **'rskill'** and **'rankinc'** can be generated in the prompt system by

MTB > correlation 'rskill' 'rankinc'

In the menu system the following sequence should be followed:

→**Stat** →**Basic Statistics** →**Correlation…** →**rskill** →**Select** →**rankinc** →**Select** →**OK**

Although rank correlation methods are more flexible than Pearson's r, the latter tends to be preferred because interval/ratio variables comprise more information than ordinal ones. One of the reasons for the widespread use in the social sciences of questionnaire items which are built up into scales or indices (and which are then treated as interval variables) is probably that stronger approaches to the investigation of relationships like Pearson's r (and regression – see below) can be employed.

REGRESSION

Regression has become one of the most widely used techniques in the analysis of data in the social sciences. It is closely connected to Pearson's r, as will become apparent at a number of points. Indeed, it shares many of the same assumptions as r, such as that relationships between variables are linear and that variables are interval. In this section, the use of regression to explore relationships between pairs of variables will be examined. It should become apparent that regression is a powerful tool for summarizing the nature of the relationship between variables and for making predictions of likely values of the dependent variable.

At this point, it is worth returning to the scatter diagrams encountered in Figures 8.1 and 8.2. Each departs a good deal from Figure 8.3 in which all of the points are on a straight line, since the points in Figures 8.1 and 8.2 are more scattered. The idea of regression is to summarize the relationship between two variables by producing a line which fits the data closely. This line is called the line of best fit. Only one line will minimize the deviations of all of the dots in a scatter diagram from the line. Some points will appear above the line, some below and a small proportion may actually be on the line. Because only one line can meet the criterion of line of best fit, it is unlikely that it can accurately be drawn by visual inspection. This is where regression comes in. Regression procedures allow the precise line of best fit to be computed. Once we know the line of best fit, we can make predictions about likely values of the dependent variable, for particular values of the independent variable.

In order to understand how the line of best fit operates, it is necessary to get to grips with the simple equation that governs its operation and how we make predictions from it. The equation is

$$y = a + bx + e$$

In this equation, y and x are the dependent and independent variables respectively. The two elements – a and b – refer to aspects of the line itself. First, a, is known as the intercept which is the point at which the line cuts the vertical axis. Second, b is the slope of the line of the best fit and is usually referred to as the regression coefficient. By the 'slope' is meant the rate at which changes in values of the independent variable (x) affect values of the dependent variable (y). In order to predict y for a given value of x, it is necessary to

1 multiply the value of x by the regression coefficient, b, and
2 add this calculation to the intercept, a.

Finally, e is referred to as an error term which points to the fact that a proportion of the variance in the dependent variable, y, is unexplained by the regression equation. In order to simplify the following explanation of regression, for the purposes of making predictions the error term is ignored and so will not be referred to below.

Consider the following example. A researcher may want to know whether managers who put in extra hours after the normal working day tend to get on better in the organization than others. The researcher finds out the average amount of time a group of twenty new managers in a firm spend working on problems after normal working hours. Two years later the managers are re-examined to find out their annual salaries. Individual's salaries are employed as an indicator of progress, since incomes often reflect how well a person is getting on in a firm. Moreover, for these managers, extra hours of work are not rewarded by overtime payments, so salaries are a real indication of progress. Let us say that the regression equation which is derived from the analysis is

$$y = 7500 + 500x$$

The line of best fit is drawn in Figure 8.10.

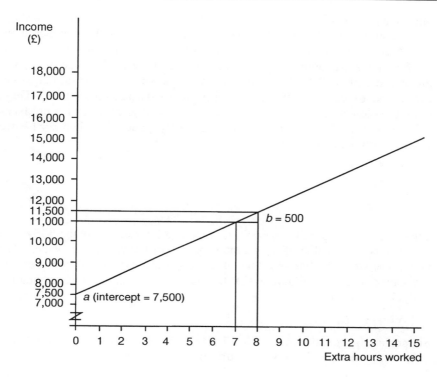

Figure 8.10   A line of best fit

The intercept, *a*, is 7500, i.e. £7500; the regression coefficient, *b*, is 500. The latter means that each extra hour worked produces an extra £500 to a manager's annual salary. We can calculate the likely annual salary of someone who puts in an extra 7 hours per week as follows:

$$y = 7500 + (500)(7)$$

which becomes

$$y = 7500 + 3500$$

which becomes

$$y = 11000 \text{ (i.e. £11,000)}.$$

For someone who works an extra 8 hours per week, the likely salary will be £11,500, i.e. $7500 + (500)(8)$. If a person does not put in any extra work, the salary is likely to be £7,500, i.e. $7500 + (500)(0)$. Thus, through regression, we are able to show how y changes for each additional increment of x (because the regression coefficient expresses how much more of y you get for each extra increment of x) and to predict the likely value of y for a given value of x. When a relationship is negative, the regression equation for the line of best fit will take the form $y = a - bx$ (see Figure 8.11). Thus, if a regression equation was $y = 50 - 2x$, each extra increment of x produces a decrease in y. If we wanted to know the likely value of y when $x = 12$, we would substitute as follows

$$y = 50 - 2x$$
$$y = 50 - (2)(12)$$
$$y = 50 - 24$$
$$y = 26$$

When a line of best fit has a positive slope and intersects with the horizontal axis at a positive value of x, the intercept, a, will have a minus value. This is because when the line is extended to the vertical axis it will intercept it at a negative point (see Figure 8.12). In this situation, the regression equation will take the form

$$y = -a + bx$$

Supposing the equation were $y = -7 + 23x$, if we wanted to know the likely value of y when $x = 3$, we would substitute as follows

$$y = -7 + 23x$$
$$y = -7 + (23)(3)$$
$$y = -7 + 69$$
$$y = 69 - 7$$
$$y = 62$$

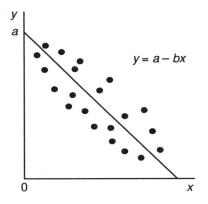

Figure 8.11   Regression: a negative relationship

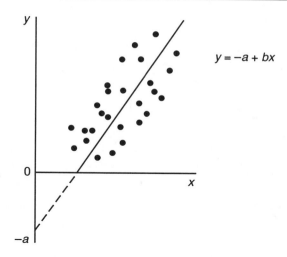

Figure 8.12   Regression: a negative intercept

As suggested at the start of this section, correlation and regression are closely connected. They make identical assumptions that variables are interval and that relationships are linear. Further, r and r^2 are often employed as indications of how well the regression line fits the data. For example, if $r = 1$, the line of best fit would simply be drawn straight through all of the points (see Figure 8.13). Where points are more scattered, the line of best fit will provide a poorer fit with the data. Accordingly, the more scatter there is in a scatter diagram, the less accurate the prediction of likely y values will be. Thus, the closer r is to 1, the less scatter there is and therefore, the better the fit between the line of best fit and the data. If the two scatter diagrams in Figures 8.6 and 8.7 are examined, the line of best fit for the left-hand diagram in each case will constitute a superior fit between data and line and will permit more accurate predictions. This can be further illustrated by reference to Figure 8.14. If we take a particular value of x, i.e. x_n, then we can estimate the likely value of y ($\hat{y}_n$) from the regression line. However, the corresponding y value for a particular case may be y_n, which is different from $\hat{y}_n$. In other words, the latter provides an estimate of y, which is likely not to be totally accurate. Clearly, the further the points are from the line, the less accurate estimates are likely to be. Therefore, where r is low, scatter will be greater and the regression equation will provide a less accurate representation of the relationship between the two variables.

On the other hand, although correlation and regression are closely connected, it should be remembered that they serve different purposes. Correlation is concerned with the degrees of relationship between variables and regression with making predictions. But they can also be usefully used in conjunction, since, unlike correlation, regression can express the

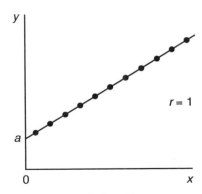

Figure 8.13 Regression: a perfect relationship

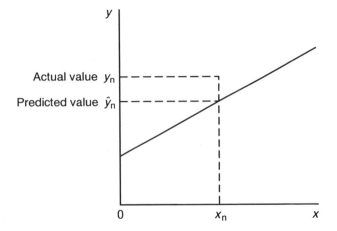

Figure 8.14 The accuracy of the line of best fit

character of relationships. Compare the two scatter diagrams in Figure 8.15. The pattern of dots is identical and each would reveal an identical level of correlation (say 0.75), but the slope of the dots in (a) is much steeper than for (b). This difference would be revealed in a larger regression coefficient for (a) and a larger intercept for (b).

The r^2 value is often used as an indication of how well the model implied by the regression equation fits the data. If we conceive of y, the dependent variable, as exhibiting variance which the independent variable goes some of the way in explaining, then we can say that r^2 reflects the proportion of the variation in y explained by x. Thus, if r^2 equals 0.74, the model is providing an explanation of 74 per cent of the variance in y.

It should be noted that although we have been talking about y as the dependent and x as the independent variable, in many instances it makes just

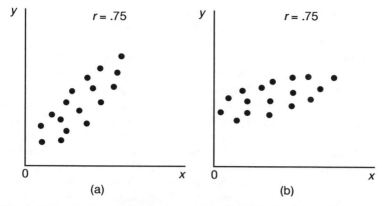

Figure 8.15 Scatter diagrams for two identical levels of correlation

as much sense to treat x as dependent and y as independent. When this is done, the regression equation will be totally different. Two other words of caution should be registered. First, regression assumes that the dispersion of points in a scatter diagram is homoscedastic, or where the pattern of scatter of the points about the line shows no clear pattern. When the opposite is the case, and the pattern exhibits heteroscedasticity, where the amount of scatter around the line of best fit varies markedly at different points, the use of regression is questionable. An example of heteroscedasticity is exhibited in Figure 8.16, which suggests that the amount of unexplained variation exhibited by the model is greater at the upper reaches of x and y. It should be noted that homoscedasticity is also a precondition of the use of Pearson's r.

Second, it should be noted that the size of a correlation coefficient and the nature of a regression equation will be affected by the amount of variance in either of the variables concerned. For example, if one variable has a

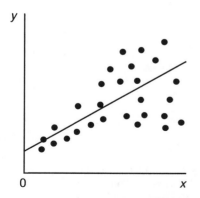

Figure 8.16 Heteroscedasticity

restricted range and the other a wider range, the size of the correlation coefficient may be reduced, but not if both were of equally wide variance.

Third, *outliers*, that is extreme values of x or y, can exert an excessive influence on the results of both correlation and regression. Consider the data in Table 8.12. We have data on twenty firms regarding their size (as measured by the number of employees) and the number of specialist functions in the organization (that is, the number of specialist areas, such as accounting, personnel, marketing, or public relations, in which at least one person spends 100 per cent of his or her time). The article by Child (1973) presents a similar variable with a maximum score of 16, which formed the idea for this example. In Table 8.12, we have an outlier − case number 20 − which is much larger than all of the other firms in the sample. It is also somewhat higher in terms of the number of specialist functions than the other firms. In spite of the fact that this is only one case its impact on estimates of both correlation and regression is quite pronounced. The Pearson's r is 0.67 and the regression equation is $y = 5.55 + 0.00472$size. If the outlier is excluded, the magnitude of r rises to 0.78 and the regression

Table 8.12 The impact of outliers: the relationship between size of firm and number of specialist functions (imaginary data)

Case no.	Size of firm (number of employees)	Number of specialist functions
1	110	3
2	150	2
3	190	5
4	230	8
5	270	5
6	280	6
7	320	7
8	350	5
9	370	8
10	390	6
11	420	9
12	430	7
13	460	3
14	470	9
15	500	12
16	540	9
17	550	13
18	600	14
19	640	11
20	2,700	16

Notes: When case 20 is included Pearson's $r = 0.67$ and the regression equation is specialization $= 5.55 + 0.00472$size. When case 20 is excluded Pearson's $r = 0.78$ and the regression equation is specialization $= 0.78 + 0.0175$size.

equation is $y = 0.78 + 0.0175\text{size}$. Such a difference can have a dramatic effect on predictions. If we wanted to know the likely value of y (number of specialist functions) for an organization of 340 employees with all twenty cases, the prediction would be 7.15; with the outlying case omitted the prediction is 6.73. Thus, this one outlying case can have an important impact upon the predictions that are generated. When such a situation arises, serious consideration has to be given to the exclusion of such an outlying case.

The purpose of this section has been to introduce the general idea of regression. In Chapter 10, it will receive a much fuller treatment, when the use of more than one independent variable will be examined, an area in which the power of regression is especially evident.

Generating basic regression analysis with Minitab

Minitab can generate a host of information relating to regression. However, much of this information is too detailed for present purposes; only some of it will be examined in Chapter 10. It is proposed to postpone a detailed treatment of generating regression information until this later chapter. The following discussion should allow the Minitab user to generate basic regression information relating to the relationship between two variables. Imagine that we want to undertake a simple regression analysis of **'routine'** and **'satis'**, with the latter as the implied dependent variable. If you are using the prompt system, the following will yield the analysis presented in Table 8.13:

MTB > regress 'satis' 1 'routine'

After the **regress** statement, the dependent variable (**'satis'**) is entered. The **1** refers to the number of independent variables, which in the case of simple bivariate regression will always be one. This is then followed by the independent variable **'routine'**.

With the menu system, the following steps will provide the information in Table 8.13.

→**S̲tat** →**R̲egression** →**R̲egression...** →satis →**Select** [satis will now appear in the **R̲esponse** box] →**routine** →**Select** [**routine** will now appear in the **Pred̲ictors** box] →**O̲K**

Thus, the dependent variable has to go into the **R̲esponse** box; the independent variable (or variables in multiple regression – see Chapter 10) is entered into the **Pred̲ictors** box.

The resulting regression equation is:

satis = 17.1 − 0.464**routine**

This implies that for every increment of **routine**, **satis** declines by 0.464. We are also given quite a large amount of extra information. We are given

Table 8.13 Regression: **satis** by **routine** (Minitab for Windows *Release 10* output from Job Survey data)

Regression Analysis

The regression equation is
satis = 17.1 − 0.464 routine

68 cases used 2 cases contain missing values

Predictor	Coef	Stdev	t-ratio	p
Constant	17.094	1.130	15.12	0.000
routine	−0.46437	0.08027	−5.79	0.000

s = 2.711   R − sq = 33.6%   R − sq(adj) = 32.6%

Analysis of Variance

SOURCE	DF	SS	MS	F	p
Regression	1	246.04	246.04	33.47	0.000
Error	66	485.18	7.35		
Total	67	731.22			

Unusual Observations

Obs.	routine	satis	Fit	Stdev.Fit	Residual	St.Resid
4	10.0	7.000	12.450	0.431	−5.450	−2.04R
13	19.0	14.000	8.271	0.552	5.729	2.16R
32	11.0	6.000	11.986	0.384	−5.986	−2.23R
50	8.0	19.000	13.379	0.549	5.621	2.12R

R denotes an obs. with a large st. resid.

the coefficient of determination, r^2, which is 33.6 per cent (see **R-sq**). This expresses the amount of variance in **'satis'** explained by the equation. Other basic useful information includes an estimation of the statistical significance of the coefficients relating to the constant in the equation and to **'routine'** using the t value and an analysis of variance which provides an F test for the equation. The p values suggest that the coefficients and the equation itself achieve a high level of statistical significance. The analysis also draws attention to 'unusual observations' based primarily on large 'standardized residuals' (**St.Resid**) being revealed (note the **R** by those in the table). A residual is the difference between the predicted value of y implied by the line of best fit and the actual value of y for a given level of x. Thus, we can see that the fourth person in the sample (Obs. 4) has a score of 10 for **'routine'** and a **'satis'** score of 7. But according to the line of best fit he or she was predicted to achieve a level of **'satis'** (**Fit**) of 12.45. Therefore, the Residual is $7 - 12.45 = -5.450$. The standardized residual merely adjusts the residual, so that in the case of multiple regression all the residuals are directly comparable. Highlighting these unusual observations is meant to alert the researcher to areas of an analysis that might warrant further investigation.

The amount of output generated by Minitab's **regress** command can be controlled, but within Minitab for Windows this can only be done from the session window. This is done by using the **brief** command *before* the **regress** command:

MTB > brief [followed by one of the following digits: **0**, **1**, **2**, or **3**]
MTB > regress 'satis' 1 'routine'

The digit after **brief** controls the output in the following way:

0 No output printed. The analysis is done and stored. It is unlikely that most users will need this option, although there is a description of a context in which it might be used in Chapter 10.
1 The regression equation, table of coefficients, r^2, and part of the analysis of variance table are provided.
2 The **brief 1** output is provided, plus the rest of the analysis of variance table and 'unusual observations' and their details. **brief 2** is the default, so that if **brief** is not specified, the output associated with **brief 2** is generated.
3 In addition to the **brief 2** output, a full table of fits and residuals is printed.

Users of Minitab and of techniques of quantitative data analysis who are not very familiar with regression techniques will probably find that **brief 1** will meet most of their needs.

A scatter diagram along with a fitted regression line and basic regression information can be generated in Minitab for Windows *Release 10*, as in Figure 8.17. To generate this output, the following command should be used with the prompt system:

%fitline 'satis' 'routine'

In other words, the dependent variable is specified after the **%fitline** command. In the Minitab for Windows *Release 10* menu system, the following sequence should be used:

→**R**egression →**F**itted Line Plot... →satis →**Select** [satis will now appear in the **Response[Y]** box] →routine →**Select** [routine will now appear in the **Predictor[X]** box] →**OK**

If only basic regression information is required or if users are new to regression procedures, this route to generating a regression equation can be very useful.

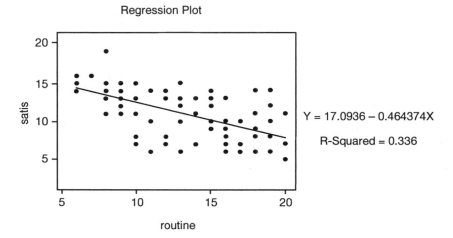

Figure 8.17 Scatter diagram: **satis** by **routine** with fitted regression line (Minitab for Windows *Release 10* output from Job Survey data)

OVERVIEW OF TYPES OF VARIABLE AND METHODS OF EXAMINING RELATIONSHIPS

In large part, the nature of the variables being analysed determines the type of analysis to be used. Crosstabulation and chi-square are most likely to occur in conjunction with nominal variables; Pearson's *r* presumes the use of interval variables; and when examining pairs of ordinal variables, rho should be employed. But what if, as can easily occur in the social sciences, pairs of variables are of different types, e.g. nominal plus ordinal or ordinal plus interval? One rule-of-thumb that can be recommended is to move downwards in measurement level when confronted with a pair of different variables. Thus, if you have an ordinal and an interval variable, rho could be used. If you have an ordinal and a nominal variable, you should use cross-tabulation and chi-square. This may mean collapsing ranks into groups (e.g. 1 to 5, 6 to 10, 11 to 15 and so on) and assigning ranks to the groupings (e.g. 1 to 5 = 1, 6 to 10 = 2, 11 to 15 = 3 and so on). If you have a nominal and an interval variable, again the combination of a contingency table and chi-square is likely to be used. As suggested in the discussion of cross-tabulation, the interval variable will need to be collapsed into groups. The chief source of concern with collapsing values of an ordinal or interval variable is that the choice of cut-off points is bound to be arbitrary and will have a direct impact on the results obtained. Accordingly, it may be better to use more than one method of grouping or to employ a fairly systematic procedure like quartiles as a means of collapsing cases into four groups.

When pairs of variables are dichotomous, the phi coefficient should be given serious consideration. Its interpretation is the same as Pearson's r, in that it varies between 0 and +1. When pairs of variables are nominal or where one variable is nominal and the other ordinal, Cramer's V can be used to test for strength of association.

The following rules-of-thumb are suggested for the various types of combination of variables that may occur:

1 Nominal – nominal. Contingency table analysis in conjunction with chi-square as a test of statistical significance can be recommended. Cramer's V can be used to test strength of association.
2 Ordinal – ordinal. Spearman's rho and its associated significance test.
3 Interval – interval. Pearson's r and regression for estimates of the strength and character of relationships respectively. Each can generate tests of statistical significance, but more detail in this regard for regression is provided in Chapter 10.
4 Dichotomous – dichotomous. Same as under 1 for nominal – nominal, except that phi could be used to measure the strength of association.
5 Interval – ordinal. If the ordinal variable assumes quite a large number of categories, it will probably be best to use rho. The interval variable will need to be rank-ordered using the **rank** procedure. Contingency table analysis may be used if there are few categories in both the ordinal and interval variables (or if categories can be 'collapsed'). If the interval variable can be relatively unambiguously identified as the dependent variable and if the ordinal variable has few categories, another approach may be to use an analysis of variance which will in turn allow an F ratio to be computed (see Chapter 7). In this way, a test of statistical significance can be provided.
6 Interval – nominal/dichotomous. Contingency table analysis plus the use of chi-square may be employed if the interval variable can be sensibly 'collapsed' into categories. This approach is appropriate if it is not meaningful to talk about which is the independent and which is the dependent variable. If the interval variable can be identified as a dependent variable, an analysis of variance could be considered.
7 Nominal – ordinal. Same as 1.

EXERCISES

1. (a) Using Minitab, how would you create a contingency table for the relationship between **'gender'** and **'prody'**, with the former variable going across, along with column percentages (Job Survey data)?
    (b) How would you assess the statistical significance of the relationship with Minitab?
    (c) In your view, is the relationship statistically significant?
    (d) What is the percentage of women who are described as exhibiting 'good' productivity?

2. A researcher carries out a study of the relationship between ethnic group and voting behaviour. The relationship is examined through a contingency table, for which the researcher computes the chi-square statistic. The value of chi-square turns out to be statistically significant at $p < 0.01$. The researcher concludes that this means that the relationship between the two variables is important and strong. Assess this reasoning.

3. (a) Using Minitab, how would you generate a matrix of Pearson's r correlation coefficients for **'income'**, **'years'**, **'satis'** and **'age'** (Job Survey data)?
    (b) Conduct an analysis using the commands from question 3 (a). Which pair of variables exhibits the largest correlation?
    (c) Taking this pair of variables, how much of the variance in one variable is explained by the other?

4. A researcher wants to examine the relationship between social class and number of books read in a year. The first hundred people are interviewed as they enter a public library in the researcher's home town. On the basis of the answers given, the sample is categorized in terms of a four-fold classification of social class: upper middle class/lower middle class/upper working class/ lower working class. Using Pearson's r, the level of correlation is found to be 0.73 which is significant at $p < 0.001$. The researcher concludes that the findings have considerable validity, especially since 73 per cent of the variance in number of books read is explained by social class. Assess the researcher's analysis and conclusions.

5. A researcher finds that the correlation between income and a scale measuring interest in work is 0.55 (Pearson's r) which is nonsignificant since p is greater than 0.05. This finding is compared to another study using the same variables and measures which found the correlation to be 0.46 and $p < 0.001$. How could this contrast arise? In other words, how could the larger correlation be nonsignificant and the smaller correlation be significant?

6. (a) What statistic or statistics would you recommend to estimate the strength of the relationship between **'prody'** and **'commit'** (Job Survey data)?
    (b) What Minitab commands would you use to generate the relevant estimates?
    (c) What is the result of using these commands?

7. The regression equation for the relationship between **'age'** and **'autonom'** (with the latter as the dependent variable) is

    autonom = 6.964 + 0.06230**age** $r = 0.28$

    (a) Explain what 6.964 means.
    (b) Explain what 0.06230 means.
    (c) How well does the regression equation fit the data?
    (d) What is the likely level of **autonom** for someone age 54?
    (e) Using Minitab, how would you generate this regression information?

Chapter 9

Multivariate analysis
Exploring differences among three or more variables

In most studies in the social sciences we collect information on more than just two variables. Although it would be possible and more simple to examine the relationships between these variables just two at a time, there are serious disadvantages to restricting oneself to this approach, as we shall see. It is preferable initially to explore these data with multivariate rather than bivariate tests. The reasons for looking at three or more variables vary according to the aims and design of a study. Consequently, we will begin by outlining four design features which only involve three variables at a time. Obviously these features may include more than three variables and the features themselves can be combined to form more complicated designs, but we shall discuss them largely as if they were separate designs. However, as has been done before, we will use one set of data to illustrate their analysis, all of which can be carried out with a general statistical model called *analysis of variance and covariance* (ANOVA and ANCOVA). The basic principles of this model are similar to those of other parametric tests we have previously discussed such as the *t* test, one-way analysis of variance, and simple regression.

MULTIVARIATE DESIGNS

Factorial design

We are often interested in the effect of two variables on a third, particularly if we believe that the two variables may influence one another. To take a purely hypothetical case, we may expect the gender of the patient to interact with the kind of treatment they are given for feeling depressed. Women may respond more positively to psychotherapy where they have an opportunity to talk about their feelings while men may react more favourably to being treated with an antidepressant drug. In this case, we are anticipating that the kind of treatment will *interact* with gender in alleviating depression. An interaction is when the effect of one variable is not the same under all the conditions of the other variable. It is often more readily understood when it is depicted in the form of a graph as in Figure 9.1. However, whether these effects are statistically significant can only be determined by testing them and not just by visually inspecting them. The vertical axis shows the amount of improvement in depression that has taken place after treatment, while the horizontal one can represent either of the other two variables. In this case it reflects the kind of treatment received. The effects of the third variable, gender, is depicted by two different kinds of points and lines in the graph itself. Men are indicated by a cross and a continuous line while women are signified by a small circle and a broken line.

An interaction is indicated when the two lines representing the third variable are not parallel. Consequently, a variety of interaction effects can exist, three of which are shown in Figure 9.2 as hypothetical possibilities. In Figure 9.2(a), men show less improvement with psychotherapy than with drugs while women derive greater benefit from psychotherapy than from the drug treatment. In Figure 9.2(b), men improve little with either treatment, while women, once again, benefit considerably more from psychotherapy than from drugs. Finally, in Figure 9.2(c), both men and women improve more with psychotherapy than with drugs, but the improvement is much greater for women than it is for men.

The absence of an interaction can be seen by the lines representing the third variable as remaining more or less parallel to one another, as is the case in the three examples in Figure 9.3. In Figure 9.3(a), both men and women show a similar degree of improvement with both treatments. In Figure 9.3(b), women improve more than men under both conditions while both treatments are equally effective. In Figure 9.3(c), women show greater benefit than men with both treatments, and psychotherapy is better than drugs.

The results of treatment and gender on their own are known as *main* effects. In these situations, the influence of the other variable is disregarded. If, for example, we wanted to examine the effect of gender, we would only

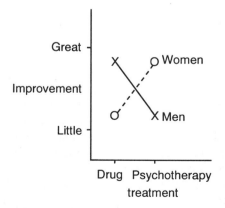

Figure 9.1 An example of an interaction between two variables

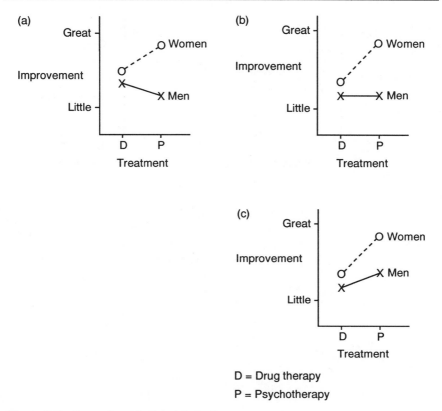

D = Drug therapy
P = Psychotherapy

Figure 9.2 Examples of other interactions

look at improvement for men and women, ignoring that of treatment. If we were interested in the effect of the kind of treatment, we would simply compare the outcome of patients receiving psychotherapy with those being given drugs, paying no heed to gender.

The variables which are used to form the comparison groups are termed *factors*. The number of groups which constitute a factor are referred to as the *levels* of that factor. Since gender consists of two groups, it is called a two-level factor. The two kinds of treatment also create a two-level factor. If a third treatment had been included such as a control group of patients receiving neither drugs nor psychotherapy, we would have a three-level factor. Studies which investigate the effects of two or more factors are known as *factorial* designs. A study comparing two levels of gender and two levels of treatment is described as a 2 × 2 factorial design. If three rather than two levels of treatment had been compared, it would be a 2 × 3 factorial design. Incidentally, a study which only looks at one factor is called a one-way or single factor design.

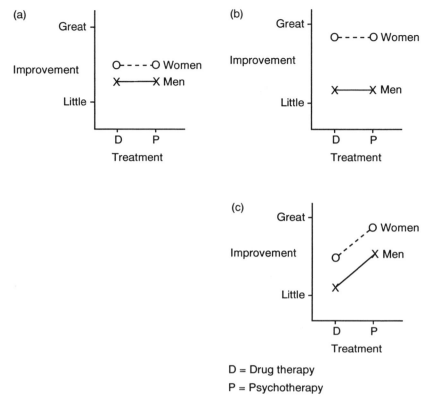

Figure 9.3 Examples of no interactions

The factors in these designs may be ones that are *manipulated* such as differing dosages of drugs, different teaching methods, or varying levels of induced anxiety. Where they have been manipulated and where subjects have been randomly assigned to different levels, the factors may also be referred to as *independent* variables since they are more likely to be unrelated to, or independent of, other features of the experimental situation such as the personality of the subjects. Variables which are used to assess the effect of these independent variables are known as *dependent* variables since the effect on them is thought to depend on the level of the variable which has been manipulated. Thus, for example, the improvement in the depression experienced by patients (i.e. the dependent variable) is believed to be partly the result of the treatment they have received (i.e. the independent variable). Factors can also be variables which have not been manipulated such as gender, age, ethnic origin, and social class. Because they cannot be separated from the individual who has them, they are sometimes referred to as *subject* variables. A study which investigated the effect of such subject variables would also be called a factorial design.

One of the main advantages of factorial designs, other than the study of interaction effects, is that they provide a more sensitive or powerful statistical test of the effect of the factors than designs which investigate just one factor at a time. To understand why this is the case, it is necessary to describe how a one-way and a two-way (i.e. a factorial) analysis of variance differ. In one-way analysis of variance, the variance in the means of the groups (or levels) is compared with the variance within them averaged across all the groups:

$$F = \frac{\text{variance between-groups}}{\text{variance within-groups}}$$

The between-groups variance is calculated by comparing the group mean with the overall or grand mean, while the within-groups variance is worked out by comparing the individual scores in the group with its mean. If the group means differ, then their variance should be greater than the average of those within them. This situation is illustrated in Figure 9.4 where the means of the three groups (M_1, M_2, and M_3) are quite widely separated causing a greater spread of between-groups variance (V_B) while the variance within the groups (V_1, V_2, and V_3) is considerably less when averaged (V_W).

Now the variance within the groups is normally thought of as error since this is the only way in which we can estimate it, while the between-groups variance is considered to consist of this error plus the effect of the factor which is being investigated. While some of the within-groups variance may be due to error such as that of measurement and of procedure, the rest of it

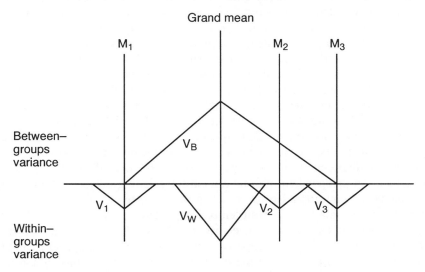

Figure 9.4   Schematic representation of a significant one-way effect

will be due to factors which we have not controlled such as gender, age, and motivation. In other words, the within-groups variance will contain error as well as variance due to other factors, and so will be larger than if it contained just error variance. Consequently, it will provide an overestimate of error. In a two-factor design, on the other hand, the variance due to the other factor can be removed from this overestimate of the error variance, thereby giving a more accurate calculation of it. If, for example, we had just compared the effectiveness of the drug treatment with psychotherapy in reducing depression, then some of the within-groups variance would have been due to gender but treated as error, and may have obscured any differential effect due to treatment.

Covariate design

Another way of reducing error variance is by removing the influence of a non-categorical variable (i.e., one which is not nominal) which we believe to be biasing the results. This is particularly useful in designs where subjects are not randomly assigned to factors, such as in the Job Survey study, or where random assignment did not result in the groups being equivalent in terms of some other important variable, such as how depressed patients were before being treated. A covariate is a variable which is linearly related to the one we are most directly interested in, usually called the *dependent* or *criterion* variable.

We will give two examples of the way in which the effect of covariates may be controlled. Suppose, for instance, we wanted to find out the relationship between job satisfaction and the two factors of gender and ethnic group in the Job Survey data and we knew that job satisfaction was positively correlated with income, so that people who were earning more were also more satisfied with their jobs. It is possible that both gender and ethnic group will also be related to income. Women may earn less than men and non-white workers may earn less than their white counterparts. If so, then the relationship of these two factors to job satisfaction is likely to be biased by their association with income. To control for this, we will remove the influence of income by covarying it out. In this case, income is the covariate. If income was not correlated with job satisfaction, then there would be no need to do this. Consequently, it is only advisable to control a covariate when it has been found to be related to the dependent variable.

In true experimental designs, we try to control the effect of variables other than the independent ones by randomly assigning subjects to different treatments or conditions. However, when the number of subjects allocated to treatments is small (say, about ten or less), there is a stronger possibility that there will be chance differences between them. If, for example, we are interested in comparing the effects of drugs with psychotherapy in treating depression, it is important that the patients in the two conditions should be similar in terms of how depressed they are before treatment begins (i.e. at *pre-test*). If the patients receiving the drug treatment were found at pre-test to be more depressed than those having psychotherapy despite random assignment, then it is possible that because they are more depressed to begin with, they will show less improvement than the psychotherapy patients. If pre-test depression is positively correlated with depression at the end of treatment (i.e. at *post-test*), then the effect of these initial differences can be removed statistically by covarying them out. The covariate in this example would be the pre-test depression scores.

Three points need to be made about the selection of covariates. First, as mentioned before, they should only be variables which are related to the dependent variable. Variables which are unrelated to it do not require to be covaried out. Second, if two covariates are strongly correlated with one another (say 0.8 or above), it is only necessary to remove one of them since the other one seems to be measuring the same variable(s). And third, with small numbers of subjects only a few covariates at most should be used, since the more covariates there are in such situations, the less powerful the statistical test becomes.

Multiple measures design

In many designs we may be interested in examining differences in more than one dependent or criterion measure. For example, in the Job Survey study, we may want to know how differences in gender and ethnic group are related to job autonomy and routine as well as job satisfaction. In the depression study, we may wish to assess the effect of treatment in more than one way. How depressed the patients themselves feel may be one measure. Another may be how depressed they appear to be to someone who knows them well, such as a close friend or informant. One of the advantages of using multiple measures is to find out how restricted or widespread a particular effect may be. In studying the effectiveness of treatments for depression, for instance, we would have more confidence in the results if the effects were picked up by a number of similar measures rather than just one. Another advantage is that although groups may not differ on individual measures, they may do so when a number of related individual measures are examined jointly. Thus, for example, psychotherapy may not be significantly more effective than the drug treatment when outcome is assessed by either the patients themselves or by their close friends, but it may be significantly better when these two measures are analysed together.

Mixed between-within design

The multiple-measures design needs to be distinguished from the repeated-measures design which we encountered at the end of Chapter 7. A multiple-measures design has two or more dependent or criterion variables such as two separate measures of depression. A repeated-measures design, on the other hand, consists of one or more factors being investigated on the same group of subjects. Measuring job satisfaction or depression at two or more points in time would be an example of such a factor. Another would be evaluating the effectiveness of drugs and psychotherapy on the same patients by giving them both treatments. If we were to do this, we would have to make sure that half the patients were randomly assigned to receiving psychotherapy first and the drug treatment second, while the other patients would be given the two treatments in the reverse order. It is necessary to counterbalance the sequence of the two conditions to control for *order effects*. It would also be advisable to check that the sequence in which the treatments were administered did not affect the results. The order effect would constitute a between-subjects factor since any one subject would only receive one of the two orders. In other words, this design would become a mixed one which included both a between-subjects factor (order) and a within-subjects one (treatment). One of the advantages of this design is that it restricts the amount of variance due to individuals, since the same treatments are compared on the same subjects.

Another example of a mixed between-within design is where we assess the dependent variable before as well as after the treatment, as in the study on depression comparing the effectiveness of psychotherapy with drugs. This design has two advantages. The first is that the pre-test enables us to determine whether the groups were similar in terms of the dependent variable before the treatment began. The second is that it allows us to determine if there has been any change in the dependent variable before and after the treatment has been given. In other words, this design enables us to discern whether any improvement has taken place as a result of the treatment and whether this improvement is greater for one group than the other.

Combined design

As was mentioned earlier, the four design features can be combined in various ways. Thus, for instance, we can have two independent factors (gender and treatment for depression), one covariate (age), two dependent measures (assessment of depression by patient and informant), and one repeated measure (pre- and post-test). These components will form the basis of the following illustration, which shall be referred to as the Depression Project. The data for it are shown in Table 9.1. There are three treatments: a no treatment control condition (coded 1 and with eight subjects); a psychotherapy treatment (coded 2 and with ten subjects); and a drug treatment (coded 3 and with twelve subjects). Females are coded as 1 and males as 2. A high score on depression indicates a greater degree of it. The patient's assessment of their depression before and after treatment is referred to as **'patpre'** and **'patpost'** respectively and the assessment

Table 9.1 The Depression Project data

'id'	'treat'	'gender'	'age'	'patpre'	'infpre'	'patpost'	'infpost'
01	1	1	27	25	27	20	19
02	1	2	30	29	26	25	27
03	1	1	33	26	25	23	26
04	1	2	36	31	33	24	26
05	1	1	41	33	30	29	28
06	1	2	44	28	30	23	26
07	1	1	47	34	30	30	31
08	1	2	51	35	37	29	28
09	2	1	25	21	24	9	15
10	2	2	27	20	21	9	12
11	2	1	30	23	20	10	8
12	2	2	31	22	28	14	18
13	2	1	33	25	22	15	17
14	2	2	34	26	23	17	16
15	2	1	35	24	26	9	13
16	2	2	37	27	25	18	20
17	2	1	38	25	21	11	8
18	2	2	42	29	30	19	21
19	3	1	30	34	37	23	25
20	3	2	33	31	27	15	13
21	3	1	36	32	35	20	21
22	3	2	37	33	35	20	18
23	3	1	39	40	38	33	35
24	3	2	41	34	31	18	19
25	3	1	42	34	36	23	27
26	3	2	44	37	31	14	11
27	3	1	45	36	38	24	25
28	3	2	47	38	35	25	27
29	3	1	48	37	39	29	28
30	3	2	50	39	37	23	24

provided by an informant before and after treatment as **'infpre'** and **'infpost'**. We shall now turn to methods of analysing the results of this kind of study using ANOVA or ANCOVA.

MULTIVARIATE ANALYSIS

Factorial design

The example we have given is the more common one in which there are unequal numbers of subjects on one or more of the factors. Although it is possible to equalize them by randomly omitting two subjects from the psychotherapy treatment and four from the drug one, this would be a waste of valuable data and so is not recommended. There are three different ways of analysing the results of factorial designs (Overall and Spiegel, 1969). All three methods produce the same result when there are equal numbers of subjects in each cell. When they are unequal, as in this case, one of them has to be selected as the preferred method since the results they give differ. The first method, referred to as the *regression* or *unweighted means* approach, assigns equal weight to the means in all cells regardless of their size. In other words, interaction effects have the same importance as main ones. This is the approach to be recommended in a true experimental design such as this one where subjects have been randomly assigned to treatments. The second method, known as the *classic experimental* or *least squares* approach, places greater weight on cells with larger numbers of subjects and is recommended for non-experimental designs in which the number of subjects in each cell may reflect its importance. This approach gives greater weight to main effects than to interaction ones. This analysis will be described at the end of this chapter. The third method, called the *hierarchical* approach, allows the investigator to determine the order of the effects. If one factor is thought to precede another, then it can be placed first. This approach should be used in non-experimental designs where the factors can be ordered in some sequential manner. If, for example, we are interested in the effect of ethnic group and income on job satisfaction, then ethnic group would be entered first since income cannot determine to which ethnic group we belong.

To determine the effect of treatment, gender and their interaction on post-test depression as seen by the patient for unequal numbers of cases in cells, we need to use the **glm** command which would take the following form:

MTB > glm patpost = treat gender treat * gender;
SUBC> means treat gender treat * gender;
SUBC> brief 1.

Glm is short for **g**eneral **l**inear **m**odel. Note that the quotation marks around the variable names can be omitted from the **glm** command. The **means** subcommand provides means and standard deviations for subjects grouped according to treatment, gender and their interaction. Specifying **1** on the **brief** subcommand restricts the output to the analysis of variance table.

The menu procedure for doing this is

→**S**tat →**A**NOVA →**G**eneral Linear Model... →**patpost** →**Select**
[this puts **patpost** in the box beside **Response:**] →box under **M**odel:
→**treat** →**Select** [this puts **treat** in this box] →**gender** →**Select** →type
treat * gender →**O**ptions... →box under **Display means for (list of
terms):** →**treat** →**Select** [this puts **treat** in this box] →**gender**
→**Select** →type **treat * gender** →**O**K

The menu system does not have the **brief 1** output option, so the default output option (**brief 2**) is produced which includes unusual observations (see Table 9.6 for an example).

The **brief 1** output is presented in Table 9.2. The F ratios in the analysis of variance table reflect the regression approach and are the most appropriate for analysing the results of this design. They are produced by dividing the adjusted mean square of an effect by the adjusted mean square of the error. For example, the F ratio for the **treat**ment effect is **23.76** which is derived by dividing the adjusted mean square (**Adj MS**) of **treat**ment (**383.97**) by the adjusted mean square of **Error** (**16.16**). This effect is significant ($p < 0.0005$) as is the interaction effect of treatment and gender ($p = 0.016$).

If we wanted F ratios for the classic experimental approach, we first need to obtain the sequential mean square for an effect by dividing its sequential sum of squares (**Seq SS**) by its degrees of freedom (**DF**). We would then divide this sequential mean square by the adjusted mean square of the error. For instance, the sequential mean square for **treat**ment is 383.97 (**767.94/2**) giving an F ratio of 23.76 (383.97/**16.16**). To determine the probability of this value, we would need to use the appropriate **invcdf** command as shown in Chapter 7. F ratios for the classical experimental approach are provided if effects are ordered as follows: (1) covariates; (2) main effects; (3) two-way interactions; (4) three-way interactions and so on.

Table 9.2 **Glm brief 1** output for the effect of **treat**ment, **gender** and their interaction on **patient**-rated **post**-treatment depression

Analysis of Variance for patpost

Source	DF	Seq SS	Adj SS	Adj MS	F	P
treat	2	767.94	767.94	383.97	23.76	0.000
gender	1	7.50	2.68	2.68	0.17	0.688
treat*gender	2	159.61	159.61	79.80	4.94	0.016
Error	24	387.92	387.92	16.16		
Total	29	1322.97				

Means for patpost

treat		Mean	Stdev
1		25.38	1.421
2		13.10	1.271
3		22.25	1.161
gender			
1		20.54	1.052
2		19.94	1.052
treat*gender			
1	1	25.50	2.010
1	2	25.25	2.010
2	1	10.80	1.798
2	2	15.40	1.798
3	1	25.33	1.641
3	2	19.17	1.641

If, for some reason, we wished to enter the interaction effect before the two main effects in the analysis of variance, we would place this term first after the equals sign on the **glm** command.

MTB > glm patpost=treat * gender treat gender;
SUBC> brief 1.

The menu sequence for doing this is

→**S̲tat** →**A̲NOVA** →**G̲eneral Linear Model...** →**patpost** →**Select**
[this puts **patpost** in the box beside **R̲esponse:**] →box under **M̲odel:**
→type **treat * gender** [this puts **treat * gender** in this box] →**treat**
→**Select** →**gender** →**Select** →**O̲K**

The **brief 1** output for this procedure is presented in Table 9.3. Note that while the adjusted sums of squares are the same in both analyses, the sequential sum of squares differs slightly for the **gender** and the **treat * gender** effect.

If we plot the means of this interaction, we can see that depression after the drug treatment is higher for women than for men, while after psychotherapy it is higher for men than for women.

We can plot the interaction in *Release 10* with the following prompt command

MTB > %interact 'treat' 'gender';
SUBC> responses 'patpost'.

The factors are listed on the **%interact** command and the dependent variable on the **responses** subcommand.

The menu sequence for doing this is

→**S̲tat** →**A̲NOVA** →**I̲nteractions Plot...** →**treat** →**Select** [this puts
treat in the box under **F̲actors :**] →**gender** →**Select** →box beside
R̲aw response data in: →**patpost** →**Select** [this puts **patpost** in this
box] →box beside **D̲isplay full interaction plot matrix** →**O̲K**

The output from this procedure is depicted in Figure 9.5.

Table 9.3 **Glm brief 1** output for the interaction effect of **treat**ment and **gender** and the main effects of **treat**ment and **gender** on **pat**ient-rated **post**-treatment depression

Analysis of Variance for patpost

Source	DF	Seq SS	Adj SS	Adj MS	F	P
treat*gender	2	164.43	159.61	79.80	4.94	0.016
treat	2	767.94	767.94	383.97	23.76	0.000
gender	1	2.68	2.68	2.68	0.17	0.688
Error	24	387.92	387.92	16.16		
Total	29	1322.97				

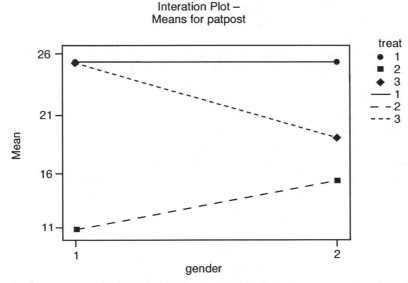

Figure 9.5   **% interact** output showing the effect of **treat**ment and **gender** on **pat**ient-rated **post**-treatment depression

Having found that there is an overall significant difference in depression for the three treatments, we need to determine where this difference lies. One way of doing this is to test for differences between two treatments at a time. If we had not anticipated certain differences between treatments, we would apply *a priori* tests such as Tukey's to do this, whereas if we had predicted them we would use unrelated *t* tests (see Chapter 7).

Covariate design

If the patients' pre-test depression scores differ for gender, treatment or their interaction and if the pre-test scores are related to the post-test ones, then the results of the previous test will be biased by this. To determine if there are such differences, we need to run a factorial analysis of variance on the patients' pre-test depression scores using the following Minitab prompt command

MTB > glm patpre = treat gender treat * gender;
SUBC> brief 1.

The menu action for doing this is

→**Stat** →**ANOVA** →**General Linear Model...** →**patpre** →**Select** [this puts **patpre** in the box beside **Response:**] →box under **Model:** →**treat** →**Select** [this puts **treat** in this box] →**gender** →**Select** →type **treat*gender** →**OK**

If we do this, we find that there is a significant effect for treatments (see the output in Table 9.4), which means that the pre-test depression scores differ between treatments.

Covariate analysis is based on the same assumptions as the previous factorial analysis plus three additional ones. First, there must be a linear relationship between the dependent variable and the covariate. If there is no such relationship, then there is no need to conduct a covariate analysis. This assumption can be tested by plotting a scatter diagram (see Chapter 8) to see if the relationship appears non-linear. If the correlation is statistically significant, then it is appropriate to carry out a covariate analysis. The statistical procedure **glm** also provides information on this (see p. 204). If the relationship is non-linear, it may be possible to transform it so that it becomes linear using a logarithmic transformation of one variable. The procedure for effecting such a transformation with Minitab involves using the appropriate **let** command.

The second assumption is that the slope of the regression lines is the same in each group or cell. If they are the same, this implies that there is no interaction between the independent variable and the covariate and that the average within-cell regression can be used to adjust the scores of the dependent variable. This information is also provided by **glm**. If this condition is not met, then the Johnson-Neyman technique should be considered. This method is not available on Minitab but a description of it may be found elsewhere (Huitema, 1980).

The third assumption is that the covariate should be measured without error. For some variables such as gender and age, this assumption can usually be justified. For others, however, such as measures of depression, this needs to be checked. This can be done by computing the alpha reliability coefficient for multi-item variables (such as job satisfaction) or test–retest correlations where this information is available. A coefficient of 0.8 or above is usually taken as indicating a reliable measure (see Cramer, 1996). This assumption is more important in non- than in true-experimental designs, where its violation may lead to either Type I or II errors. In true-experimental designs, the violation of this assumption only leads to loss of

Table 9.4 **Glm brief 1** output for the effect of **treat**ment, **gender** and their interaction on **pat**ient-rated **pre**-treatment depression

Analysis of Variance for patpre

Source	DF	Seq SS	Adj SS	Adj MS	F	P
treat	2	686.47	686.47	343.24	33.14	0.000
gender	1	3.33	4.23	4.23	0.41	0.529
treat*gender	2	3.47	3.47	1.74	0.17	0.847
Error	24	248.58	248.58	10.36		
Total	29	941.87				

power. As there are no agreed or simple procedures for adjusting covariates for unreliability, these will not be discussed.

To determine if the second assumption, that the slope of the regression lines is the same in each cell, is met we need to use the following commands

MTB > glm patpost = treat patpre treat ∗ patpre;
SUBC> covariates patpre;
SUBC> brief 1.

The dependent variable **patpost** is listed first after the **glm** keyword, followed by an equals sign and the two variables and their interaction. It is the significance of this interaction that we are solely concerned with in this analysis. The **covariance** subcommand specifies that **patpre** is to be the covariate in this analysis while **1** on the **brief** subcommand restricts the output to the analysis of covariance table.

The menu sequence for doing this is

→**S̲tat** →**ANOVA** →**G̲eneral Linear Model...** →**patpost** →**Select** [this puts **patpost** in the box beside **R̲esponse:**] →box under **M̲odel:** →**treat** [this puts **treat** in this box] →**patpre** →**Select** →type **treat ∗ patpre** →box under **C̲ovariates [optional]:** →**patpre** →**Select** →**O̲K**

The **brief 1** output from this procedure is presented in Table 9.5. The interaction between the independent variable of **treat**ment and the covariate of **patpre** is not significant since p is **0.793**. This means that the slope of the regression line in each of the cells is similar and the second assumption is met. Therefore, we can proceed with the main analysis.

To find out the effect of treatment on patient-reported post-treatment depression covarying patient-reported pre-test depression, we use the following commands

MTB > glm patpost = treat patpre;
SUBC> covariates patpre;
SUBC> means treat.

Table 9.5 **Glm brief 1** output showing the test of homogeneity of slope of regression line within cells

Analysis of Variance for patpost

Source	DF	Seq SS	Adj SS	Adj MS	F	P
treat	2	767.94	16.91	8.45	0.81	0.458
patpre	1	298.65	299.44	299.44	28.58	0.000
treat∗patpre	2	4.91	4.91	2.45	0.23	0.793
Error	24	251.47	251.47	10.48		
Total	29	1322.97				

We are not now interested in the effect of the interaction between treatment and the covariate, so we omit this interaction term from the **glm** command. We include the **means** subcommand because we want to know the means of the three treatments adjusted for the effect of the covariate. We leave out the **brief** subcommand since we wish to display the covariate coefficient.

The menu procedure for doing this is

→**Stat** →**ANOVA** →**General Linear Model...** →**patpost** →**Select** [this puts **patpost** in the box beside **Response:**] →box under **Model:** →**treat** [this puts **treat** in this box] →**patpre** →**Select** →box under **Covariates [optional]:** →**patpre** →**Select** →**Options...** →box under **Display means for (list of terms):** →**treat** →**Select** [this puts **treat** in this box] →**OK**

The output from this procedure is shown in Table 9.6. The coefficient for the covariate **patpre** (**1.0814**) is statistically significant ($p < 0.0005$). This means that the first assumption is also satisfied which is that there is a significant linear relationship between the dependent variable and the covariate. The analysis of the covariance table shows there is a significant **treat**ment effect when pre-treatment depression is covaried out ($p < 0.0005$). Comparing the unadjusted means in Table 9.2 with the adjusted ones in Table 9.6 indicates that controlling for pre-treatment depression has little effect on the mean for the control group, which remains at about 25. However, it makes a considerable difference to the means of the two treatment conditions, reversing their order so that patients who received psychotherapy report themselves as being more depressed than those given the drug treatment. The Bryant-Paulson *post-hoc* test for determining whether this difference is statistically significant is described in Stevens (1992).

Multiple measures design

So far, we have analysed only one of the two dependent measures, the patient's self-report of depression. Analysing the two dependent measures together has certain advantages. First, it reduces the probability of making Type I errors (deciding there is a difference when there is none) when making a number of comparisons. The probability of making this error is usually set at 0.05 when comparing two groups on one dependent variable. If we made two such independent comparisons, then the p level would increase to about 0.10. Since the comparisons are not independent, this probability is higher. Second, analysing the two dependent measures together provides us with a more sensitive measure of the effects of the independent variables.

This analysis is only available from *Release 9* onwards. To determine the effect of **treat**ment on **pat**ient-reported and **inf**ormant-reported **post-**

Table 9.6 **Glm** output testing the effect of **treat**ment on **pat**ient-reported **post**-treatment depression covarying **pat**ient **pre**-treatment depression

Factor	Levels	Values		
treat	3	1	2	3

Analysis of Variance for patpost

Source	DF	Seq SS	Adj SS	Adj MS	F	P
treat	2	767.94	339.16	169.58	17.20	0.000
patpre	1	298.65	298.65	298.65	30.29	0.000
Error	26	256.38	256.38	9.86		
Total	29	1322.97				

Term	Coeff	Stdev	t-value	P
Constant	−12.107	5.907	−2.05	0.051
patpre	1.0814	0.1965	5.50	0.000

Unusual Observations for patpost

Obs.	patpost	Fit	Stdev.Fit	Residual	St.Resid
23	33.0000	27.2063	1.2778	5.7937	2.02R
26	14.0000	23.9622	0.9584	−9.9622	−3.33R

R denotes an obs. with a large st. resid.

Means for Covariates

Covariate	Mean	Stdev
patpre	30.27	5.699

Adjusted Means for patpost

treat	Mean	Stdev
1	25.53	1.111
2	19.66	1.551
3	16.68	1.359

treatment patient depression taken together and separately, we would use the following commands:

MTB > glm patpost infpost = treat;
SUBC> manova;
SUBC> brief 1.

The two dependent measures **patpost** and **infpost** are listed after the **glm** keyword, followed by the equals sign and the independent variable **treat**. The **manova** subcommand performs the four following multivariate tests: Wilk's test, Lawley-Hotelling test, Pillai's test and Roy's largest root test.

The menu action for doing this is

→**Stat** →**A**NOVA →**G**eneral **Linear Model... →patpost →Select**
[this puts **patpost** in the box beside **R**esponse:] →**infpost** →**Select**
→box under **M**odel: →**treat** [this puts **treat** in this box] →box beside
Include multivariate ANOVA →**O**K

The **brief 1** output from this procedure is shown in Table 9.7. The results
of the two univariate tests are presented first and indicate a significant
treatment effect ($p < $**0.0005**) for the two measures examined separately. The
three multivariate tests which provide a probability value also demonstrate a
significant treatment effect ($p < $**0.0005**) when the two measures are taken
together. To determine which treatments differ significantly from one
another, it would be necessary to carry out a series of unrelated t tests or
post hoc tests as discussed previously.

Mixed between-within design

To be able to carry out with Minitab an analysis of variance on the data from a
mixed between-within design, it is necessary to have a *balanced* design which
contains an equal number of subjects in the different conditions. Consequently,

Table 9.7 **Glm brief 1** output testing the effect of **treat**ment on **pat**ient- and
informant-reported **post**-treatment depression taken separately and together

General Linear Model

Analysis of Variance for patpost

Source	DF	Seq SS	Adj SS	Adj MS	F	P
treat	2	767.94	767.94	383.97	18.68	0.000
Error	27	555.03	555.03	20.56		
Total	29	1322.97				

Analysis of Variance for infpost

Source	DF	Seq SS	Adj SS	Adj MS	F	P
treat	2	652.14	652.14	326.07	11.50	0.000
Error	27	765.72	765.72	28.36		
Total	29	1417.87				

MANOVA for treat $s = 2$ $m = -0.5$ $n = 12.0$

CRITERION	TEST STATISTIC	F	DF	P
Wilk's	0.39350	7.724	(4, 52)	0.000
Lawley-Hotelling	1.51298	9.456	(4, 50)	0.000
Pillai's	0.61765	6.032	(4, 54)	0.000
Roy's	1.49402			

if we wanted to carry out this kind of analysis on the Depression Project data, we need to have eight subjects in each of the three treatments by randomly dropping the data of two subjects in the second condition (say, 13 and 15) and four in the third condition (say, 19, 20, 21 and 23). To determine, for example, whether there is a significant difference between the three conditions in improvement in depression as assessed by the patient before (**patpre**) and after (**patpost**) treatment, we have to create four new columns. Note that since the data of the subjects are grouped together according to our independent variable **treat**, it is not necessary to re-order the data as we need to do for the analysis of the data in the combined design below.

The first column contains the pre-test depression scores stacked on top of the post-test depression scores which we do with the following command:

MTB > stack 'patpre' 'patpost' c9

We shall call this first new column **'pat'** which is short for patient

MTB > name c9 'pat'

The menu sequence for doing this is

→**Manip** →**Stack...** →**patpre** →**Select** [this puts **patpre** in the first box below **Stack the following blocks:**] →second box under **Stack the following blocks:** →**patpost** →**Select** [this puts **patpost** in this box] →box under **Store results in blocks:** and in it type **pat** →**OK**

The second new column comprises the code which distinguishes the pre-test scores (coded as **1**) from the post-test scores (coded **2**). It consists of 24 **1**'s and 24 **2**'s and can be formed with the following **set** command

MTB > set c10
DATA> (1:2)24
DATA> end

The numbers to be repeated are placed within parentheses. The colon represents consecutive numbers between **1** and **2** (i.e. only 1 and 2 in this case). The number **24** after the closing parenthesis means the first number **1** is repeated 24 times after which the second number **2** is repeated 24 times. There must be no space between this number and the closing bracket.

We shall call this new column **'test'** for time of testing

MTB > name c10 'test'

The third new column indicates which of these pre- and post-test scores comes from which of the three conditions and can be produced by stacking **'treat'** twice

MTB > stack 'treat' 'treat' c11

We can call this new column **'treat2'** to distinguish it from **'treat'**.

The menu sequence for doing this is

→**Manip** →**Stack...** →**treat** →**Select** →second box under **Stack the following blocks:** →**treat** →**Select** →box under **Store results in blocks:** and in it type **treat2** →**OK**

The fourth new column indicates that there are eight subjects in each condition. It consists of six sets of eight subjects and is produced with the following **set** command

MTB > set c12
DATA> 6(1:8)
DATA> end

The numbers to be repeated are placed within parentheses. The colon represents consecutive numbers between **1** and **8**. The number **6** before the opening parenthesis means the sequence 1 to 8 is repeated 6 times. There must be no space between this number and the opening bracket.

We shall call this fourth new column **'subjects'**.

To carry out an analysis of variance on this balanced mixed design we use the following **anova** command

MTB > anova pat=treat2 test subjects treat2 * test treat2 * subjects

The dependent variable **pat** is listed after the **anova** keyword followed by an equals sign and the effects we want to test which include three main effects (**treat2**, **test** and **subjects**) and two interactions (**treat2 * test** and **treat2 * subjects**). The quotes around the variable names can be omitted from the **anova** command.

The menu action for doing this is

→**Stat** →**ANOVA** →**Balanced ANOVA...** →**pat** →**Select** [this puts **pat** in the box beside **Response:**] →box under **Model:** →**treat2** →**Select** [this puts **treat2** in this box] →**test** →**Select** →**subjects** →**Select** →type **treat2 * test** →type **treat2 * subjects** →**OK**

The output from this procedure is shown in Table 9.8. The effect that we are interested in is the interaction between **treat2** (i.e. the three treatments) and **test** (i.e. the two times of testing) which with an F ratio of **20.22** is statistically significant with a p of **0.0005** or less. This F ratio is formed by dividing the mean square of this interaction term (**88.08**) by the mean square of the error term (**4.36**). The result of 20.20 differs slightly from the figure of **20.22** shown in Table 9.8 due to the fact that Minitab calculates these statistics using values with more decimal places than those shown in the output.

Table 9.8 **Anova** output for a balanced mixed between- and within-subjects design

Factor	Type	Levels	Values							
treat2	fixed	3	1	2	3					
test	fixed	2	1	2						
subjects	fixed	8	1	2	3	4	5	6	7	8

Analysis of Variance for pat

Source	DF	SS	MS	F	P
treat2	2	1000.67	500.33	114.83	0.000
test	1	1160.33	1160.33	266.31	0.000
subjects	7	337.33	48.19	11.06	0.000
treat2*test	2	176.17	88.08	20.22	0.000
treat2*subjects	14	128.67	9.19	2.11	0.059
Error	21	91.50	4.36		
Total	47	2894.67			

To display the means of the patients' pre-test and post-test depression scores we use the following **table** command

MTB > table 'treat2' 'test';
SUBC> count;
SUBC> means 'pat'.

The menu sequence for doing this is

→**S**tat →**T**ables →**C**ross Tabulation... →**treat2** →**Select** [this puts **treat2** in the box under **Classification Variables**] →**test** →**Select** →box beside **Coun**t**s** [this puts a cross in this box] →**S**ummaries... →**pat** →**Select** [this puts **pat** in the box under **Associated variables:**] →box beside **Means** [this puts a cross in this box] →**OK**

The first variable **'treat2'** forms the rows of the table while the second variable **'test'** makes up its columns. The **count** subcommand counts the number of observations in each cell while the **means** subcommand gives the mean for the variable **'pat'** for each cell, each row and each column.

The output from this procedure is presented in Table 9.9. We can see that the amount of improvement shown by the three groups of patients is not the same. Least improvement has occurred in the group receiving no treatment (**30.125 – 25.375** = 4.75), while patients being administered the drug treatment exhibit the most improvement (**36.000 – 22.000** = 14.000).

Statistical differences in the amount of improvement shown in the three treatments could be further examined using **oneway** analysis of variance where the dependent variable is the computed difference between pre- and post-test patient depression.

Table 9.9 Means of patients' pre-test and post-test depression for the three treatments in the Depression Project

ROWS:	treat2	COLUMNS:	test
	1	2	ALL
1	8 30.125	8 25.375	16 27.750
2	8 24.125	8 13.375	16 18.750
3	8 36.000	8 22.000	16 29.000
ALL	24 30.083	24 20.250	48 25.167

CELL CONTENTS –

COUNT
pat:MEAN

Combined design

As pointed out earlier on, it is possible to combine some of the above analyses. To show how this can be done, we shall look at the effect of two between-subject factors (treatment and gender) and one within-subject one (pre- to post-test or time) on two dependent variables (depression as assessed by the patient and an informant), covarying out the effects of age which we think might be related to the pre- and post-test measures.

To do this we first need to ensure that each cell has the same number of cases as every other cell. In other words, one of the cases dropped at random from the second condition of psychotherapy must be male (say, 13) and one female (say, 18) while two of the cases in the third treatment of drugs must be male (say, 19 and 21) and two female (say, 20 and 23). We can check that this has been done using the appropriate **table** and **count** command.

Next we have to re-arrange the data so that the data for, say, males is grouped together within each of the three treatments. We do this with the following **sort** command

MTB > sort c1-c8 c9-c16;
SUBC> by 'treat' 'gender'.

The data in columns **1** to **8** are to be arranged in ascending order according to the two variables **'treat'** and **'gender'** and these re-arranged data are to be put into columns **9** to **16**. Rows are sorted initially by the first variable (**'treat'**) on the **by** subcommand, and then, within that, by the second variable (**'gender'**).

The menu action for doing this is

→**Manip** →**Sort...** →**c1-c8** →**Select** [this puts **c1-c8** in the box under Sort **c**olumn(s): →box under **Store sorted column(s) in:** and in it type **c9-c16** →box beside first **S**ort by column: →**treat** →**Select** →box beside second **S**ort by column: →**gender** →**Select** →**O**K

We shall name columns **9** to **16** by adding **s** (for sorted) to the beginning of each of their original names as follows

MTB > name c9 'sid' c10 'streat' c11 'sgender' c12 'sage' &
CONT> c13 'spatpre' c14 'sinfpre' c15 'spatpost' c16 &
CONT> 'sinfpost'

Note that a line within a Minitab session can contain up to 160 characters. If the information we wish to put on a command exceeds this number, then we can continue on to subsequent lines by adding an ampersand (**&**) at or before the end of the line and press return. The **CONT>** prompt will appear as shown above.

Output of the data in columns **9** to **16** is presented in Table 9.10.

Table 9.10 Subsample of the Depression Project data containing four men and four women in each of three treatments sorted according to treatment and then gender

ROW	sid	streat	sgender	sage	spatpre	sinfpre	spatpost	sinfpost
1	1	1	1	27	25	27	20	19
2	3	1	1	33	26	25	23	26
3	5	1	1	41	33	30	29	28
4	7	1	1	47	34	30	30	31
5	2	1	2	30	29	26	25	27
6	4	1	2	36	31	33	24	26
7	6	1	2	44	28	30	23	26
8	8	1	2	51	35	37	29	28
9	9	2	1	25	21	24	9	15
10	11	2	1	30	23	20	10	8
11	15	2	1	35	24	26	9	13
12	17	2	1	38	25	21	11	8
13	10	2	2	27	20	21	9	12
14	12	2	2	31	22	28	14	18
15	14	2	2	34	26	23	17	16
16	16	2	2	37	27	25	18	20
17	23	3	1	39	40	38	33	35
18	25	3	1	42	34	36	23	27
19	27	3	1	45	36	38	24	25
20	29	3	1	48	37	39	29	28
21	24	3	2	41	34	31	18	19
22	26	3	2	44	37	31	14	11
23	28	3	2	47	38	35	25	27
24	30							

Next we need to create seven new columns in order to perform the within-subjects analysis on the pretest-posttest difference.

The variable **c17**, called **'pat'**, consists of patient-assessed pre-test and post-test depression scores and is formed by stacking **'patpre'** on **'patpost'**

MTB > stack 'patpre' 'patpost' 'pat'

The menu procedure for doing this is

→**Manip** →**Stack...** →**patpre** →**Select** →second box under **Stack the following blocks:** →**patpost** →**Select** →box under **S**t**ore results in blocks:** and in it type **pat** →**OK**

The variable **c18**, named **'inf'**, comprises informant-assessed pre-test and post-test depression scores and is produced by stacking **'infpre'** on **'infpost'**

MTB > stack 'infpre' 'infpost' 'inf'

The menu procedure for doing this is

→**Manip** →**Stack...** →**infpre** →**Select** →second box under **Stack the following blocks:** →**infpost** →**Select** [this puts **infpost** in this box] →box under **Store results in blocks:** and in it type **inf** →**OK**

The variable **c19**, named **'test'**, provides the code for identifying pre-test (coded **1**) and post-test (coded **2**) scores and consists of 24 **1**'s and 24 **2**'s. As explained previously, it can be created using the following **set** command

MTB > set c19
DATA> (1:2)24
DATA> end

The variable **c20**, called **'subjects'**, specifies the number of cases in each cell and identifies the data coming from the same cases. It consists of 12 sets of the four consecutive numbers **1 2 3 4** which can be produced using the previously described **set** command as follows

MTB > set c20
DATA> 12(1:4)
DATA> end

The variable **c21**, called **'streat2'**, provides the code for denoting the three treatments of the stacked pre- and post-test scores and is produced using the **stack** command.

The variable **c22**, named **'sgender2'**, gives the code for signifying the gender of the stacked pre- and post-test scores and is formed with the **stack** command.

The variable **c23**, named **'sage2'**, provides the age of the stacked pre- and post-test scores and is created with the **stack** command.

The output shown in Table 9.11 lists the values of the variables stored in columns **17** to **23**.

Table 9.11 Variables and their values for the combined design **ancova** analysis

ROW	pat	inf	test	subjects	streat2	sgender2	sage2
1	25	27	1	1	1	1	27
2	26	25	1	2	1	1	33
3	33	30	1	3	1	1	41
4	34	30	1	4	1	1	47
5	29	26	1	1	1	2	30
6	31	33	1	2	1	2	36
7	28	30	1	3	1	2	44
8	35	37	1	4	1	2	51
9	21	24	1	1	2	1	25
10	23	20	1	2	2	1	30
11	24	26	1	3	2	1	35
12	25	21	1	4	2	1	38
13	20	21	1	1	2	2	27
14	22	28	1	2	2	2	31
15	26	23	1	3	2	2	34
16	27	25	1	4	2	2	37
17	40	38	1	1	3	1	39
18	34	36	1	2	3	1	42
19	36	38	1	3	3	1	45
20	37	39	1	4	3	1	48
21	34	31	1	1	3	2	41
22	37	31	1	2	3	2	44
23	38	35	1	3	3	2	47
24	39	37	1	4	3	2	50
25	20	19	2	1	1	1	27
26	23	26	2	2	1	1	33
27	29	28	2	3	1	1	41
28	30	31	2	4	1	1	47
29	25	27	2	1	1	2	30
30	24	26	2	2	1	2	36
31	23	26	2	3	1	2	44
32	29	28	2	4	1	2	51
33	9	15	2	1	2	1	25
34	10	8	2	2	2	1	30
35	9	13	2	3	2	1	35
36	11	8	2	4	2	1	38
37	9	12	2	1	2	2	27
38	14	18	2	2	2	2	31
39	17	16	2	3	2	2	34
40	18	20	2	4	2	2	37
41	33	35	2	1	3	1	39
42	23	27	2	2	3	1	42
43	24	25	2	3	3	1	45
44	29	28	2	4	3	1	48
45	18	19	2	1	3	2	41
46	14	11	2	2	3	2	44
47	25	27	2	3	3	2	47
48	23	24	2	4	3	2	50

Table 9.12 **Ancova** output for **pat**ient-assessed depression in the combined design

Factor	Levels	Values			
streat2	3	1	2	3	
sgender2	2	1	2		
test	2	1	2		
subjects	4	1	2	3	4

Analysis of Covariance for pat

Source	DF	ADJ SS	MS	F	P
Covariates	1	0.00	0.00	0.00	1.000
streat2	2	123.54	61.77	23.93	0.000
sgender2	1	0.00	0.00	0.00	1.000
test	1	1150.52	1150.52	445.79	0.000
subjects	3	21.45	7.15	2.77	0.073
streat2*sgender2	2	63.06	31.53	12.22	0.001
streat2*test	2	159.54	79.77	30.91	0.000
streat2*subjects	6	45.78	7.63	2.96	0.037
sgender2*test	1	7.52	7.52	2.91	0.106
sgender2*subjects	3	7.86	2.62	1.01	0.410
streat2*sgender2*test	2	69.04	34.52	13.38	0.000
streat2*sgender2*subjects	6	126.57	21.10	8.17	0.000
Error	17	43.87	2.58		
Total	47	3297.48			

Covariate	Coeff	Stdev	t-value	P
sage2	0.1250	1191157	0.000000	1.000

The following **ancova** command is used for carrying out the analysis for this combined design

MTB > ancova pat inf=streat2 sgender2 test subjects &
CONT> streat2*sgender2 streat2*test streat2*subjects &
CONT> sgender2 * test sgender2 * subjects streat2 * sgender2 * test &
CONT> streat2 * sgender2 * subjects;
SUBC> covariates sage2.

Note that the covariate **sage2** is only listed on the **covariates** subcommand. It is not possible to perform a multivariate test on **pat** and **inf** together with the **ancova** command.

The menu sequence for doing this is

→**Stat** →**ANOVA** →**Balanced ANOVA...** →**pat** →**Select** [this puts **pat** in the box beside **Response:**] →**inf** →**Select** →box under **Model:** →**streat2** →**Select** [this puts **streat2** in this box] →**sgender2** →**Select** →**test** →**Select** →**subjects** →**Select** →type **streat2 * gender** →type

streat2 * test →type streat2 * subjects →type sgender2 * test →type
sgender2 * subjects →type streat2 * sgender2 * test →type streat2
* sgender2 * subjects →box under Covariates [optional]: →sage2
→Select →OK

The output from this procedure is shown separately for patient-assessed
depression in Table 9.12 and informant-assessed depression in Table 9.13.
The effect we are interested in is the interaction between treatment, gender
and time of testing (streat2 * sgender2 * test). This effect is statistically
significant for patient-assessed depression ($p < 0.0005$) but not for
informant-assessed depression ($p = 0.115$). To interpret these results, it
would be necessary to compute the mean pre- and post-treatment patient
depression scores, adjusted for age, for men and women in the three
treatments which we could do by adding the following means subcommand

MTB > means streat2 * sgender2 * test

The menu sequence for doing this is

→Options... →box under Display means for (list of terms):
→streat2 * sgender2 * test →Select [this puts streat2 * sgender2 *
test in this box] →OK

Additional analyses would have to be conducted to test these interpretations, as described previously.

Table 9.13 **Ancova** output for **inf**ormant-assessed depression in the combined
design

Analysis of Covariance for inf

Source	DF	ADJ SS	MS	F	P
Covariates	1	0.000	0.000	0.00	1.000
streat2	2	125.380	62.690	7.98	0.004
sgender2	1	0.000	0.000	0.00	1.000
test	1	784.083	784.083	99.85	0.000
subjects	3	14.883	4.961	0.63	0.605
streat2*sgender2	2	217.500	108.750	13.85	0.000
streat2*test	2	136.792	68.396	8.71	0.002
streat2*subjects	6	67.685	11.281	1.44	0.258
sgender2*test	1	3.000	3.000	0.38	0.545
sgender2*subjects	3	40.600	13.533	1.72	0.200
streat2*sgender2*test	2	38.625	19.313	2.46	0.115
streat2*sgender2*subjects	6	148.951	24.825	3.16	0.029
Error	17	133.500	7.853		
Total	47	2907.667			

Covariate	Coeff	Stdev	t-value	P
sage2	0.1245	2077787	0.000000	1.000

EXERCISES

1. What are the two main advantages in studying the effects of two rather than one independent variable?

2. What is meant when two variables are said to interact?

3. How would you determine whether there was a significant interaction between two independent variables?

4. A colleague is interested in the relationship between alcohol, anxiety and gender on performance. Participants are randomly assigned to receiving one of four increasing dosages of alcohol. In addition, they are divided into three groups of low, moderate, and high anxiety. Which is the dependent variable?

5. How many factors are there in this design?

6. How many levels of anxiety are there?

7. How would you describe this design?

8. If there are unequal numbers of subjects in each group and if the variable names for alcohol, anxiety, gender, and performance are **alcohol**, **anxiety**, **gender**, and **perform** respectively, what is the Minitab procedure for examining the effect of the first three variables on performance?

9. You are interested in examining the effect of three different methods of teaching on learning to read. Although subjects have been randomly assigned to the three methods, you think that differences in intelligence may obscure any effects. How would you try to control statistically for the effects of intelligence?

10. What is the Minitab procedure for examining the effect of three teaching methods on learning to read, covarying out the effect of intelligence when the names for these three variables are **methods**, **read**, and **intell** respectively?

11. You are studying what effect physical attractiveness has on judgments of intelligence, likeability, honesty, and self-confidence. Participants are shown a photograph of either an attractive or unattractive person and are asked to judge the extent to which this person has these four characteristics. How would you describe the design of this study?

12. If the names of the five variables in this study are **attract**, **intell**, **likeable**, **honesty**, and **confid** respectively, what Minitab procedure would you use for analysing the results of this study?

13. What kind of design would this be called if participants had been presented with photographs of both the attractive and the unattractive person?

14. What would the appropriate Minitab procedure be for analysing the results of this study?

15. Suppose that in the Depression Study described in this chapter, patients had been followed up three months after the experiment had ended to find out how depressed they were. What would the appropriate Minitab commands be for comparing pre- with post-treatment depression and post-treatment with follow-up depression? These three variables are respectively called **'pre'**, **'post'** and **'fol'**.

Chapter 10

Multivariate analysis

Exploring relationships among three or more variables

In this chapter we will be concerned with a variety of approaches to the examination of relationships when more than two variables are involved. Clearly, these concerns follow on directly from those of Chapter 8, in which we focused upon bivariate analysis of relationships. In the present chapter, we will be concerned to explore the reasons for wanting to analyse three or more variables in conjunction, that is, why multivariate analysis is an important aspect of the examination of relationships among variables.

The basic rationale for multivariate analysis is to allow the researcher to discount the alternative explanations of a relationship that can arise when a survey/correlational design has been employed. The experimental researcher can discount alternative explanations of a relationship through the combination of having a control group as well as an experimental group (or through a number of experimental groups) and random assignment (see Chapter 1). The absence of these characteristics, which in large part derives from the failure or inability to manipulate the independent variable in a survey/ correlational study, means that a number of potentially confounding factors may exist. For example, we may find a relationship between people's self-assigned social class (whether they describe themselves as middle or working class) and their voting preference (Conservative or Labour). But there are a number of problems that can be identified with interpreting such a relationship as causal. Could the relationship be spurious? This possibility could arise because people of higher incomes are both more likely to consider themselves middle class *and* to vote Conservative. Also, even if the relationship is not spurious, does the relationship apply equally to young and old? We know that age affects voting preferences, so how does this variable interact with self-assigned social class in regard to voting behaviour? Such a finding would imply that the class−voting relationship is moderated by age. The problem of spuriousness arises because we cannot make some people think they are middle class and others working class and then randomly assign subjects to the two categories. If we wanted to establish whether a moderated relationship exists whereby age moderated the class−voting relationship with an experimental study, we would use a factorial design (see Chapter 9). Obviously, we are not able to create such experimental conditions, so when we investigate this kind of issue through surveys, we have to recognize the limitations of inferring causal relationships from our data. In each of the two questions about the class–voting relationship, a third variable – income and age respectively – potentially contaminates the relationship and forces us to be sceptical about it.

The procedures to be explained in this chapter are designed to allow such contaminating variables to be discounted. This is done by imposing 'statistical controls' which allow the third variable to be 'held constant'. In this way we can examine the relationship between two variables by *partialling out* and thereby *controlling* the effect of a third variable. For example, if we believe that income confounds the relationship between self-assigned social class and voting, we examine the relationship between social class and voting for each income level in our sample. The sample might reveal four income levels, so we examine the class–voting relationship for each of these four income levels. We can then ask whether the relationship between class and voting persists for each income level or whether it has been eliminated for all or some of these levels. The third variable (i.e. the one that is controlled) is often referred to as the *test factor* (e.g. Rosenberg, 1968), but the term *test variable* is preferred in the following discussion.

The imposition of statistical controls suffers from a number of disadvantages. In particular, it is only possible to control for those variables which occur to you as potentially important and which are relatively easy to measure. Other variables will constitute further contaminating factors, but whose effects are unknown. Further, the time order of variables collected by means of a survey/correlational study cannot be established through multivariate analysis, but has to be inferred. In order to make inferences about the likely direction of cause and effect, the researcher must look to probable directions of causation (e.g. education precedes current occupation) or to theories which suggest that certain variables are more likely to precede others. As suggested in Chapter 1, the generation of causal inferences from survey/correlational research can be hazardous, but in the present chapter we will largely side-step these problems which are not capable of easy resolution in the absence of a panel study.

The initial exposition of multivariate analysis will solely emphasize the examination of three variables. It should be recognised that many examples of mutivariate analysis, particularly those involving correlation and regression techniques, go much further than this. Many researchers refer to the relationship between two variables as the *zero order relationship*; when a third variable is introduced, they refer to the *first order relationship*, that is the relationship between two variables when one variable is held constant; and when two extra variables are introduced, they refer to the *second order relationship* when two variables are held constant.

MULTIVARIATE ANALYSIS THROUGH CONTINGENCY TABLES

In this section, we will examine the potential of contingency tables as a means of exploring relationships among three variables. Four contexts in which such analysis can be useful are provided: testing for spuriousness, testing for intervening variables, testing for moderated relationships, and examining multiple causation. Although these four notions are treated in connection with contingency table analysis, they are also relevant to the correlation and regression techniques which are examined later.

Testing for spuriousness

The idea of spuriousness was introduced in Chapter 1 in the context of a discussion about the nature of causality. In order to establish that there exists a relationship between two variables it is necessary to show that the relationship is non-spurious. A spurious relationship exists when the relationship between two variables is not a 'true' relationship, in that it only appears because a third variable causes each of the variables making up the pair. In Table 10.1 a bivariate contingency table is presented which derives from an imaginary study of 500 manual workers in twelve firms. The table seems to show a relationship between the presence of variety in work and job satisfaction. For example, 80 per cent of those performing varied work are satisfied, as against only 24 per cent of those whose work is not varied. Thus there is a difference (d_1) of 56 per cent (i.e. $80 - 24$) between those performing varied work and those not performing varied work in terms of job satisfaction. Contingency tables are not normally presented with the

Table 10.1 Relationship between work variety and job satisfaction (imaginary data)

		Work variety			
		Varied work		*Not varied work*	
	Satisfied	(200)	1 80% $d_1 =$	24% 56%	(60) 2
Job satisfaction					
	Not satisfied	(50)	3 20% $d_2 =$	76% 56%	(190) 4

differences between cells inserted, but since these form the crux of the multivariate contingency table analysis, this additional information is provided in this and subsequent tables in this section.

Could the relationship between these two variables be spurious? Could it be that the size of the firm (the test variable) in which each respondent works has 'produced' the relationship (see Figure 10.1)? It may be that size of firm affects both the amount of variety of work reported and levels of job satisfaction. In order to examine this possibility, we partition our sample into those who work in large firms and those who work in small firms. There are 250 respondents in each of these two categories. We then examine the relationship between amount of variety in work and job satisfaction for each category. If the relationship is spurious we would expect the relationship between amount of variety in work and job satisfaction largely to disappear. Table 10.2 presents such an analysis. In a sense, what one is doing here is to present two separate tables: one examining the relationship between amount of variety in work and job satisfaction for respondents from large firms and one examining the same relationship for small firms. This notion is symbolized by the double line separating the analysis for large firms from the analysis for small firms.

What we find is that the relationship between amount of variety in work and job satisfaction has largely disappeared. Compare d_1 in Table 10.1 with both d_1 and d_2 in Table 10.2. Whereas d_1 in Table 10.1 is 56 per cent, implying a large difference between those whose work is varied and those whose work is not varied in terms of job satisfaction, the corresponding percentage differences in Table 10.2 are 10 and 11 per cent for d_1 and d_2 respectively. This means that when size of firm is controlled, the difference in terms of job satisfaction between those whose work is varied and those whose work is not varied is considerably reduced. This analysis implies that there is not a true relationship between variety in work and job satisfaction, because when size of firm is controlled the relationship between work variety and job satisfaction is almost eliminated. We can suggest that size of firm seems to affect both variables. Most respondents reporting varied work come from large firms ([cell1 + cell5] − [cell3 + cell7]) and most respondents who are satisfied come from large firms ([cell1 + cell2] − [cell3 + cell4]).

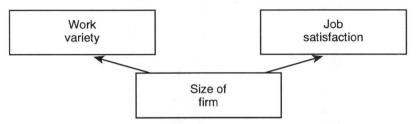

Figure 10.1   Is the relationship between work variety and job satisfaction spurious?

Table 10.2 A spurious relationship: the relationship between work variety and job satisfaction, controlling for size of firm (imaginary data)

Job satisfaction	Large firms		Small firms	
	Varied work	Not varied work	Varied work	Not varied work
Satisfied	1 (190) 95% $d_1=$	2 (42) 85% 10%	3 (10) 20% $d_2=$	4 (18) 9% 11%
Not satisfied	5 (10) 5% $d_3=$	6 (8) 15% 10%	7 (40) 80% $d_4=$	8 (182) 91% 11%

What would Table 10.2 look like if the relationship between variety in work and job satisfaction was not spurious when size of firm is controlled? Table 10.3 presents the same analysis but this time the relationship is not spurious. Again, we can compare d_1 in Table 10.1 with both d_1 and d_2 in Table 10.3. In Table 10.1, the difference between those who report variety in their work and those who report no variety is 56 per cent (i.e. d_1), whereas in Table 10.3 the corresponding differences are 55 per cent for large firms (d_1) and 45 per cent for small firms (d_2) respectively. Thus, d_1 in Table 10.3 is almost exactly the same as d_1 in Table 10.1, but d_2 is 11 percentage points smaller (i.e. $56 - 45$). However, this latter finding would not be sufficient to suggest that the relationship is spurious because the difference between those who report varied work and those whose work is not varied is still large for both respondents in large firms and those in small firms. We do not expect an exact replication of percentage differences when we carry out such controls. Similarly, as suggested in the context of the discussion of Table 10.2, we do not need percentage differences to disappear completely in order to infer that a relationship is spurious. When there is an in-between reduction in percentage differences (e.g. to around half of the original difference), the relationship is probably partially spurious, implying that part of it is caused by the third variable and the other part is indicative of a 'true' relationship. This would have been the interpretation if the original d_1 difference of 56 per cent had fallen to around 28 per cent for respondents from both large firms and from small firms.

Testing for intervening variables

The quest for intervening variables is different from the search for potentially spurious relationships. An intervening variable is one that is both a product of the independent variable and a cause of the dependent variable. Taking the data examined in Table 10.1, the sequence depicted in Figure 10.2 might be imagined. The analysis presented in Table 10.4 strongly suggests that the level of people's interest in their work is an intervening variable. As with Tables 10.2 and 10.3, we partition the sample into two groups (this time those who report that they are interested and those

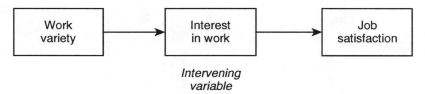

Figure 10.2 Is the relationship between work variety and job satisfaction affected by an intervening variable?

Table 10.3 A non-spurious relationship: the relationship between work variety and job satisfaction, controlling for size of firm (imaginary data)

Job satisfaction	Large firms		Small firms	
	Varied work	Not varied work	Varied work	Not varied work
Satisfied	1 (166) 83% $d_1 =$	2 (14) 28% 55%	3 (34) 68% $d_2 =$	4 (46) 23% 45%
Not satisfied	5 (34) 17% $d_3 =$	6 (36) 72% 55%	7 (16) 32% $d_4 =$	8 (154) 77% 45%

Table 10.4 A intervening variable: the relationship between work variety and job satisfaction, controlling for interest in work (imaginary data)

Job satisfaction	Interested		Not interested	
	Varied work	Not varied work	Varied work	Not varied work
Satisfied	1 (185) 93% $d_1=$	2 (40) 80% 13%	3 (15) 30% $d_2=$	4 (20) 10% 20%
Not satisfied	5 (15) 7% $d_3=$	6 (10) 20% 13%	7 (35) 70% $d_4=$	8 (180) 90% 20%

reporting no interest in their work) and examine the relationship between work variety and job satisfaction for each group. Again, we can compare d_1 in Table 10.1 with d_1 and d_2 in Table 10.4. In Table 10.1 d_1 is 56 per cent, but in Table 10.4 d_1 and d_2 are 13 per cent and 20 per cent respectively. Clearly, d_1 and d_2 in Table 10.3 have not been reduced to zero (which would suggest that the whole of the relationship was through interest in work), but they are also much lower than the 56 per cent difference in Table 10.1. If d_1 and d_2 in Table 10.4 had remained at or around 56 per cent, we would conclude that interest in work is not an intervening variable.

The sequence in Figure 10.2 suggests that variety in work affects the degree of interest in work that people experience which in turn affects their level of job satisfaction. This pattern differs from that depicted in Figure 10.1 in that if the analysis supported the hypothesized sequence, it suggests that there is a relationship between amount of variety in work and job satisfaction, but the relationship is not direct. The search for intervening variables is often referred to as *explanation* and it is easy to see why. If we find that a test variable acts as an intervening variable, we are able to gain some explanatory leverage on the bivariate relationship. Thus, we find that there is a relationship between amount of variety in work and job satisfaction and then ask why that relationship might exist. We speculate that it may be because those who have varied work become more interested in their work which heightens their job satisfaction.

It should be apparent that the computation of a test for an intervening variable is identical to a test for spuriousness. How, then, do we know which is which? If we carry out an analysis like those shown in Tables 10.2, 10.3 and 10.4, how can we be sure that what we are taking to be an intervening variable is not in fact an indication that the relationship is spurious? The answer is that there should be only one logical possibility, that is, only one that makes sense. If we take the trio of variables in Figure 10.1, to argue that the test variable – size of firm – could be an intervening variable would mean that we would have to suggest that a person's level of work variety affects the size of the firm in which he or she works – an unlikely scenario. Similarly, to argue that the trio in Figure 10.2 could point to a test for spuriousness, would mean that we would have to accept that the test variable – interest in work – can affect the amount of variety in a person's work. This too makes much less sense than to perceive it as an intervening variable.

One further point should be registered. It is clear that controlling for interest in work in Table 10.4 has not totally eliminated the difference between those reporting varied work and those whose work is not varied in terms of job satisfaction. It would seem, therefore, that there are aspects of the relationship between amount of variety in work and job satisfaction that are not totally explained by the test variable, interest in work.

Testing for moderated relationships

A moderated relationship occurs when a relationship is found to hold for some categories of a sample but not others. Diagrammatically this can be displayed as in Figure 10.3. We may even find the character of a relationship can differ for categories of the test variable. We might find that one category (those who report varied work) exhibit greater job satisfaction, but for another category of people the reverse may be true (i.e. varied work seems to engender lower levels of job satisfaction than work that is not varied).

Table 10.5 looks at the relationship between variety in work and job satisfaction for men and women. Once again, we can compare d_1 (56 per cent) in Table 10.1 with d_1 and d_2 in Table 10.5, which are 85 per cent and 12 per cent respectively. The bulk of the 56 percentage points difference between those reporting varied work and those reporting that work is not varied in Table 10.1 appears to derive from the relationship between variety in work and job satisfaction being far stronger for men than women and there being more men (300) than women (200) in the sample. Table 10.5 demonstrates the importance of searching for moderated relationships in that they allow the researcher to avoid inferring that a set of findings pertains to a sample as a whole, when in fact it only really applies to a portion of that sample. The term *interaction effect* is often employed to refer to the situation in which a relationship between two variables differs substantially for categories of the test variable. This kind of occurrence was also addressed in Chapter 9. The discovery of such an effect often inaugurates a new line of inquiry in that it stimulates reflection about the likely reasons for such variations.

The discovery of moderated relationships can occur by design or by chance. When they occur by design, the researcher has usually anticipated the possibility that a relationship may be moderated (though he or she may be wrong of course). They can occur by chance when the researcher conducts a test for an intervening variable or a test for spuriousness and finds a marked contrast in findings for different categories of the test variable.

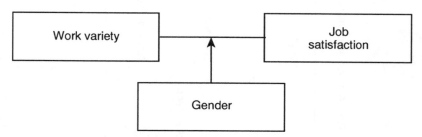

Figure 10.3 Is the relationship between work variety and job satisfaction moderated by gender?

Table 10.5 A moderated relationship: the relationship between work variety and job satisfaction, controlling for gender (imaginary data)

Job satisfaction	Men		Women	
	Varied work	Not varied work	Varied work	Not varied work
Satisfied	1 95% (143) $d_1 =$	2 10% (15) 85%	3 57% (57) $d_2 =$	4 45% (45) 12%
Not satisfied	5 5% (7) $d_3 =$	6 90% (135) 85%	7 43% (43) $d_4 =$	8 55% (55) 12%

Multiple causation

Dependent variables in the social sciences are rarely determined by one variable alone, so that two or more potential independent variables can usefully be considered in conjunction. Figure 10.4 suggests that whether someone is allowed participation in decision-making at work also affects their level of job satisfaction. It is misleading to refer to participation in decision-making as a test variable in this context, since it is really a second independent variable. What, then, is the impact of amount of variety in work on job satisfaction when we control the effects of participation?

Again, we compare d_1 in Table 10.1 (56 per cent) with d_1 and d_2 in Table 10.6. The latter are 19 and 18 per cent respectively. This suggests that although the effect of amount of variety in work has not been reduced to zero or nearly zero, its impact has been reduced considerably. Participation in decision-making appears to be a more important cause of variation in job satisfaction. For example, compare the percentages in cells 1 and 3 in Table 10.6: among those respondents who report that they perform varied work, 93 per cent of those who experience participation exhibit job satisfaction, whereas only 30 per cent of those who do not experience participation are satisfied.

One reason for this pattern of findings is that most people who experience participation in decision-making also have varied jobs, that is (cell1 + cell5) − (cell2 + cell6). Likewise, most people who do not experience participation have work which is not varied, that is (cell4 + cell8) − (cell3 + cell7). Could this mean that the relationship between variety in work and job satisfaction is really spurious, when participation in decision-making is employed as the test variable? The answer is that this is unlikely, since it would mean that participation in decision-making would have to cause variation in the amount of variety in work, which is a less likely possibility (since technological conditions tend to be the major influence on variables like work variety). Once again, we have to resort to a combination of intuitive logic and theoretical reflection in order to discount such a possibility. We will return to this kind of issue in

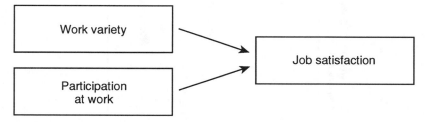

Figure 10.4   Does work variety have a greater impact on job satisfaction than participation at work?

Table 10.6 Two independent variables: the relationship between work variety and job satisfaction, controlling for participation at work (imaginary data)

	Participation		Little or no participation	
	Varied work	Not varied work	Varied work	Not varied work
Job satisfaction				
Satisfied	1 (185) 93% $d_1=$	2 (37) 74% 19%	3 (15) 30% $d_2=$	4 (23) 12% 18%
Not satisfied	5 (15) 7% $d_3=$	6 (13) 26% 19%	7 (35) 70% $d_4=$	8 (177) 88% 18%

the context of an examination of the use of multivariate analysis through correlation and regression.

Using Minitab to perform multivariate analysis through contingency tables

Taking the Job Survey data, we might want to examine the relationship between **'skill'** and **'ethnicgp'**, holding **'gender'** constant (i.e. as a test variable). Assuming that we want cell frequencies and column percentages, the following commands would be required in the prompt system:

MTB > table 'skill' 'gender' 'ethnicgp';
SUBC> counts;
SUBC> colpercents;
SUBC> layout 1 2.

The order in which the variables are specified in the first line and the **layout** subcommand in the last line are key here. Thus, the variable by which a relationship is to be broken down, which in this case is **'gender'**, has to be the second of the three variables stipulated. Chi-square is not available with the **layout** subcommand.

With the menu system, the following sequence will yield the same results:

→Stat →Tables →Cross Tabulation... →skill →Select [skill should now be in the **Classification Variables:** box] →gender →Select [**gender** should now be in the **Classification Variables:** box] →ethnicgp → Select [skill should now be in the **Classification Variables:** box] → [if the boxes by **Counts** and **Column Percents** do not have a tick in them, you should *click* once on each of these boxes] →Options... →type 1 in the box in the middle of the clause **Use the first ... classification variables for rows** and type 2 in the box in the middle of the clause **and the next ... for columns** →OK →OK

The resulting table will produce two contingency tables crosstabulating **'skill'** by **'ethnicgp'** – one for men and one for women.

MULTIVARIATE ANALYSIS AND CORRELATION

Although the use of contingency tables provides a powerful tool for multivariate analysis, it suffers from a major limitation, namely that complex analyses with more than three variables require large samples, especially when the variables include a large number of categories. Otherwise, there is the likelihood of very small frequencies in many cells (and indeed the likelihood of many empty cells) when a small sample is employed. By contrast, correlation and regression can be used to conduct multivariate analyses on fairly small samples, although their use in relation to very small samples is limited. Further, both correlation and regression provide easy to interpret indications of the relative strength of relationships. On the other hand, if one or more variables are nominal, multivariate analysis through contingency tables is probably the best way forward for most purposes.

The partial correlation coefficient

One of the main ways in which the multivariate analysis of relationships is conducted in the social sciences is through the partial correlation coefficient. This test allows the researcher to examine the relationship between two variables while holding one other or more variables constant. It allows tests for spuriousness, tests for intervening variables, and multiple causation to be investigated. The researcher must stipulate the anticipated logic that underpins the three variables in question (e.g. test for spuriousness) and can then investigate the effect of the test variable on the original relationship. Moderated relationships are probably better examined by computing Pearson's r for each category of the test variable (e.g. for both men and women, or young, middle-aged, and old) and then comparing the rs.

The partial correlation coefficient is computed by first calculating the Pearson's r for each of the pairs of possible relationships involved. Thus, if the two variables concerned are x and y, and t is the test variable (or second independent variable in the case of investigating multiple causation), the partial correlation coefficient computes Pearson's r for x and y, x and t, and y and t. Because of this, it is necessary to remember that all the restrictions associated with Pearson's r apply to variables involved in the possible computation of the partial correlation coefficient (e.g. variables must be interval).

There are three possible effects that can occur when partial correlation is undertaken: the relationship between x and y is unaffected by t; the relationship between x and y is totally explained by t; and the relationship between x and y is partially explained by t. Each of these three possibilities can be illustrated with Venn diagrams (see Figure 10.5). In the first case (a), t is only related to x, so the relationship between x and y is unchanged, because t can only have an impact on the relationship between x and y if it affects *both* variables. In the second case (b), all of the relationship between x and y (the cross-hatched area) is encapsulated by t. This would mean that the relationship between x and y when t is controlled would be zero. What usually occurs is that the test variable, t, partly explains the relationship between x and y, as in the case of (c) in Figure 10.5. In this case, only part of the relationship between x and y is explained by t (the shaded area which is overlapped by t). This would mean that the partial correlation coefficient will be lower than the Pearson's r for x and y. This is the most normal outcome of calculating the partial correlation coefficient. If the first order

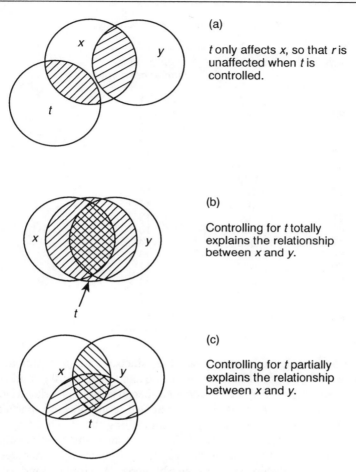

(a)

t only affects *x*, so that *r* is
unaffected when *t* is
controlled.

(b)

Controlling for *t* totally
explains the relationship
between *x* and *y*.

(c)

Controlling for *t* partially
explains the relationship
between *x* and *y*.

Figure 10.5   The effects of controlling for a test variable

correlation between x and y when t is controlled is considerably less than the
zero order correlation between x and y, the researcher must decide (if he or
she has not already done so) whether: (a) the $x-y$ relationship is spurious,
or at least largely so; or (b) whether t is an intervening variable between x
and y; or (c) whether t is best thought of as a causal variable which is
related to x and which largely eliminates the effect of x on y. These are the
three possibilities represented in Figures 10.1, 10.2 and 10.4 respectively.

As an example, consider the data in Table 10.7. We have data on eighteen
individuals relating to three variables: age, income and a questionnaire scale
measuring support for the market economy, which goes from a minimum of
5 to a maximum of 25. The correlation between income and support for the
market economy is 0.64. But could this relationship be spurious? Could it be

Table 10.7 Income, age and support for the market economy (imaginary data)

Subject	Age	Income	Support for market economy
1	20	9,000	11
2	23	8,000	9
3	28	12,500	12
4	30	10,000	14
5	32	15,000	10
6	34	12,500	13
7	35	13,000	16
8	37	14,500	14
9	37	14,000	17
10	41	16,000	13
11	43	15,500	15
12	47	14,000	14
13	50	16,500	18
14	52	12,500	17
15	54	14,500	15
16	59	15,000	19
17	61	17,000	22
18	63	16,500	18

that age should be introduced as a test variable, since we might anticipate that older people are both more likely to earn more and to support the market economy? This possibility can be anticipated because age is related to income (0.76) and to support (0.83). When we compute the partial correlation coefficient for income and support controlling the effects of age, the level of correlation falls to 0.01. This means that the relationship between income and support for the market economy is spurious. When age is controlled, the relationship falls to nearly zero. A similar kind of reasoning would apply to the detection of intervening variables and multiple causation.

Partial correlation with Minitab

Partial correlation cannot be generated directly with Minitab. In order to compute partial correlation coefficients with Minitab either of two routes can be followed. With the first route, it is necessary first to compute the Pearson r coefficients for the variables concerned and then substitute those coefficients in the following formula:

$$r_{12.3} = \frac{r_{12} - (r_{13} \times r_{23})}{\sqrt{(1 - r_{13}^2) \times (1 - r_{23}^2)}}$$

In this equation, $r_{12.3}$ refers to the partial correlation coefficient between variables 1 and 2, holding 3 constant (i.e. partialling out its effect). If we want to calculate the correlation between **'age'** and **'income'** holding **'years'** constant, we will first have to use the **correlation** command in Minitab. With the prompt system, the following simple command will provide the correlation coefficients:

MTB > correlation 'age' 'years' 'income'

In the Minitab for Windows menu system:

→**Stat** →**Basic Statistics** →**Correlation...** →**age** →**Select** →**years**
→**Select** →**income** →**Select** [age, years, and income should be in the
Variables: box] →**OK**

The correlation between **'age'** and **'income'** (r_{12}) is 0.618; for **'age'** and **'years'** (r_{13}) it is 0.808; and for **'income'** and **'years'** (r_{23}) it is 0.342. Substituting in the formula we then have:

$$r_{12.3} = \frac{0.618 - (0.808 \times 0.342)}{\sqrt{(1 - 0.808^2) \times (1 - 0.342^2)}}$$
$$= 0.62$$

Thus, the correlation between **'age'** and **'income'** is unaffected by **'years'**, since the computed partial correlation coefficient of 0.62 is almost identical to the zero order correlation between **'age'** and **'income'**. We have just computed a 'first order' partial correlation coefficient, i.e. one in which a single variable has been held constant. If two variables are to be held constant, for example, both **'years'** and **'satis'**, 'second order' partial correlation coefficients will be needed. To do this the first order correlation coefficients need to be computed and substituted in the above equation (see Cramer, 1994b, for a fuller exposition).

The alternative route is through the **regression** procedure and is probably easiest with the prompt system. The commands and the output are presented in Table 10.8. Essentially, this route involves storing the residuals from the two regression commands and then correlating the two residuals which have been stored as **c45** and **c46** respectively. The **regression** output has been controlled using **brief 0** (see Chapter 8). Using **brief 0** means that no regression output will be generated on the screen, but the residuals will be stored, as requested. Since it is not necessary to examine the regression output in this particular context, there seems little point generating it. However, it is then necessary to restore the default, **brief 2**, in order for the **correlation** output to be printed. The resulting partial correlation coefficient, 0.644, is very slightly different from that produced through the other route, 0.62, and almost certainly the difference derives from rounding errors. In

Table 10.8 Computing the partial correlation coefficient for **age** and **income** holding **years** constant (Minitab for Windows *Release 10* output from Job Survey data using the prompt system)

```
MTB > brief 0
MTB > regress 'age' 1 'years';
SUBC> residuals c45.
MTB > regress 'income' 1 'years';
SUBC> residuals c46.
MTB > brief 2
MTB > correlation c45 c46.
```

Correlations (Pearson)

Correlation of C45 and C46 = 0.644

order to establish whether the correlation is statistically significant, the table in Appendix I should be consulted using number of cases − 3 (i.e. $n − 3$) as the number of degrees of freedom.

REGRESSION AND MULTIVARIATE ANALYSIS

Nowadays regression, in the form of multiple regression, is the most widely used method for conducting multivariate analysis, particularly when more than three variables are involved. In Chapter 8 we previously encountered regression as a means of expressing relationships among pairs of variables. In this chapter, the focus will be on the presence of two or more independent variables.

Consider first of all, a fairly simple case in which there are three variables, that is two independent variables. The nature of the relationship between the dependent variable and the two independent variables is expressed in a similar manner to the bivariate case explored in Chapter 8. The analogous equation for mutivariate analysis is

$$y = a + b_1 x_1 + b_2 x_2 + e$$

where x_1 and x_2 are the two independent variables, a is the intercept, b_1 and b_2 are the regression coefficients for the two independent variables, and e is an error term which points to the fact that a proportion of the variance in the dependent variable, y, is unexplained by the regression equation. As in Chapter 8, the error term is ignored.

In order to illustrate the operation of multiple regression we can return to the data in Table 10.7. The regression equation for these data is

$$support = 5.913 + 0.21262age + 0.000008income$$

where 5.913 is the intercept (a), 0.21262 is the regression coefficient for the first independent variable, age (x_1), and 0.000008 is the regression coefficient for the second independent variable, income (x_2). Each of the two regression coefficients estimates the amount of change that occurs in the dependent variable (support for the market economy) for a one unit change in the independent variable. Moreover, the regression coefficient expresses the amount of change in the dependent variable with the effect of all other independent variables in the equation partialled out (i.e. controlled). Thus, if we had an equation with four independent variables, each of the four regression coefficients would express the unique contribution of the relevant variable to the dependent variable (with the effect in each case of the three other variables removed). This feature is of considerable importance, since the independent variables in a multiple regression equation are almost always related to each other.

Thus, every extra year of a person's age increases support for the market economy by 0.21262, and every extra £1,000 increases support by 0.000008. Moreover, the effect of age on support is with the effect of income removed, and the effect of income on support is with the effect of age removed. If we wanted to predict the likely level of support for the market economy of someone aged 40 with an income of £17,500, we would substitute as follows:

$$y = 5.913 + (0.21262)(40) + (0.000008)(17500)$$
$$= 5.913 + 8.5048 + 0.014$$
$$= 14.56$$

Thus, we would expect that someone with an age of 40 and an income of £17,500 would have a score of 14.56 on the scale of support for the market economy.

While the ability to make such predictions is of some interest to social scientists, the strength of multiple regression lies primarily in its use as a means of establishing the relative importance of independent variables to the dependent variable. However, we cannot say that simply because the regression coefficient for age is larger than that for income that this means that age is more important to support for the market economy than income. This is because age and income derive from different units of measurement that cannot be directly compared. In order to effect a comparison it is necessary to standardize the units of measurement involved. This can be done by multiplying each regression coefficient by the product of dividing the standard deviation of the relevant independent variable by the standard deviation of the dependent variable. The result is known as a *standardized regression coefficient* or *beta weight*. A possibly simpler approach is to standardize the relevant variables and then to perform the regression on the standardized variables. This is done by a simple procedure through which each value of a variable is subtracted from that variable's mean and then divided by the variable's standard deviation.

In the following example we will want to treat **'satis'** as the dependent variable and **'routine'**, **'autonom'** and **'income'** as the independent variables. The three independent variables were chosen because they are all known to be related to **'satis'**, as revealed by the relevant correlation coefficients. However, it is important to ensure that the independent variables are not too highly related to each other. The Pearson's r between each pair of independent variables should not exceed 0.80; otherwise the independent variables that show a relationship at or in excess of 0.80 may be suspected of exhibiting *multicollinearity*. Multicollinearity is usually regarded as a problem because it means that the regression coefficients may be unstable. This implies that they are likely to be subject to considerable variability from sample to sample. In any case, when two variables are very highly correlated, there seems little point in treating them as separate entities.

Standardized regression coefficients in a regression equation employ the same standard of measurement and can therefore be compared to establish which of two or more independent variables is the more important factor in relation to the dependent variable. They essentially tell us how many standard deviation units the dependent variable will change for a one unit change in the independent variable.

We can now take an example from the Job Survey data in order to illustrate some of these points. When the previous multiple regression analysis is carried out, the following equation is generated:

satis $= -2.243 + 0.57327$**autonom** $+ 0.0012787$**income**
$- 0.16989$**routine**

Thus, if we wanted to predict the likely **'satis'** score of someone with an **'autonom'** score of 16, an **'income'** of £8,000, and a **'routine'** score of 8, the calculation would proceed as follows:

satis $= -2.243 + (0.57327)(16) + (0.0012787)(8000) - (0.16989)(8)$
$= -2.243 + 9.17232 + 10.2296 - 1.35912$
$= 15.7998$

However, it is the relative impact of each of these variables on **'satis'** that provides the main area of interest for many social scientists. Table 10.9 presents the regression coefficients for the three independent variables remaining in the equation and the corresponding standardized regression coefficients. Although **'autonom'** provides the largest unstandardized and standardized regression coefficients, the case of **'income'** demonstrates the danger of using unstandardized coefficients in order to infer the magnitude of the impact of independent variables on the dependent variable. The variable **'income'** provides the smallest unstandardized coefficient (0.0012787), but

Table 10.9 Comparison of unstandardized and standardized regression coefficients with **satis** as the dependent variable

Independent variables	Unstandardized regression coefficients	Standardized regression coefficients
autonom	0.57327	0.47847
income	0.0012787	0.38627
routine	−0.16989	−0.21114

the second largest standardized coefficient (0.38625). As pointed out earlier, the magnitude of an unstandardized coefficient is affected by the nature of the measurement scale for the variable itself. The variable **'income'** has a range from 0 to 10,500, whereas a variable like **'routine'** has a range of only 4 to 20. When we examine the standardized regression coefficients, we can see that **'autonom'** has the greatest impact on **'satis'** and **'income'** the next highest. The variable **'routine'** has the smallest impact which is negative, indicating that more **'routine'** engenders less **'satis'**.

We can see here some of the strengths of multiple regression and the use of standardized regression coefficients. In particular, the latter allow us to examine the effects of each of a number of independent variables on the dependent variable. Thus, the standardized coefficient for **'autonom'** means that for each one unit change in **'autonom'**, there is a standard deviation change in **'satis'** of 0.47873, with the effects of **'income'** and **'routine'** on **'satis'** partialled out.

One of the questions that we may ask is how well the independent variables explain the dependent variable. In just the same way that we were able to use r^2 (the coefficient of determination) as a measure of how well the line of best fit represents the relationship between the two variables, we can compute the multiple coefficient of determination (R^2) for the collective effect of all of the independent variables. The R^2 value for the equation as a whole is 0.71, implying that only 29 per cent of the variance in **'satis'** (i.e. $100 - 71$) is not explained by the three variables in the equation. In addition, Minitab will produce an adjusted R^2. The technical reasons for this variation should not overly concern us here, but the basic idea is that the adjusted version provides a more conservative estimate than the ordinary R^2 of the amount of variance in **'satis'** that is explained. The adjusted R^2 takes into account the number of independent variables involved. The magnitude of R^2 is bound to be inflated by the number of independent variables associated with the regression equation. The adjusted R^2 corrects for this by adjusting the level of R^2 to take account of the number of independent variables.

Statistical significance and multiple regression

A useful statistical test that is related to R^2 is the F ratio. The F ratio test generated by Minitab is based on the multiple correlation (R) for the analysis. The multiple correlation, which is of course the square root of the coefficient of determination, expresses the correlation between the dependent variable (**'satis'**) and all of the independent variables collectively (i.e. **'autonom'**, **'routine'**, and **'income'**). The multiple R for the multiple regression analysis under consideration is 0.85. The F ratio test allows the researcher to test the null hypothesis that the multiple correlation is zero in the population from which the sample (which should be random) was taken. For our computed equation, $F = 53.03$ (see Table 10.10) and the significance level is 0.0000 (which means $p < 0.00005$), suggesting that it is extremely improbable that R in the population is zero.

The calculation of the F ratio is useful as a test of statistical significance for the equation as a whole, since R reflects how well the independent variables collectively correlate with the dependent variable. If a test of the statistical significance of the individual regression coefficients is required, a different test must be used. Minitab will produce a test of the statistical significance of individual regression coefficients through the calculation of a t value for each coefficient and an associated two-tailed significance test. As the output in Table 10.10 indicates, the significance levels for **'autonom'** and **'income'** were 0.000, and for **'routine'** 0.009. These are consistent with the previous analysis using the F ratio and suggest that the coefficients for **'income'**, **'autonom'** and **'routine'** are highly unlikely to be zero in the population.

Multiple regression and Minitab

The regression program within Minitab can create a large amount of output which can be controlled through **brief** (see Chapter 8, page 185). The default for the **regression** program is **brief 2** and for most users of multiple regression with Minitab, this will probably generate the right amount of detail. In other words, for most purposes there will probably be little need to specify the amount of output required. The output for the regression analysis used as an illustration in the previous section (in which **'satis'** is the dependent variable and **'autonom'**, **'routine'**, and **'income'** are the independent variables) is presented in Table 10.10.

The output in Table 10.10 can be produced through the prompt system with the following command:

MTB > regress 'satis' 3 'income' 'autonom' 'routine'

Thus, after **regress** the dependent variable (**'satis'**) is specified. This is followed by a number which refers to the number of independent variables being used (in this case **3**). Then the three independent variables – **'income'**, **'autonom'**, and **'routine'** – are specified. If **brief** has not been specified, the default output (**brief 2**) will be generated.

Table 10.10   Sample multiple regression output using unstandardized variables (Minitab for Windows *Release 10*)

Regression Analysis

The regression equation is
satis = −2.24 + 0.573 autonom − 0.170 routine + 0.00128 income

66 cases used 4 cases contain missing values

Predictor	Coef	Stdev	t-ratio	p
Constant	−2.243	2.391	−0.94	0.352
autonom	0.57327	0.09616	5.96	0.000
routine	−0.16989	0.06273	−2.71	0.009
income	0.0012787	0.0002400	5.33	0.000

s = 1.787   R − sq = 72.0%   R − sq (adj) = 70.6%

Analysis of Variance

SOURCE	DF	SS	MS	F	p
Regression	3	508.20	169.40	53.03	0.000
Error	62	198.06	3.19		
Total	65	706.26			

SOURCE	DF	SEQ SS
autonom	1	368.33
routine	1	49.16
income	1	90.71

Unusual Observations

Obs.	autonom	satis	Fit	Stdev.Fit	Residual	St.Resid
4	7.0	7.000	10.556	0.455	−3.556	−2.06R
10	8.0	13.000	8.618	0.303	4.382	2.49R
31	10.0	14.000	10.148	0.289	3.852	2.18R
46	10.0	13.000	9.339	0.378	3.661	2.10R
51	10.0	7.000	11.169	0.248	−4.169	−2.36R

R denotes an obs. with a large st. resid.

With the menu system, the following steps will provide the information in Table 10.10.

→**S̲tat** →**R̲egression** →**R̲egression...** →satis →**Select** [**satis** will now appear in the **R̲esponse:** box] →**income** →**Select** [**income** will now appear in the **Predictors:** box] →**autonom** →**Select** [**autonom** will now appear in the **Predictors:** box] →**routine** →**Select** [**routine** will now appear in the **Predi̲ctors:** box] →**O̲K**

The procedure yields the following information which relates to aspects of regression that have been covered above:

1 The regression equation is specified with the coefficients rounded to make it easier to read.
2 The number of cases on which the analysis is based (66) and the number of missing cases (4) are specified.
3 A table showing the coefficient (**Coef**) and the t-ratio and the statistical significance level (**p**) for each coefficient. The t-ratios for the coefficients relating to the three independent variables are all statistically significant, but the t-ratio relating to the constant is not.
4 The R^2 is given (**R-sq**) and the adjusted R^2 (**R-sq(adj)**). The former is given as 72.0 per cent, suggesting that the multiple correlation (R) is 0.85. The adjusted R^2 is very slightly lower at 70.6 per cent.
5 The F ratio for the model and the significance level of F are produced. Also, an analysis of variance table is produced, which can be interpreted in the same way as the ANOVA procedure described in Chapter 7. The analysis of variance table has not been discussed in the present chapter because it is not necessary to an understanding of regression for our present purposes.
6 There is then a list of Unusual Observations.

It must be remembered that the regression coefficients in this output are unstandardized regression coefficients. If *standardized* regression coefficients (beta weights) are wanted, as noted above, two possibilities present themselves. First, it can be done by multiplying each regression coefficient by the product of dividing the standard deviation of the relevant independent variable by the standard deviation of the dependent variable. We know that the unstandardized regression coefficient for **'autonom'** is 0.57327. Using the Minitab **describe** command, we can establish that the standard deviation for **'autonom'** is 2.757 and for **'satis'** it is 3.304. Therefore, the standardized regression coefficient for **'autonom'** will be

$$0.57327 \times \frac{2.757}{3.304} = 0.478$$

Thus the standardized regression for **'autonom'** is 0.478.

Alternatively, we can standardize all the relevant variables and then perform the regression on the standardized variables. This is done by subtracting from each value of a variable that variable's mean and then dividing by the variable's standard deviation. All four variables will need to be standardized. To create standardized variables which we will call **'satiss'**, **'routines'**, **'autonoms'**, and **'incomes'**, the following procedure needs to be followed.

Table 10.11   Sample multiple regression output using standardized variables (Minitab for Windows *Release 10*)

Regression Analysis

The regression equation is
satiss = 0.0050 + 0.478 autonoms − 0.211 routines + 0.386 incomes

66 cases used 4 cases contain missing values

Predictor	Coef	Stdev	t-ratio	p
Constant	0.00496	0.06666	0.07	0.941
autonoms	0.47847	0.08026	5.96	0.000
routines	−0.21114	0.07796	−2.71	0.009
incomes	0.38627	0.07249	5.33	0.000

s = 0.5410   **R − sq = 72.0%**   **R − sq(adj) = 70.6%**

Analysis of Variance

SOURCE	DF	SS	MS	F	p
Regression	3	46.565	15.522	53.03	0.000
Error	62	18.147	0.293		
Total	65	64.713			

SOURCE	DF	SEQ SS
autonoms	1	33.750
routines	1	4.504
incomes	1	8.311

Unusual Observations

Obs.	autonoms	satiss	Fit	Stdev.Fit	Residual	St.Resid
4	−0.87	−1.1618	−0.0853	0.1378	−1.0766	−2.06R
10	−0.50	0.6544	−0.6721	0.0918	1.3264	2.49R
31	0.22	0.9571	−0.2089	0.0876	1.1660	2.18R
46	0.22	0.6544	−0.4539	0.1145	1.1082	2.10R
51	0.22	−1.1618	0.1002	0.0751	−1.2620	−2.36R

R denotes an obs. with a large st. resid.

With the prompt system, the following command should be used:

MTB > center 'satis' 'routine' 'autonom' 'income' c61 c62 c63 c64
MTB > name c61 'satiss' c62 'routines' c63 'autonoms' c64 'incomes'

In other words, we stipulate after **center** the four variables to be standardized and then stipulate the four new names for them. We then need to use the **regression** command as previously outlined. With the prompt system, we would type:

MTB > regress 'satiss' 3 'incomes' 'autonoms' 'routines'

In the Minitab for Windows menu system, the following sequence should be used to standardize the variables:

→**Calc** →**Standardize…** →**satis** →**Select** →**routine** →**Select** →**autonom** →**Select** →**income** →**Select** [**satis, routine, autonom** and **income** should now be in the **Input column(s):** box.] →**Store results in:** box and click once. →type **satiss routines autonoms incomes** →make sure that the circle by **Subtract mean and divide by std. Dev.** is filled with a black dot. If it is not, click once in the box →**OK**

The following sequence should then be used to perform the regression on the standardized variables:

→**Stat** →**Regression** →**Regression…** →**satiss** →**Select** [**satiss** will now appear in the **Response:** box] →**incomes** →**Select** [**incomes** will now appear in the **Predictors:** box] →**autonoms** →**Select** [**autonoms** will now appear in the **Predictors:** box] →**routines** →**Select** [**routines** will now appear in the **Predictors:** box] →**OK**

The relevant output is shown in Table 10.11. The format of the output is basically the same as Table 10.10 in which the same regression analysis was performed but with unstandardized variables.

PATH ANALYSIS

The final area to be examined in this chapter, path analysis, is an extension of the multiple regression procedures explored in the previous section. In fact, path analysis entails the use of multiple regression in relation to explicitly formulated causal models. Path analysis cannot establish causality; it cannot be used as a substitute for the researcher's views about the likely causal linkages among groups of variables. All it can do is to examine the pattern of relationships between three or more variables, but can neither confirm nor reject the hypothetical causal imagery.

The aim of path analysis is to provide quantitative estimates of the causal connections between sets of variables. The connections proceed in one direction and are viewed as making up distinct paths. These ideas can best be explained with reference to the central feature of a path analysis – the path diagram. The path diagram makes explicit the likely causal connections between variables. An example is provided in Figure 10.6 which takes four variables employed in the Job Survey: **'age'**, **'income'**, **'autonom'**, and **'satis'**. The arrows indicate expected causal connections between variables. The model moves from left to right implying causal priority to those variables closer to the left. Each p denotes a causal path and hence a path coefficient that will need to be computed. The model proposes that **'age'** has a direct effect on **'satis'** (p_1). But indirect effects of **'age'** on **'satis'** are also proposed: **'age'** affects **'income'** (p_5) which in turn affects **'satis'** (p_6); **'age'**

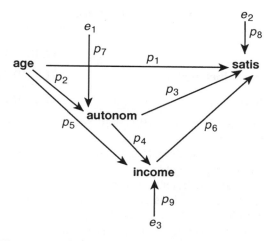

Figure 10.6   Path diagram for **satis**

affects **'autonom'** (p_2) which in turn affects **'satis'** (p_3); and **'age'** affects **'autonom'** (p_2) again, but this time affects **'income'** (p_4) which in turn affects **'satis'** (p_6). In addition, **'autonom'** has a direct effect on **'satis'** (p_3) and an indirect effect whereby it affects **'income'** (p_4) which in turn affects **'satis'** (p_6). Finally, **'income'** has a direct effect on **'satis'** (p_6), but no indirect effects. Thus, a direct effect occurs when a variable has an effect on another variable without a third variable intervening between them; an indirect effect occurs when there is a third intervening variable through which two variables are connected.

In addition, **'income'**, **'autonom'** and **'satis'** have further arrows directed to them from outside the nexus of variables. These refer to the amount of unexplained variance for each variable respectively. Thus, the arrow from e_1 to **'autonom'** (p_7) refers to the amount of variance in **'autonom'** that is not accounted for by **'age'**. Likewise, the arrow from e_2 to **'satis'** (p_8) denotes the amount of error arising from the variance in **'satis'** that is not explained by **'age'**, **'autonom'** and **'income'**. Finally, the arrow from e_3 to **'income'** (p_9) denotes the amount of variance in **'income'** that is unexplained by **'age'** and **'autonom'**. These error terms point to the fact that there are other variables that have an impact on **'autonom'** and **'satis'**, but which are not included in the path diagram.

In order to provide estimates of each of the postulated paths, path coefficients are computed. A path coefficient is a standardized regression coefficient. The path coefficients are computed by setting up *structural equations*, that is equations which stipulate the structure of hypothesized relationships in a model. In the case of Figure 10.6, three structural equations will be required – one for **'autonom'**, one for **'satis'** and one for **'income'**. The three equations will be:

$$\text{autonom} = x_1\text{age} + e_1 \qquad\qquad\qquad \text{(Eq. 10.1)}$$

$$\text{satis} = x_1\text{age} + x_2\text{autonom} + x_3\text{income} + e_2 \qquad\qquad \text{(Eq. 10.2)}$$

$$\text{income} = x_1\text{age} + x_2\text{autonom} + e_3 \qquad\qquad\qquad \text{(Eq. 10.3)}$$

The standardized coefficient for **'age'** in (Eq. 10.1) will provide p_2. The coefficients for **'age'**, **'autonom'** and **'income'** in (Eq. 10.2) will provide p_1, p_3 and p_6 respectively. Finally, the coefficients for **'age'** and **'autonom'** in (Eq. 10.3) will provide p_5 and p_4 respectively.

Thus, in order to compute the path coefficients, it is necessary to treat the three equations as multiple regression equations and the resulting standardized regression coefficients provide the path coefficients. The intercepts in each case are ignored. It is preferable to remove the constant altogether by typing in the following command in the prompt system before doing a regression analysis (regardless of whether the regression analysis will be done in the prompt or the menu system):

MTB > noconstant

However, if this is done the output will not include an R^2 value which is an important component of a path diagram (see below), since the computation of the error term is based on it. The R^2 value could be calculated by running **regress** for each equation with a constant (so that R^2 can be computed) and then running each equation without a constant. Thus, each of the three equations has to be run twice – once with a constant to generate an estimate of R^2 and once without to compute the standardized coefficients with the constant removed.

The three error terms are calculated by taking the R^2 for each equation away from 1 and taking the square root of the result of this subtraction.

To compute the three equations with Minitab we will need to standardize all four variables. We can call these four variables **'autonoms'**, **'ages'**, **'incomes'**, and **'satiss'**. Of these four variables, only **'ages'** has not been created thus far. We can standardize this variable with the prompt system as follows:

MTB > center 'age' c65
MTB > name c65 'ages'

In other words, we stipulate after **center** the variable to be standardized and then the new name for it.

In the Minitab for Windows menu system the following sequence should be used:

→**Calc** →**Standardize...** →**age** →**Select** [age should now be in the **Input column(s):** box] →**Store results in:** box →type **ages** →make sure that the circle by **Su̲btract mean and divide by std. Dev.** is filled with a black dot. If it is not, click once in the box →**O̲K**

Once all the variables have been standardized, the three equations can be generated with the following commands:

For equation (10.1):

With the prompt system, we would type:

MTB > regress 'autonoms' 1 'ages'

With Minitab for Windows the following steps will be required:

→**S̲tat   →R̲egression   →R̲egression...   →autonoms   →Select** [**autonoms** will now appear in the **R̲esponse:** box] →**ages** →**Select** [**ages** will now appear in the **Predi̲ctors:** box] →**O̲K**

For equation (10.2), with the prompt system, we would type:

MTB > regress 'satiss' 3 'incomes' 'autonoms' 'ages'

With the Minitab for Windows menu system, the following steps will be required:

→**S̲tat →R̲egression →R̲egression... →satiss →Select** [**satiss** will now appear in the **R̲esponse:** box] →**incomes →Select** [**incomes** will now appear in the **Predi̲ctors:** box] →**autonoms →Select** [**autonoms** will now appear in the **Predi̲ctors:** box] →**ages →Select** [**ages** will now appear in the **Predi̲ctors:** box] →**O̲K**

For equation (10.3), with the prompt system, we would type:

MTB > regress 'incomes' 2 'autonoms' 'ages'

With the Minitab for Windows menu system, the following steps will be required:

→**S̲tat →R̲egression →R̲egression... →incomes →Select** [**incomes** will now appear in the **R̲esponse:** box] →**autonoms →Select** [**autonoms** will now appear in the **Predi̲ctors:** box] →**ages →Select** [**ages** will now appear in the **Predi̲ctors:** box] →**O̲K**

The crucial information in the Minitab output for these three equations will be the standardized regression coefficient for each variable and the R^2 (for the error term paths). If we take the results of the third equation, we find that the standardized coefficients for **'autonom'** and **'age'** are 0.21681 and 0.56818 respectively and the R^2 is 0.426. Thus for p_4, p_5 and p_9 in the path diagram (Figure 10.7) we substitute 0.22, 0.57, and 0.76 (the latter being the square root of $1 - 0.426$). All of the relevant path coefficients have been inserted in Figure 10.7.

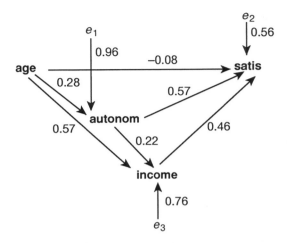

Figure 10.7   Path diagram for **satis** with path coefficients

Since the path coefficients are standardized, it is possible to compare them directly. We can see that **'age'** has a very small negative direct effect on **'satis'**, but it has a number of fairly pronounced positive indirect effects on **'satis'**. In particular, there is a strong sequence that goes from **'age'** to **'income'** ($p_5 = 0.57$) to **'satis'** ($p_6 = 0.46$).

Many researchers recommend calculating the overall impact of a variable like **'age'** on **'satis'**. This would be done as follows. We take the direct effect of **'age'** (-0.08) and add to it the indirect effects. The indirect effects are gleaned by multiplying the coefficients for each path from **'age'** to **'satis'**. The paths from **'age'** to **'income'** to **'satis'** would be calculated as $(0.57)(0.46) = 0.26$. For the paths from **'age'** to **'autonom'** to **'satis'** we have $(0.28)(0.57) = 0.16$. Finally, the sequence from **'age'** to **'autonom'** to **'income'** to **'satis'** yields $(0.28)(0.22)(0.46) = 0.03$. Thus the total indirect effect of **'age'** on **'satis'** is $0.26 + 0.16 + 0.03 = 0.45$. For the total effect of **'age'** on **'satis'**, we add the direct effect and the total indirect effect, i.e. $-0.08 + 0.45 = 0.37$. This exercise suggests that the indirect effect of **'age'** on **'satis'** is inconsistent with its direct effect, since the former is slightly negative and the indirect effect is positive. Clearly, an appreciation of the intervening variables **'income'** and **'autonom'** is essential to an understanding of the relationship between **'age'** and **'satis'**.

The effect of **'age'** on **'satis'** could be compared with the effect of other variables in the path diagram. Thus, the effect of **'autonom'** is made up of the direct effect (0.57) plus the indirect effect of **'autonom'** to **'income'** to **'satis'**, i.e. $0.57 + (0.22)(0.46)$, which equals 0.67. The effect of **'income'** on **'satis'** is made up only of the direct effect, which is 0.46, since there is no indirect effect from **'income'** to **'satis'**. Thus, we have three *effect* *coefficients* as they are often called (e.g. Pedhazur, 1982) – 0.37, 0.67, and 0.46 for **'age'**, **'autonom'** and **'income'** respectively – implying that **'autonom'** has the largest overall effect on **'satis'**.

Sometimes, it is not possible to specify the causal direction between all of the variables in a path diagram. In Figure 10.8 **'autonom'** and **'routine'** are deemed to be correlates; there is no attempt to ascribe causal priority to one or the other. The link between them is indicated by a curved arrow with two heads. Each variable has a direct effect on **'absence'** (p_5 and p_4). In addition, each variable has an indirect effect on **'absence'** through **'satis'**: **'autonom'** to **'satis'** (p_1) and **'satis'** to **'absence'** (p_3); **'routine'** to **'satis'** (p_2) and **'satis'** to **'absence'** (p_3). In order to generate the necessary coefficients, we would need the Pearson's *r* for **'autonom'** and **'routine'** and the standardized regression coefficients from two equations:

$$\textbf{satis} = a + x_1\textbf{autonom} + x_2\textbf{routine} + e_1 \qquad \text{(Eq. 10.4)}$$

$$\textbf{absence} = a + x_1\textbf{autonom} + x_2\textbf{routine} + x_3\textbf{satis} + e_2 \qquad \text{(Eq. 10.5)}$$

We could then compare the total causal effects of both **'autonom'**, **'routine'** and **'satis'**. The total effect would be made up of the direct effect plus the total indirect effect. The total effect of each of these three variables on **'absence'** would be:

Total effect of **autonom** = $(p_5) + (p_1)(p_3)$
Total effect of **routine** = $(p_4) + (p_2)(p_3)$
Total effect of **satis** = p_3

These three total effects can then be compared to establish which has the greater overall effect on absence. However, with complex models involving a large number of variables, the decomposition of effects using the foregoing procedures can prove unreliable and alternative methods have to be employed (Pedhazur, 1982).

Path analysis has become a popular technique because it allows the relative impact of variables within a causal network to be estimated. It

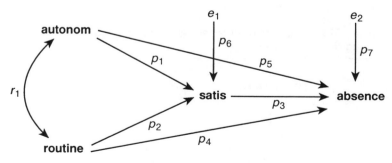

Figure 10.8 Path diagram for **absence**

forces the researcher to make explicit the causal structure that is believed to undergird the variables of interest. On the other hand, it suffers from the problem that it cannot confirm the underlying causal structure. It tells us what the relative impact of the variables upon each other is, but cannot validate that causal structure. Since a cause must precede an effect, the time order of variables must be established in the construction of a path diagram. We are forced to rely on theoretical ideas and our common sense notions for information about the likely sequence of the variables in the real world. Sometimes these conceptions of time ordering of variables will be faulty and the ensuing path diagram will be misleading. Clearly, while path analysis has much to offer, its potential limitations should also be appreciated. In this chapter, it has only been feasible to cover a limited range of issues in relation to path analysis and the emphasis has been upon the use of examples to illustrate some of the relevant procedures, rather than a formal presentation of the issues. Readers requiring more detailed treatments should consult Land (1969), Pedhazur (1982) and Davis (1985).

EXERCISES

1. A researcher hypothesizes that women are more likely than men to support legislation for equal pay between the sexes. The researcher decides to conduct a social survey and draws a sample of 1,000 individuals among whom men and women are equally represented. One set of questions asked directs the respondent to indicate whether he or she approves of such legislation. The findings are provided in Table 10E.1. Is the researcher's belief that women are more likely than men to support equal pay legislation confirmed by the data in Table 10E.1?

2. Following from Question 1, the researcher controls for age and the results of the analysis are provided in Table 10E.2. What are the implications of this analysis for the researcher's view that men and women differ in support for equal pay legislation?

Table 10E.1 The relationship between approval of equal-pay legislation and gender

	Men (*percentage*)	Women (*percentage*)
Approve	58	71
Disapprove	42	29
	100	100
N =	500	500

Table 10E.2 The relationship between approval of equal-pay legislation and gender holding age constant

	Under 35		35 and over	
	Men (percentage)	Women	Men (percentage)	Women
Approve	68	92	48	54
Disapprove	32	8	52	46
	100	100	100	100
N =	250	250	250	250

3. What Minitab commands would be required to examine the relationship between **'ethnicgp'** and **'commit'**, controlling for **'gender'**?

4. A researcher is interested in the correlates of the number of times that people attend religious services during the course of a year. On the basis of a sample of individuals, he finds that income correlates fairly well with frequency of attendance (Pearson's $r = 0.59$). When the researcher controls for the effects of age the partial correlation coefficient is found to be 0.12. Why has the size of the correlation fallen so much?

5. What Minitab commands would you need to correlate **'income'** and **'satis'**, controlling for **'age'**?

6. Consider the following regression equation and other details:

$$y = 7.3 + 2.3x_1 + 4.1x_2 - 1.4x_3 \qquad R^2 = 0.78 \qquad F = 21.43, \qquad p < 0.01$$

   (a) What value would you expect y to exhibit if $x_1 = 9$, $x_2 = 22$, and $x_3 = 17$?
   (b) How much of the variance in y is explained by x_1, x_2, and x_3?
   (c) Which of the three independent variables exhibits the largest effect on y?
   (d) What does the negative sign for x_3 mean?

7. What Minitab commands would you need to provide the data for the multiple regression equations on p. 249? In considering the commands, you should bear in mind that the information is required for a path analysis.

8. Turning to the first of the two equations referred to in Question 7 (i.e. the one with **'satis'** as the dependent variable),
   (a) How much of the variance in **'satis'** do the two variables account for?
   (b) Are the individual regression coefficients for **'autonom'** and **'routine'** statistically significant?
   (c) What is the standardized regression coefficient for **'routine'**?

9. Examine Figure 10.8. Using the information generated for Questions 7 and 8, which variable has the largest overall effect on **'absence'** – is it **'autonom'**, **'routine'** or **'satis'**?

Chapter 11

Aggregating variables
Exploratory principal-components analysis

Many of the concepts we use to describe human behaviour seem to consist of a number of different aspects. Take, for example, the concept of job satisfaction. When we say we are satisfied with our job, this statement may refer to various feelings we have about our work, such as being keen to go to it every day, not looking for other kinds of jobs, being prepared to spend time and effort on it, and having a sense of achievement about it. If these different components contribute to our judgement of how satisfied we are with our job, we would expect them to be interrelated. In other words, how eager we are to go to work should be correlated with the feeling of accomplishment we gain from it and so on. Similarly, the concept of job routine may refer to a number of interdependent characteristics such as how repetitive the work is, how much it makes us think about what we are doing, the number of different kinds of tasks we have to carry out each day and so on. Some people may enjoy repetitive work while others may prefer a job which is more varied. If this is the case, we would expect job satisfaction to be unrelated to job routine. To determine this, we could ask people to describe their feelings about their job in terms of these characteristics and see to what extent those aspects which reflect satisfaction are correlated with one another and are unrelated to those which represent routine. Character-istics which go together constitute a *factor* and *factor analysis* refers to a number of related statistical techniques which help us to determine them.

These techniques are used for three main purposes. First, as implied above, they can assess the degree to which items, such as those measuring job satisfaction and routine, are tapping the same concept. If people respond in similar ways to questions concerning job satisfaction as they do to those about job routine, this implies that these two concepts are not seen as being conceptually distinct by these people. If, however, their answers to the job-satisfaction items are unrelated to their ones to the job-routine items, this suggests that these two feelings can be distinguished. In other words, factor analysis enables us to assess the *factorial validity* of the questions which make up our scales by telling us the extent to which they seem to be measuring the same concepts or variables.

Second, if we have a large number of variables, factor analysis can determine the degree to which they can be reduced to a smaller set. Suppose, for example, we were interested in how gender and ethnic group were related to attitudes towards work. To measure this, we generate from our own experience twelve questions similar to those used in the Job Survey to reflect the different feelings we think people hold towards their job. At this stage, we have no idea that they might form three distinct concepts (i.e. job satisfaction, autonomy, and routine). To analyse the relationship of gender and ethnic group to these items, we would have to conduct twelve separate analyses. There would be two major disadvantages to doing this. First, it would make it more difficult to understand the findings since we would have to keep in mind the results of twelve different tests. Second, the more statistical tests we carry out, the more likely we are to find that some of them will be significant by chance. It is not possible to determine the likelihood of this if the data come from the same sample.

The third use to which factor analysis has been put is related to the previous one but is more ambitious in the sense that it is aimed at trying to make sense of the bewildering complexity of social behaviour by reducing it to a more limited number of factors. A good example of this is the factor analytic approach to the description of personality by psychologists such as Eysenck and Cattell (for example, Eysenck and Eysenck, 1969; Cattell, 1973). There is a large number of ways in which the personality of people varies. For example, there are hundreds of words describing personality characteristics listed in a dictionary. Many of these terms seem to refer to similar aspects. For example, the words 'sociable', 'outwardgoing', 'gregarious', and 'extraverted' all describe individuals who like the company of others. If we ask people to describe themselves or someone they know well in terms of these and other words, and we factor analyse this information, we will find that these characteristics will group themselves into a smaller number of factors. In fact, a major factor that emerges is one called sociability or extraversion. Some people, then, see factor analysis as a tool to bring order to the way we see things by determining which of them are related and which of them are not.

Two uses of factor analysis can be distinguished. The one most commonly reported is the *exploratory* kind in which the relationships between various variables are examined without determining the extent to which the results fit a particular model. *Confirmatory* factor analysis, on the other hand, compares the solution found against a hypothetical one. For example, if we expected the four items measuring job satisfaction in the Job Survey to form one factor, then we could assess the degree to which they did so by comparing the results of our analysis with a hypothetical solution in which this was done perfectly. Although there are techniques for making these kinds of statistical comparisons (for example, Bentler, 1993; Jöreskog and Sörbom, 1989), they are not available with Minitab. Consequently, we shall

Table 11.1 **Correlation** output of a correlation matrix for job satisfaction and routine items

Correlations (Pearson)

	satis1	satis2	satis3	satis4	routine1	routine2	routine3
satis2	−0.439						
satis3	0.439	−0.314					
satis4	−0.442	0.470	−0.543				
routine1	−0.468	0.521	−0.301	0.404			
routine2	−0.465	0.472	−0.213	0.398	0.693		
routine3	−0.393	0.434	−0.293	0.407	0.787	0.621	
routine4	−0.351	0.463	−0.247	0.283	0.725	0.507	0.638

confine our discussion to the exploratory use of factor analysis. We will illustrate its use with an analysis of the job satisfaction and routine items in the Job Survey, in which we will describe the decisions to be made, followed by the commands to carry these out.

CORRELATION MATRIX

The initial step is to compute a correlation matrix for the eight items which make up the two scales of job satisfaction and routine. If there are no statistically significant correlations between these items, then this means that they are unrelated and that we would not expect them to form one or more factors. In other words, it would not be worthwhile to go on to conduct a factor analysis. Consequently, this should be the first stage in deciding whether to carry one out.

The Minitab prompt command for performing a correlation is **correlation** and so the command for producing this matrix is

MTB>correlation c8-c11 c16-c19

The menu procedure for doing this is

→**Stat** →**Basic Statistics** →**Correlation...** →**c8-c11**
→**Select** [this puts **c8-c11** in the box under **Variables:**]
→**c16-c19** →**Select** →**OK**

The output for this procedure is shown in Table 11.1. With a sample of 68, a correlation of about 0.24 is significant at the 0.05 two-tailed level. As all but one of the correlations are higher than this value, this suggests that the data may constitute one or more factors.

SAMPLE SIZE

Second, how reliable the factors are which emerge from a factor analysis depends on the size of the sample, although there is no consensus on what this should be. There is agreement, however, that there should be more subjects than variables. Gorsuch (1983), for example, has proposed an absolute minimum of five subjects per variable and not less than 100 individuals per analysis. Although factor analysis can be carried out on samples smaller than this to describe the relationships between the variables, not much confidence should be placed that these same factors would emerge in a second sample. Consequently, if the main purpose of a study is to find out what factors underlie a group of variables, it is essential that the sample should be sufficiently large to enable this to be done reliably.

PRINCIPAL COMPONENTS

The two most widely used forms of factor analysis are *principal-components* and *factor* analysis (also called *principal-axis factoring*). There are other kinds of methods such as alpha, image, and maximum likelihood factoring (which is also available on *Release 9* onwards) but these are used much less frequently. Because of this and the need to keep the discussion brief, we will outline only the first technique.

Principal-components analysis is primarily concerned with describing the variation or variance which is shared by the scores of people on three or more variables. This variance is referred to as *common variance* and needs to be distinguished from two other kinds of variance. *Specific variance* describes the variation which is specific or unique to a variable and which is not shared with any other variable. *Error variance*, on the other hand, is the variation due to the fluctuations which inevitably result from measuring something. If, for example, you weigh yourself a number of times in quick succession, you will find that the readings will vary somewhat, despite the fact that your weight could not have changed in so short a time. These fluctuations in measurement are known as error variance. So the total variation that we find in the scores of an instrument (such as an item or test) to assess a particular variable can be divided or partitioned into common, specific and error variance.

Total variance = Common variance + Specific variance + Error variance

Since principal-components analysis cannot distinguish specific from error variance, they are combined to form *unique variance*. In other words, the total variance of a test consists of its common and its unique variance.

This idea may be illustrated with the relationship between three variables, x, y, and z, as displayed in the Venn diagram in Figure 11.1. The overlap between any two of the variables and all three of them represents common variance (the shaded areas), while the remaining unshaded areas constitute the unique variance of each of the three variables.

In principal-components analysis, all the variance of a score or variable is analysed, including its unique variance. In other words, it is assumed that the test used to assess the variable is perfectly reliable and without error.

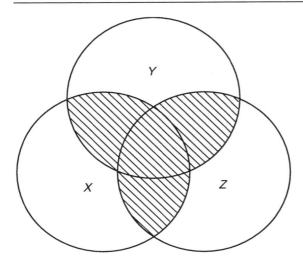

Figure 11.1 Common and unique variance

Since principal-components analysis examines the total variance of a test, this is set at 1, while for principal-axis factoring it varies between 0 and 1. The variance of a test to be explained is known as its *communality*.

The first component that is extracted accounts for the largest amount of variance shared by the tests. The second component consists of the next largest amount of variance which is not related to or explained by the first one. In other words, these two components are unrelated or *orthogonal* to one another. The third component extracts the next largest amount of variance, and so on. There are as many components as variables, although the degree of variance which is explained by successive components becomes smaller and smaller. In other words, the first few components are the most important ones.

The Minitab prompt command and subcommand for producing just the principal components, their communality, their variance (or *eigenvalue*) and (more accurately) the proportion of variance they account for is

MTB > factor c8-c11 c16-c19;
SUBC> brief 1.

This subcommand suppresses the display of the component score coefficients which we do not require.

The menu procedure for doing this is

→<u>S</u>tat →<u>M</u>ultivariate →<u>F</u>actor Analysis... →c8-c11 →Select [this puts **c8-c11** in the box under **<u>V</u>ariables:**] →c16-c19 →Select →<u>O</u>K

The **brief 1** output for this procedure is presented in Table 11.2. The output for the menu system is slightly different in format. The relationship

Table 11.2 **Principal components brief 1** output of the principal components, their communality and variance

Factor Analysis

Principal Component Factor Analysis of the Correlation Matrix

Unrotated Factor Loadings and Communalities

68 cases used   2 cases contain missing values

Variable	Factor1	Factor2	Factor3	Factor4	Factor5	Factor6
satis1	0.673	−0.306	0.375	−0.468	0.259	−0.139
satis2	−0.706	0.087	−0.406	−0.521	−0.165	−0.152
satis3	0.524	−0.691	−0.361	−0.054	0.137	0.289
satis4	−0.671	0.506	0.077	−0.192	0.363	0.345
routine1	−0.873	−0.310	0.113	0.050	−0.002	−0.036
routine2	−0.771	−0.242	−0.234	0.170	0.377	−0.174
routine3	−0.814	−0.296	0.253	0.076	0.112	−0.083
routine4	−0.744	−0.364	0.235	−0.111	−0.352	0.225
Variance	4.2485	1.2084	0.6281	0.5792	0.5238	0.3341
% Var	0.531	0.151	0.079	0.072	0.065	0.042

Variable	Factor7	Factor8	Commnlty
satis1	0.091	0.018	1.000
satis2	−0.081	−0.019	1.000
satis3	−0.112	0.005	1.000
satis4	−0.012	0.015	1.000
routine1	−0.059	0.348	1.000
routine2	0.291	−0.076	1.000
routine3	−0.357	−0.185	1.000
routine4	0.248	−0.103	1.000
Variance	0.3049	0.1730	8.0000
% Var	0.038	0.022	1.000

between each item (or test) and a principal component (or factor) is expressed as a correlation or *loading*. So, **satis1** correlates or loads **0.673** with **Factor1**. The variance accounted for by the first factor is **4.2485** or 53.1 (**0.531**) per cent of the total variance. The total variance explained by the eight components is simply the sum of their eigenvalues, which in this case is 8. The proportion of variance accounted for by any one factor is its eigenvalue divided by the sum of the eigenvalues, which is multiplied by 100 to convert it to a percentage. Thus, for example, the proportion of variance due to the first factor is about 4.25/8 or 0.531, which multiplied by 100 equals 53.1.

NUMBER OF COMPONENTS TO BE RETAINED

Since the object of principal-components analysis is to reduce the number of variables we have to handle, this would not be achieved if we used all of them. Consequently, the next step is to decide how many components we should keep. This really is a question of how many of the smaller components we should retain, since we would obviously keep the first few which explain most of the variance. There are two main criteria used for deciding which components to exclude. The first, known as *Kaiser's criterion*, is to select those components which have an eigenvalue greater than one. Since the total variance that any one variable can have has been standardized as one, what this means, in effect, is that a component which explains less variance than a single variable is excluded. From Table 11.2, we can see that only the first two components have eigenvalues greater than one.

The second method is the graphical *scree test* proposed by Cattell (1966). In this method, a graph is drawn of the descending variance accounted for by the components initially extracted.

The Minitab prompt command and subcommand for storing the eigenvalues in a new column (and the eigenvectors in a matrix) are

MTB > factor c8-c11 c16-c19;
SUBC> eigen c25 m1;
SUBC> brief 1.

The menu sequence for doing this is

→**Stat** →**Multivariate** →**Factor Analysis...** →**c8-c11** →**Select** [this puts **c8-c11** in the box under **Variables:**] →**c16-c19** →**Select** →**Storage...** →box beside **Eigenvalues:** and in it type **c25** →box beside **Eigenmatrix:** and in it type **m1** →**OK**

To plot the eigenvalues in **c25** against the eight principal components, we create a further column containing values from one to eight.

MTB > set c26
DATA> 1:8
DATA> end

With the **plot** command, we then plot **c25** against **c26**.

MTB > plot c25 ∗ c26

The menu procedure for doing this is

→**Graph** →**Plot...** →**c25** →**Select** [this puts **c25** in the Y column of the box under **Graph variables:**] →**c26** →**Select** [this puts **c26** in the X column of this box] →**OK**

The output for this procedure is depicted in Figure 11.2. The plot typically shows a break between the steep slope of the initial components and the

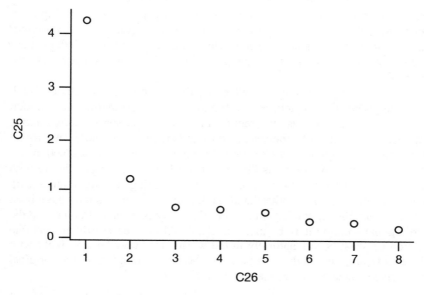

Figure 11.2 Scree test of eigenvalues

gentle one of the later components. The term 'scree', in fact, is a geological one for describing the debris found at the bottom of a rocky slope and implies that these components are not very important. The components to be retained are those which lie before the point at which the eigenvalues seem to level off. This occurs after the first two components in this case, both of which also have eigenvalues greater than one. In other words, both criteria suggest the same number of components in this example. Which criterion to use may depend on the size of the average communalities and the number of variables and subjects. The Kaiser criterion has been recommended for situations where the number of variables is less than 30 and the average communality is greater than 0.70 or when the number of subjects is greater than 250 and the mean communality is greater than or equal to 0.60 (Stevens, 1992).

ROTATION OF COMPONENTS

The first components extracted from an analysis are those which account for the maximum amount of variance. As a consequence, what they represent may not be easy to interpret since items will not correlate as highly with them as they might. In fact, most of the items will fall on the first component, although their correlations with it may not be that high. In order to increase the interpretability of components, they are rotated to maximize the loadings of some of the items. These items can then be used to identify the meaning of the component. A number of ways have been developed to rotate components. The two most commonly used methods are *orthogonal* rotation which produces components which are unrelated to or independent of one another, and *oblique* rotation in which the components are correlated.

There is some controversy as to which of these two kinds of rotation is the more appropriate. The advantage of orthogonal rotation is that the information the components provide is not redundant, since a person's score on one component is unrelated to their score on another. For example, if we found two orthogonal components which we interpreted as being job satisfaction and routine, then what this means is that in general how satisfied people are with their job is not related to how routine they see it as being. The disadvantage of orthogonal rotation, on the other hand, is that the components may have been forced to be unrelated, whereas in real life they may be related. In other words, an orthogonal solution may be more artificial and not necessarily an accurate reflection of what occurs naturally in the world. This may be less likely with oblique rotation, although it should be borne in mind that the original components in an analysis are made to be orthogonal.

ORTHOGONAL ROTATION

Only orthogonal rotation is available on Minitab. To produce a *varimax* orthogonal rotation of the first two principal-components, we use the following command and subcommands

MTB > fact c8-c11 c16-c19;
SUBC> nfac=2;
SUBC> sort;
SUBC> vmax;
SUBC> brief 1.

The first subcommand (**nfac=2**) specifies that the number of **fac**tors to be extracted is **2**. The components extracted are always the largest ones. The second subcommand (**sort**) orders the loadings so that the items with the highest absolute correlations with the first component are displayed first, followed by the items with the highest absolute loadings on the second component and so on. This ordering makes it easier to see which items correlate the highest with which components.

The menu action for doing this is

→**S**tat →**M**ultivariate →**F**actor Analysis... →**c8-c11** →**Select** [this puts **c8-c11** in the box under **Variables:**] →**c16-c19** →**Select** →box beside **Number of factors to extract:** and in it type **2** →**V**arimax [when the circle beside it will have its centre filled] →**Sort loadings** [when a cross will be put in the box beside it] →**OK**

The **brief 1** output for this procedure is shown in Table 11.3. In terms of the orthogonally rotated solution, five items (**routine1**, **routine3**, **routine4**, **routine2** and **satis2**) load on the first component, while three items (**satis3**, **satis4** and **satis1**) correlate most highly with the second component. The items which load most strongly on the first component are listed or grouped together first and are ordered in terms of the size of their correlations. The items which correlate most strongly with the second component form the second group on the second component. If there had been a third component, then the items which loaded most highly on it would constitute the

Table 11.3 **Principal components brief 1** output of unsorted and sorted item loadings on the two orthogonally rotated components

Factor Analysis

Principal Component Factor Analysis of the Correlation Matrix

Rotated Factor Loadings and Communalities
Varimax Rotation

68 cases used   2 cases contain missing values

Variable	Factor1	Factor2	Commnlty
satis1	−0.379	0.634	0.546
satis2	0.531	−0.473	0.506
satis3	−0.037	0.866	0.752
satis4	0.264	−0.798	0.706
routine1	0.894	−0.243	0.859
routine2	0.772	−0.240	0.653
routine3	0.837	−0.220	0.749
routine4	0.819	−0.124	0.686
Variance	3.2635	2.1934	5.4569
% Var	0.408	0.274	0.682

Sorted Rotated Factor Loadings and Communalities

Variable	Factor1	Factor2	Commnlty
routine1	0.894	−0.243	0.859
routine3	0.837	−0.220	0.749
routine4	0.819	−0.124	0.686
routine2	0.772	−0.240	0.653
satis2	0.531	−0.473	0.506
satis3	−0.037	0.866	0.752
satis4	0.264	−0.798	0.706
satis1	−0.379	0.634	0.546
Variance	3.2635	2.1934	5.4569
% Var	0.408	0.274	0.682

third group on the third component, and so on. From the items loading most highly on them, the first component appears to be a measure of job routine and the second component a measure of job satisfaction.

Although the data are made up, if we obtained a result like this with real data it would suggest that the way in which people answered the job-routine items was not related to the way they responded to the job-satisfaction ones, with the exception of **satis2**. In other words, the two groups of items seem to be factorially distinct. The loadings of items on components can be positive or negative: for example, the **satis2** item has a positive correlation with the first component while **satis1** is negatively correlated with it. In fact, this item appears to be a reflection of both these components, since it correlates quite highly with both of them. Consequently, if we wanted to have a purer measure of job satisfaction, it would be advisable to omit it from this scale.

In general, the meaning of a component is determined by the items which load most highly on it. Which items to ignore when interpreting a component is arguable. It may not be appropriate to use the significance level of the component loading since this depends on the size of the sample. In addition, the appropriate level to use is complicated by the fact that a large number of correlations have been computed on data which come from the same subjects. Conventionally, items or variables which correlate less than 0.3 with a component are omitted from consideration since they account for less than 9 per cent of the variance and so are not very important. An alternative criterion to use is the correlation above which no item correlates highly with more than one component. The advantage of this rule is that components are interpreted in terms of items unique to them. Consequently, their meaning should be less ambiguous. According to these two rules, component 1 comprises all four of the routine items whereas component 2 contains only **satis3** and **satis4**. However, the use of these two conventions in conjunction produces a highly stringent set of criteria for deciding which variables should be included in which components. Many researchers ignore the second convention and emphasize all loadings of 0.3 and above regardless of whether any variables are thereby implicated in more than one component.

The amount and proportion of variance that each of the orthogonally rotated components accounts for is also shown in the output. The first component explains about 41 (**0.408**) per cent of the variance and the second component about 27 (**0.274**) per cent.

EXERCISES

1. You have developed a questionnaire to measure anxiety which consists of ten items. You want to know whether the items constitute a single factor. To find this out, would it be appropriate to carry out a factor analysis on the ten items?

2. If you were to carry out a factor analysis on ten items or variables, what would be the minimum number of subjects or cases you would use?

3. What is the unique variance of a variable?

4. How does principal-components analysis differ from principal-axis factoring?

5. How many components are there in a principal-components analysis?

6. Which component accounts for most of the variance?

7. Why are not all the components extracted?

8. Which criterion is most commonly used to determine the number of components to be extracted?

9. What is meant by a loading?

10. Why are components rotated?

11. What is the main advantage of orthogonal rotation?

Appendix I

Critical values of the Pearson Product Moment Correlation Coefficient

df = N − 2	Level of significance for one-tailed test		
	0.05	0.025	0.01
	Level of significance for two-tailed test		
	0.10	0.05	0.02
1	0.9877	0.9969	0.9995
2	0.9000	0.9500	0.9800
3	0.8054	0.8783	0.9343
4	0.7293	0.8114	0.8822
5	0.6694	0.7545	0.8329
6	0.6215	0.7067	0.7887
7	0.5822	0.6664	0.7498
8	0.5494	0.6319	0.7155
9	0.5214	0.6021	0.6851
10	0.4973	0.5760	0.6581
11	0.4762	0.5529	0.6339
12	0.4575	0.5324	0.6120
13	0.4409	0.5139	0.5923
14	0.4259	0.4973	0.5742
15	0.4124	0.4821	0.5577
16	0.4000	0.4683	0.5425
17	0.3887	0.4555	0.5285
18	0.3783	0.4438	0.5155
19	0.3687	0.4329	0.5034
20	0.3598	0.4227	0.4921
25	0.3233	0.3809	0.4451
30	0.2960	0.3494	0.4093
35	0.2746	0.3246	0.3810
40	0.2573	0.3044	0.3578
45	0.2428	0.2875	0.3384
50	0.2306	0.2732	0.3218
60	0.2108	0.2500	0.2948
70	0.1954	0.2319	0.2737
90	0.1726	0.2050	0.2422
100	0.1638	0.1946	0.2301

Source: Taken from Table VII of Fisher and Yates, *Statistical Tables for Biological, Agricultural and Medical Research*, published by Longman Group UK Ltd, 1974, and reproduced by permission of the authors and publishers.

Appendix II

Critical values for the Spearman Rank-Order Correlation Coefficient

	Significance level for a one-tailed test at		
	0.05	0.025	0.005
	Significance level for a two-tailed test at		
N	0.10	0.05	0.01
5	0.900	1.000	
6	0.829	0.886	1.000
7	0.715	0.786	0.929
8	0.620	0.715	0.881
9	0.600	0.700	0.834
10	0.564	0.649	0.794
11	0.537	0.619	0.764
12	0.504	0.588	0.735
13	0.484	0.561	0.704
14	0.464	0.539	0.680
15	0.447	0.522	0.658
16	0.430	0.503	0.636
17	0.415	0.488	0.618
18	0.402	0.474	0.600
19	0.392	0.460	0.585
20	0.381	0.447	0.570
21	0.371	0.437	0.556
22	0.361	0.426	0.544
23	0.353	0.417	0.532
24	0.345	0.407	0.521
25	0.337	0.399	0.511
26	0.331	0.391	0.501
27	0.325	0.383	0.493
28	0.319	0.376	0.484
29	0.312	0.369	0.475
30	0.307	0.363	0.467

Answers to exercises

CHAPTER 1

1. These forms of analysis concentrate upon one, two and three or more variables respectively.

2. It is necessary in order to ensure that members of experimental and control groups are as alike as possible. If members of the experimental and control groups are alike any contrasts that are found between the two groups cannot be attributed to differences in the membership of the two groups; instead, it is possible to infer that it is the experimental stimulus (Exp) that is the source of the differences between the two groups.

3. The reasoning is faulty. First, those who read the quality dailies and those who read the tabloids will differ from each other in ways other than the newspapers that they read. In other words, people cannot be treated as though they have been randomly assigned to two experimental treatments – qualities and tabloids. Second, the causal inference is risky because it is possible that people with a certain level of political knowledge are more likely to read certain kinds of newspaper, rather than the type of newspaper affecting the level of political knowledge.

CHAPTER 2

1. Since not all possible religious affiliations have been included (e.g. Baha'i, Zoroastrianism), it is important to have a further option in which these can be placed. This can be called 'Other'.

2. The most convenient way of coding this information is to assign a number to each option, such as 1 for Agnostic, 2 for Atheist, and so on.

3. This information should be coded as missing. In other words, you need to assign an asterisk to data that are missing.

4. If this happened very infrequently, then one possibility would be to code this kind of response as missing. Since the answer is not truly missing, an alternative course of action would be to record one of the two answers. There are a number of ways this could be done. First, the most common category could be chosen. Second, one of the two answers could be selected at random. Third, using other information we could try

and predict which of the two was the most likely one. If there were a large number of such multiple answers, then a separate code could be used to signify them.

5. If we provide an identification number for each subject and if Agnostics are coded as 1 and Atheists as 2, your data file should look something like this:

   01 1 25
   02 1 47
   03 2 33
   04 2 18

In other words, the information for the same participant is placed in a separate row, while the information for the same variable is placed in the same column(s).

6. Two columns as we have to include the 'Other' category.

7. There are usually no more than 80 columns to a line.

8. Eight characters.

CHAPTER 3

1. With the prompt system

   MTB > **copy** relevant variables;
   SUBC> use 'ethnicgp' = 4.

   With the menu system

   →**Manip** →**Copy Columns...** →relevant variables →**Select** [this puts them in the box under **Copy from columns:**] →box under **To columns:** and type new variables in it →**Use Rows...** →**Use rows with column equal to [eg, −4.5 −2:3 14):** →box beside it →**ethnicgp** →**Select** →type 4 [which goes in the box below] →**OK** →**OK**

2. With the prompt system

   MTB > **let c30 = ('ethnicgp' = 2 or 'ethnicgp' = 4) and ('gender' = 2) and ('age' le 25)**
   MTB > **copy** relevant variables;
   SUBC> use c30 = 1.

   With the menu system

   →**Calc** →**Mathematical Expressions...** →type c30 in the box beside **Variable [new or modified]:** →box under **Expression:** and in it type **('ethnicgp' = 2 or 'ethnicgp' = 4) and ('gender' = 2) and ('age' le 25)** →**OK**

   →**Manip** →**Copy Columns...** →relevant variables →**Select** [this puts them in the box under **Copy from columns:**] →box under **To columns:** →type new names of variables →**Use Rows...** →**Use rows with column equal to [eg, −4.5 −2:3 14]** →box beside it →**c30** →**Select** →type 1 [which goes in the box below] →**OK** →**OK**

3. With the prompt system

   MTB >code (2) 1 (3 4) 2 'skill' new column

   With the menu system

   →**M**anip →**C**ode Data **V**alues... →**skill** →**Select** [this puts **skill** in the box under **C**ode data from columns:] →box under **I**nto columns: and type name of variable in it →first box beneath O**r**iginal values [eg, 1 : 4 12]: and in it type 2 →first corresponding box under **N**ew: and in it type 1 →second box under O**r**iginal values [eg, 1 : 4 12]: and in it type 3 and 4 →second corresponding box under **N**ew: and in it type 2 →**O**K

4. With the prompt system

   MTB > code (1 : 4999) 1 (5000 : 9999) 2 (10000 : 50000) 'income' new column

   With the menu system

   →**M**anip →**C**ode Data **V**alues... →**income** →**Select** [this puts **income** in the box beneath **C**ode data from columns:] →box under **I**nto columns: and type new variable in it →first box under O**r**iginal values [eg, 1 : 4 12]: and in it type **1:4999** →first corresponding box under **N**ew: and in it type **1** →second box under O**r**iginal values [eg, 1 : 4 12]: and in it type **5000:9999** →second corresponding box under **N**ew: and in it type **2** →third box under O**r**iginal values [eg, 1 : 4 12]: and in it type **10000:50000** →third corresponding box under **N**ew: and in it type **3** →**O**K

5. With the prompt system

   MTB > **name** new column **'days'**
   MTB > **let 'days' = 'weeks' ∗ 7**

   With the menu system

   →**C**alc →**M**athematical **E**xpressions... →type **days** in the box beside **V**ariable [new or modified]: →box under **E**xpression: and in it type ('weeks' ∗ 7) →**O**K

CHAPTER 4

1. (b).

2. It forces the researcher to think about the breadth of the concept and the possibility that it comprises a number of distinct components.

3. (a) dichotomous
   (b) nominal
   (c) ordinal
   (d) interval/ratio.

4. Interval.

5. External reliability.

6. Internal reliability.

7. (a).

CHAPTER 5

1. If you are using the prompt system:

   MTB > tally 'prody';
   SUBC> counts;
   SUBC> percents.

   If you are using the menu system:

   →**Stat** →**Tables** →**Tally...** →**incgrp** →**select** →[make sure that there is a cross in the relevant boxes in the windows by both **Counts** and **Percents**. If crosses are not present, simply *click* once in each or either box.] →**OK**

2. 17.39 per cent.

3. (c)

4. You will need to find the first and third quartiles. With the prompt system:

   MTB >describe 'satis'

   With the menu system:

   →**Stat** →**Basic Statistics** →**Descriptive Statistics...** →**satis** →**select** →**OK**

5. 6 (i.e. 14 − 8).

6. It takes all values in a distribution into account and is easier to interpret in relation to the mean which is more commonly employed as a measure of central tendency than the median.

7. Between 4.23 and 17.446. Some 95.44 per cent of cases will probably lie within this range.

CHAPTER 6

1. A representative sample is one which accurately mirrors the population from which it was drawn. A random sample is a type of sample which aims to enhance the likelihood of achieving a representative sample. However, due to a number of factors (such as sampling error or non-response), it is unlikely that a random sample will be a representative sample.

2. Because it enhances the likelihood that the groups (i.e. strata) in the population will be accurately represented.

3. When a population is highly dispersed, the time and cost of interviewing can be reduced by multistage cluster sampling.

4. No. Quite aside from the problems of non-response and sampling error, it is unlikely that the Yellow Pages provide a sufficiently complete and accurate sampling frame.

5. Since there are only two possible outcomes (heads and tails) and the coin was flipped four times, the probability of finding the particular sequence you did would be one out of sixteen ($2 \times 2 \times 2 \times 2$) or 0.0625.

6. No. Even if the coin was unbiased, you would still have a one in sixteen chance that you would obtain four heads in a row.

7. The probability of obtaining any sequence of two heads and two tails is six out of sixteen or 0.375 since six such sequences are possible. In other words, this is the most likely outcome.

8. Since there are only two outcomes to each question (true and false), the most likely score for someone who has no general knowledge is 50 points (0.5×100 which is the mean of the probability distribution).

9. Once again, there are only two outcomes for each person (butter or margarine). The probability of guessing correctly is 0.5. Since fifty people took part, the mean or most likely number of people guessing correctly would be twenty-five.

10. The null hypothesis would be that there was no difference in talkativeness between men and women.

11. The non-directional hypothesis would be that men and women differ in talkativeness. In other words, the direction of the difference is not stated.

CHAPTER 7

1. A chi-square test should be used since there are two unrelated categorical variables (i.e. shop and type of book) and the number of books sold in any one category is fixed. In other words, the number of books in this case is a frequency count.

2. The null hypothesis is that the number of books sold according to shop or type of book does not differ from that expected by chance.

3. With the prompt system

   MTB > chisquare 'shop1' 'shop2'

   With the menu system

   →**Stat** →**Tables** →**Chisquare Test...** →**shop1** →**Select** [this puts **shop1** in the box under **Columns containing the table:**] →**shop2** →**Select** →**OK**

4. We would use a two-tailed level of significance in this case and in others involving a comparison of three or more cells since it is not possible to determine the direction of any differences as all differences have been made positive by being squared.

5. Since the value 0.25 is greater than the conventional criterion or cut-off point 0.05, we would conclude that the number of books sold did not differ significantly according to shop or type of book. A probability value of 0.25 means that we could expect to obtain this result by chance one out of four times. To be more certain that our result is not due to chance, it is customary to expect the finding to occur at or less than five times out of a hundred.

6. A finding with a probability level of 0.0001 would not mean that there had been a greater difference in the number of books sold than one with a probability level of 0.037. It would simply mean that the former finding was less likely to occur (once in 10,000 times) than the latter one (thirty-seven out of a thousand times).

7. A binomial test would be used to determine if there had been a significant difference.

8. If we specify the direction of the difference in the number of books sold between the two shops, we would use a one-tailed level of significance.

9. You would simply divide the two-tailed level by 2, which in this case would give a one-tailed level of 0.042.

10. It would be inappropriate to analyse these data with a binomial test since it does not take account of the number of men and women who reported not having this experience. In other words, it does not compare the proportion of men with the proportion of women reporting this experience. Consequently, it is necessary to use a chi-square test for two samples. Note, however, that it would have been possible to have used a binomial test if the proportion of people falling in love in one sample was compared with that in the other. However, it may be simpler to use chi-square.

11. Since the number of close friends a person has is a ratio measure and the data being compared come from two unrelated samples (men and women), an unrelated t test should be used.

12. The pooled variance estimate is used to interpret the results of a t test when the variances do not differ significantly from one another.

13. You would use a repeated-measure test since the average number of books sold is an interval/ratio measure which can vary between the ten shops, and the cases (i.e. the ten shops) are the same for the three time-periods.

CHAPTER 8

1. (a)

```
MTB > table 'prody' 'gender';
SUBC> counts;
SUBC> colpercents;
SUBC> chisquare.
```

With the menu system:

→**Stat** →**Tables** →**Cross Tabulation...** →**prody** →**select** →**gender** →**select** → [ensure that there is a mark in the small boxes by Cou**n**ts and **C**olumn percents. If no mark is present, *click once* in the relevant boxes. Also, *click on* the box by **Chisquare analysis**. A cross will appear in each box that has been chosen.] →**OK**

(b) Chi-square would probably be the best choice.
(c) With $(x^2 = 1.183$ and $p > .05$, the relationship would be regarded as non-significant.
(d) 35.48 per cent.

2. The reasoning is faulty. Chi-square cannot establish the strength of a relationship between two variables. Also, statistical significance is not the same as substantive significance, so that the researcher would be incorrect in believing that the presence of a statistically significant chi-square value indicates that the relationship is important.

3. (a) With the prompt system:

MTB > correlation 'income' 'years' 'satis' 'age'

With the menu system:

→**Stat** →**Basic Statistics** →**Correlation...** →**income** →**select** →**years** →**select** →**satis** →**select** →**age** →**select** →**OK**

(b) The correlation between income and years $(r = 0.81)$.
(c) 66 per cent.

4. There is a host of errors. The researcher should not have employed r to assess the correlation, since social class is an ordinal variable. The amount of variance explained is 53.3 per cent, not 73 per cent. Finally, the causal inference (i.e. that social class explains the number of books read) is risky with a correlational/survey design of this kind.

5. The statistical significance of r is affected not just by the size of r, but also by the size of the sample. As sample size increases, it becomes much easier for r to be statistically significant. The reason, therefore, for the contrast in the findings is that the sample size for the researcher's study, in which $r = 0.55$ and $p > 0.05$, is smaller than the one which found a smaller correlation but was statistically highly significant.

6. (a) Since these two variables are ordinal, a measure of rank correlation will probably be most appropriate.
   (b) First, they will need to be ranked. The procedure for doing this can be found on p. 175. Assuming that the ranked variables have been called **'rprody'** and **'rcommit'**, the following command would be used with the prompt system:

MTB > correlation 'rprody' 'rcommit'

With the menu system:

→**S̲tat** →**B̲asic Statistics** →**C̲orrelation...** →**rprody** →**select** →**rcommit**
→**select** →**O̲K**

(c) rho = 0.31.

7. (a) The intercept.
   (b) The regression coefficient. For each extra year, **autonom** increases by .0623.
   (c) Not terribly well. Only 28 per cent of the variance in **autonom** is explained
       by **age**.
   (d) 10.308.
   (e) With the prompt system:

MTB > regress 'autonom' 1 'age'

With the menu system:

→**S̲tat** →**R̲egression** →**R̲egression...** →**autonom** →**select** →**age** →**select**
→**O̲K**

CHAPTER 9

1. One advantage is that a more accurate measure of error variance is provided.
   The other is to examine interaction effects between the two variables.

2. An interaction is where the effect of one variable is not the same under all the
   conditions of the other variable.

3. You would conduct an analysis of variance (ANOVA) to determine whether
   the interaction between the two variables was significant.

4. Performance is the dependent variable since the way in which it is affected by
   alcohol, anxiety and gender is being investigated.

5. There are three factors, i.e. alcohol, anxiety and gender.

6. There are three levels of anxiety.

7. It can be described as a $4 \times 3 \times 2$ factorial design.

8. With the prompt system

MTB > glm perform=alcohol anxiety gender alcohol * anxiety &
CONT> alcohol * gender anxiety * gender alcohol * anxiety * gender

With the menu system

→**S̲tat** →**A̲NOVA** →**G̲eneral Linear Model...** →**perform** →**Select** [this
puts **perform** in the box beside **R̲esponse:**] →box under **M̲odel:**
→**alcohol** →**Select** [this puts **alcohol** in this box] →**anxiety** →**Select**
→**gender** →**Select** →type alcohol * anxiety →type alcohol * gender
→type anxiety * gender →type alcohol * anxiety * gender →**O̲K**

9. First, you would find out if there were any differences in intelligence between the three conditions, using one-way analysis of variance. If there were no significant differences, then you could assume that the effect of intelligence is likely to be equal in the three conditions and that there is no need to control for it statistically. If you had found that there were significant differences in intelligence between the three conditions, you would need to determine if there was any relationship between intelligence and the learning to read measure. If such a relationship existed, you could control for the effect of intelligence by conducting an analysis of covariance.

10. With the prompt system

   MTB > glm read=methods intell;
   SUBC> covariates intell.

   With the menu system

   →**Stat** →**ANOVA** →**General Linear Model...** →**read** →**Select** [this puts **read** in the box beside **Response:**] →box under **Model:** →**methods** →**Select** [this puts **methods** in this box] →**intell** →**Select** →box under **Covariates [optional]:** →**intell** →**Select** →**OK**

11. It is a between-subjects design with multiple measures.

12. With the prompt system

   MTB > glm intell likeable honesty confid = attract;
   SUBC> manova.

   With the menu system

   →**Stat** →**ANOVA** →**General Linear Model...** →**intell** →**Select** [this puts **intell** in the box beside **Response:**]→**likeable** →**Select** →**honesty** →**Select** →**confid** →**Select** →box under **Model:** →**attract** [this puts **attract** in this box] →box beside **Include multivariate ANOVA** →**OK**

13. It is a within-subjects or repeated-measures design with multiple measures.

14. You would have to distinguish the ratings of the attractive face from those of the unattractive one which you could do with a column called **attract** where the attractive face was coded **1** and the unattractive face **2**. You would also need another column which we could call **subjects** and which consecutively numbers the cases in the same order for the two faces.
   With the prompt system

   MTB > anova intell likeable honesty confid = attract subjects

   With the menu system

   →**Stat** →**ANOVA** →**Balanced ANOVA...** →**intell** →**Select** [this puts **intell** in the box beside **Response:**] →**likeable** →**Select** →**honesty** →**Select** →**confid** →**Select** →box under **Model:** →**attract** [this puts **attract** in this box] →**subjects** →**Select** →**OK**

15. With the prompt system

MTB > let c30 = 'pre'-'post'
MTB > let c31 = 'post'-'fol'
MTB > ttest c30 c31

With the menu system

→**Calc** →**Mathematical Expressions...** →**c30** →**Select** [this puts **c30** in the box beside **Variable [new or modified]:**] →box under **Expression:** and in it type **'pre'-'post'** →**OK**
→**Calc** →**Mathematical Expressions...** →**c31** →**Select** [this puts **c31** in the box beside **Variable [new or modified]:**] →box under **Expression:** and in it type **'post'-'fol'** →**OK**
→**Stat** →**Basic Statistics** →**1-Sample t...** →**c30 c31** →**Select** [this puts **c30 c31** in the box beside **Variables:**] →**OK**

CHAPTER 10

1. To a large extent, in that 71 per cent of women support equal pay legislation, as against 58 per cent of men.

2. Table 10E.2 suggests that the relationship between sex and approval for equal pay legislation is moderated by age. For respondents under the age of 35, there is greater overall support for legislation, and the difference between men and women is greater than in Table 10E.1. Among those who are 35 and over, the overall level of approval is lower and the difference between men and women is much less than in Table 10E.1. Clearly, the relationship between sex and approval for equal pay legislation applies to the under-35s in this imaginary example, rather than to those who are 35 or over.

3. In the prompt system:

MTB > table 'commit' 'gender' 'ethnicgp';
SUBC> counts;
SUBC> colpercents;
SUBC> layout 1 2.

In the menu system:

→**Stat** →**Tables** →**Cross Tabulation...** →**commit** →**Select** →**gender** →**Select** →**ethnicgp** →**Select** →[if the boxes by **Counts** and **Column Percents** do not have a tick in them, you should *click* once on each of these boxes] →**Options...** →type **1** in the box in the middle of the clause **Use the first ... classification variables for rows** and type **2** in the box in the middle of the clause **and the next ... for columns** →**OK** →**OK**

4. The main possibility is that the relationship between income and attendance at religious services is spurious. Age is probably related to both income and attendance. However, it should also be noted that the relationship between income and attendance does not disappear entirely when age is controlled.

5. In the prompt system:

   MTB > brief 0
   MTB > regress 'income' 1 'age';
   SUBC> residuals c60.
   MTB > regress 'satis' 1 'age';
   SUBC> residuals c61.
   MTB > brief 2
   MTB > correlation c60 c61

6. (a) 94.4.
   (b) 78 per cent.
   (c) This was a trick question. Since the three regression coefficients presented in the equation are unstandardized, it is not possible to compare them to determine which independent variable has the largest effect on y. In order to make such an inference, standardized regression coefficients would be required.
   (d) For every one unit change in x_3, y decreases by 1.4.

7. You will need to work with the *standardized* variables (see pp. 242–4 for the procedure for creating these). In the prompt system:

   MTB > regress 'satiss' 2 'autonoms' 'routines'
   MTB > regress 'absences' 3 'satiss' 'autonoms' 'routines'

   In the menu system:

   →**Stat** →**Regression** →**Regression...** →satiss →**Select** →autonoms →**Select** →routines →**Select** →**OK**
   →**Stat** →**Regression** →**Regression...** →absences →**Select** →satiss →**Select** →autonoms →**Select** →routines →**Select** →**OK**

8. (a) According to the adjusted R^2, 59.1 per cent of the variance in **satis (satiss)** is explained by **autonom (autonoms)** and **routine (routines)**.
   (b) Yes. The t values for **autonom (autonoms)** and **routine (routines)** are significant at $p < 0.0000$ and $p < 0.0002$ respectively.
   (c) −0.29106.

9. The largest effect coefficient is for **satis** (−0.50). The effect coefficients for **autonom** and **routine** respectively were −0.115 and −0.02.

CHAPTER 11

1. No. If you were to do this, you would be examining the way in which your anxiety items were grouped together. In other words, you may be analysing the component structure of anxiety itself. To find out if your ten items assessed a single component of anxiety, you would need to include items which measured other variables such as sociability.

2. At least 50–100 cases.

3. This is the variance which is not shared with other variables.

4. Principal-components analysis analyses all the variance of a variable while principal-axis factoring analyses the variance it shares with the other variables.

5. There are as many components as variables.

6. The first component always accounts for the largest amount of variance.

7. This would defeat the aim of principal-components analysis which is to reduce the number of variables which need to be examined. The smaller components may account for less variance than that of a single variable.

8. Kaiser's criterion which extracts components with an eigenvalue greater than one.

9. A loading is a measure of association between a variable and a component.

10. Components are rotated to increase the loading of some items and to decrease that of others so as to make the components easier to interpret.

11. The advantage of orthogonal rotation is that since the components are uncorrelated with one another, they provide the minimum number of components required to account for the relationships between the variables.

Bibliography

Bentler, P. M. (1993), *EOS Structural Equations Program Manual*, Los Angeles: BMDP Statistical Software Inc.

Blauner, R. (1964), *Alienation and Freedom: the Factory Worker and his Industry*, Chicago: University of Chicago Press.

Bohrnstedt, G. W. and Knoke, D. (1982), *Statistics for Social Data Analysis*, Itasca, IL: F. E. Peacock.

Boneau, C. (1960), 'The effects of violations of assumptions underlying the t test', *Psychological Bulletin* 57: 49–64.

Brayfield, A. and Rothe, H. (1951), 'An index of job satisfaction', *Journal of Applied Psychology* 35: 307–11.

Bridgman, P. W. (1927), *The Logic of Modern Physics*, London: Macmillan.

Bryman, A. (1985), 'Professionalism and the clergy', *Review of Religious Research* 26: 253–60.

Bryman, A. (1986), *Leadership and Organizations*, London: Routledge.

Bryman, A. (1988a), *Quantity and Quality in Social Research*, London: Routledge.

Bryman, A. (1988b), 'Introduction: "inside" accounts and social research in organizations', in A. Bryman (ed.), *Doing Research in Organizations*, London: Routledge.

Bryman, A. (1989), *Research Methods and Organization Studies*, London: Routledge.

Bryman, A. and Cramer, D. (1990), *Quantitative Data Analysis for Social Scientists*, London: Routledge.

Bryman, A. and Cramer, D. (1994), *Quantitative Data Analysis for Social Scientists* (rev. ed.), London: Routledge.

Campbell, D. T. and Fiske, D. W. (1959), 'Convergent and discriminant validation by the multitrait-multimethod index', *Psychological Bulletin* 56: 81–105.

Cattell, R. B. (1966), 'The meaning and strategic use of factor analysis', in R. B. Cattell (ed.), *Handbook of Multivariate Experimental Psychology*, Chicago: Rand McNally.

Cattell, R. B. (1973), *Personality and Mood by Questionnaire*, San Francisco: Jossey-Bass.

Child, J. (1973), 'Predicting and understanding organization structure', *Administrative Science Quarterly* 18: 168–85.

Cohen, L. and Holliday, M. (1982), *Statistics for Social Scientists*, London: Harper & Row.

Conover, W. J. (1980), *Practical Nonparametric Statistics* (2nd ed.), New York: Wiley.

Cramer, D. (1994a), 'Psychological distress and Neuroticism: A two-wave panel study', *British Journal of Medical Psychology* 67: 333–42.

Cramer, D. (1994b), *Introducing Statistics for Social Research: Step-by-Step Calculations and Computer Techniques Using SPSS*, London and New York: Routledge.

Cramer, D. (1996), *Basic Statistics for Social Research: Step-by-Step Calculations and Computer Techniques Using Minitab*, London and New York: Routledge.

Cronbach, L. J. and Meehl, P. E. (1955), 'Construct validity in psychological tests', *Psychological Bulletin* 52: 281–302.

Davis, J. A. (1985), *The Logic of Causal Order*, Sage University Paper Series on Quantitative Applications in the Social Sciences, series no. 55, Beverly Hills, CA: Sage.

Durkheim, E. (1952), *Suicide: a Study in Sociology*, London: Routledge & Kegan Paul.

Eysenck, H. J. and Eysenck, S. B. G. (1969), *Personality Structure and Measurement*, London: Routledge & Kegan Paul.

Freeman, L. C. (1965), *Elementary Applied Statistics: For Students of Behavioral Science*, New York: Wiley.

Games, P. and Lucas, P. (1966), 'Power of the analysis of variance of independent groups on non-normal and normally transformed data', *Educational and Psychological Measurement* 26: 311–27.

Glock, C. Y. and Stark, R. (1965), *Religion and Society in Tension*, Chicago: Rand McNally.

Gorsuch, R. L. (1983), *Factor Analysis*, Hillsdale, NJ: Lawrence Erlbaum.

Gould, S. J. (1991) 'The median isn't the message', *Bully for Brontosaurus: Reflections in Natural History*, London: Hutchison Radius.

Goyder, J. (1988), *The Silent Minority: Non-Respondents on Social Surveys*, Oxford: Polity Press.

Hall, R. H. (1968), 'Professionalization and bureaucratization', *American Sociological Review* 33: 92–104.

Hirschi, T. (1969), *Causes of Delinquency*, Berkeley: University of California Press.

Huff, D. (1973), *How to Lie with Statistics*, Harmondsworth: Penguin.

Huitema, B. (1980), *The Analysis of Covariance and Alternatives*, New York: Wiley.

Jackson, P. R. (1983), 'An easy to use BASIC program for agreement among many raters', *British Journal of Clinical Psychology* 22: 145–6.

Jenkins, G. D., Nadler, D. A., Lawler, E. E. and Cammann, C. (1975), 'Structured observations: an approach to measuring the nature of jobs', *Journal of Applied Psychology* 60: 171–81.

Jöreskog, K. G. and Sörbom, D. (1989) *LISREL 7: A Guide to the Program and Applications* (2nd ed.), Chicago: SPSS Inc.

Labovitz, S. (1970), 'The assignment of numbers to rank order categories', *American Sociological Review* 35: 515–24.

Labovitz, S. (1971), 'In defense of assigning numbers to ranks', *American Sociological Review* 36: 521–2.

Land, K. C. (1969), 'Principles of path analysis', in E. F. Borgatta and G. F. Bohrnstedt (eds), *Sociological Methodology 1969*, San Francisco: Jossey-Bass.

Lazarsfeld, P. F. (1958), 'Evidence and inference in social research', *Daedalus* 87: 99–130.

Locke, E. A. and Schweiger, D. M. (1979), 'Participation in decision-making: one more look', in B. M. Staw (ed.), *Research in Organizational Behavior*, vol. 1, Greenwich, CT: JAI Press.

Lord, F. M. (1953), 'On the statistical treatment of football numbers', *American Psychologist* 8: 750–1.

Marshall, G., Newby, H., Rose, D., and Vogler, C. (1988), *Social Class in Modern Britain*, London: Unwin Hyman.

Maxwell, S. E. (1980), 'Pairwise multiple comparisons in repeated measures designs', *Journal of Educational Statistics* 5: 269–87.

McNemar, Q. (1969) *Psychological Statistics* (4th edition), New York: Wiley.

Merton, R. K. (1967), *On Theoretical Sociology*, New York: Free Press.

Minitab Inc. (1989), *MINITAB Reference Manual Release 7*, State College, PA: Minitab Inc.

Minitab Inc. (1991), *MINITAB Reference Manual PC Version Release 8*, State College, PA: Minitab Inc.

Minitab Inc. (1992), *MINITAB Reference Manual Release 9*, State College, PA: Minitab Inc.

Minitab Inc. (1995), *MINITAB Reference Manual Release 10Xtra for Windows and Macintosh*, State College, PA: Minitab Inc.

Mitchell, T. R. (1985), 'An evaluation of the validity of correlational research conducted in organizations', *Academy of Management Review* 10: 192–205.

Mosteller, F. and Tukey, J. W. (1977) *Data Analysis and Regression*, Reading, MA: Addison-Wesley.

Murray, I. (1995) 'How your council rates in the efficiency league', *The Times* 30 March: 32.

O'Brien, R. M. (1979), 'The use of Pearson's r with ordinal data', *American Sociological Review* 44: 851–7.

Overall, J. E. and Spiegel, D. K. (1969), 'Concerning least squares analysis of experimental data', *Psychological Bulletin* 72: 311–22.

Pedhazur, E. J. (1982), *Multiple Regression in Behavioral Research: Explanation and Prediction* (2nd ed.), New York: Holt, Rinehart & Winston.

Rosenberg, M. (1968), *The Logic of Survey Analysis*, New York: Basic Books.

Siegal, S. (1956), *Nonparametric Statistics for the Behavioral Sciences*, New York: McGraw-Hill.

Siegel, S. and Castellan, Jr., N. J. (1988) *Nonparametric Statistics for the Behavioral Sciences* (2nd ed.), New York: McGraw-Hill.

Snizek, W. E. (1972), 'Hall's professionalism scale: an empirical reassessment', *American Sociological Review* 37: 10–14.

Stevens, J. (1992), *Applied Multivariate Statistics for the Social Sciences* (2nd ed.), Hillsdale, NJ: Lawrence Erlbaum.

Stevens, J. P. (1979), 'Comment on Olson: choosing a test statistic in multivariate analysis of variance', *Psychological Bulletin* 86: 728–37.

Stevens, S. S. (1946), 'On the theory of scales of measurement', *Science* 103: 677–80.

Tukey, J. W. (1977), *Exploratory Data Analysis*, Reading, MA: Addison-Wesley.

Walker, H. (1940), 'Degrees of freedom', *Journal of Educational Psychology* 31: 253–69.

Wilcox, R. R. (1987), 'New designs in analysis of variance', *Annual Review of Psychology*, 38: 29–60.

Zeller, R. A. and Carmines, E. G. (1980), *Measurement in the social sciences*, New York: Cambridge University Press.

Index